She Found Her Voice

JENNIFER PAYLOR

Printed in the UK

Published by Ginio Publishing

Distributed by Ingram Spark

FIRST EDITION
ISBN 978-1-8384183-0-4
eISBN 978-1-8384183-1-1

ACKNOWLEDGEMENTS

My very sincere thanks to Mandi/Mum, John, Lucy, Stuart, Paddy Whack, my literary buddy, Pip, and my editor, Jessica and book designer, Kathy for dedicating their time, energy and expertise to helping me produce this final version of *She Found Her Voice*. Writing a book was a lot more challenging than I expected and I am glad that I enrolled in the Self-Publishing School. I would also like to thank my many family members and friends who read, encouraged me and promoted this book so that Mum's legacy can be widely valued.

THE FAMILY

Noel and Enid are parents to Mandi and she has two brothers David and Ant

Mandi married Peter and had four children, Nick, Jen, Lucy and Jo

Nick married Paige and had three children Matthew, Sarah and Katie

Jen married Richard and had three children Emma, Mark (Badger) and Sam

Lucy married Stuart and had four children Ben, Charlie, Jen and Tom

Jo married Nicola (Nick Nack/Paddy Whack) and had three children, William, Jamie (Loubird) and Freddie

Sarah is married to James with Sebastian and Josh

Katie is married to Russell

Emma is married to Charlie with Bella and Matilda

Mark is married to Jen

Sam is married to India

Jen has recently been remarried to John

Young Mandi with her family. Ant. Enid. Noel and David (from left to right) and Pookie the Peke

Mandi the mum with Nick. Jen. Lucy and Jo. her children and Peter

Mandi - her life ahead

Marrying her beloved Peter

50 years later

Young love!

Mandi - Mum. Gran and Great Gran(GG)

Lucy said: "Mum gave or taught me many things:

☆ *An absolute love of living by finding pleasure in the simplest of things at any age and stage*

☆ *The capacity to communicate and truly understand other people*

☆ *It's OK to break rules—follow what you believe with respect and reason—even having two boyfriends in your eighties!*

☆ *Caring about others is fundamental and is a key motivation and purpose in life*

☆ *Just have fun! Laughter is the best medicine!*

☆ *Acceptance and no judgement are good*

☆ *Treat kings and garbage men the same*

☆ *Wacky is good and a bit of bonkers is just fun*

☆ *Life is short and we need to grab it*

☆ *There is a greater power and an afterlife*

☆ *It is OK to be real and expose a bit of yourself as it sets people at ease*

☆ *Being out of control is part of life, but hard work helps*

☆ *Being perfect is just not real, so don't stress*

☆ *Reality is that some people are just ugly—pray for them!*

☆ *You can fart pretty much anywhere!*

☆ *International language difficulties can be managed by repetition, volume and a generic French accent!*

☆ *Being self-reliant is important*

☆ *Getting pissed is just great sometimes!*

☆ *Unconditional love is to be treasured*

☆ *Forgiveness is strength and freedom*

☆ *Adventures are cool*

☆ *Artistic talent doesn't need to be recognised to be enjoyed and developed*

'She is a special lady and I love her to bits for just being herself!'

CONTENTS

There is a time for everything
and a season for every activity under the heavens:

What profit hath he that worketh in that wherein he laboureth?
I know that there is no good in them,
but for a man to rejoice and to do good in his life.

— ADAPTED FROM ECCLESIASTES 3:1-8 —

FOREWORD

My mum, Mandi, is eighty-five now, but no one believes it. Born between the Great Wars, a schoolgirl, nurse, wife, mother, counsellor and widow and now taking part in the fight against the coronavirus, Mandi has lived her roles.

First impressions tell you that this is a woman who is not done with living and before too long, you are finding out about her boyfriends or catching up on the latest stories. You will be invited to a cup of tea and a piece of delicious homemade cake or a large glass of fine wine if 'the time is right on the ever-right clock'. She will take the greatest interest in your life and get out her diaries, either recent or past, to share. Maybe this will be a story that chimes with what you are saying. Maybe it will be a story to learn from. Or maybe it will just be a good old yarn or a naughty story that will make you belly laugh.

Very soon, you will feel as though you have known her forever.

Mandi's diaries are an absolute gold mine of international and national history as well as family and personal anecdotes over the times and seasons of this ordinary, extraordinary woman's life. She keeps them in her kitchen in a large chest she uses to sit on when she needs to create more seating for her parties. There are some fifty of them, each a book in itself, telling the story of each day of each year, from about the age of seventeen onwards. There are hundreds of letters too. Quite a number of the diaries have been lost on the way, but those that have survived, together with lots of conversations and other contributions, helped me piece together her colourful, compassionate and creative life, which spans both tradition and emancipation until she found her voice.

I am not just saying this because I am her daughter, Jen; I am saying it because Mandi's life in itself is well worth reading about and because she is humble enough, generous enough, brave enough and wise enough to let others take what they want from her joy and despair, living and learning, and use it to guide their own choices and feel stronger.

This book in itself is the ultimate evidence of my Mum, Mandi, as I call her in the book, finding her own voice. She braves your critique just as she had to brave so much critique in her life, but as we see in cultures that value their elderly more than we English do, those who have truly lived have so much to give to those who have much to learn.

A TIME FOR WAR
AND A TIME FOR PEACE

With her buoyant, blond locks bouncing as she ran and her cheeks puffed up from the effort, Mandi raced down the path as fast as she could to help her brothers milk Jane, the goat. She loved any time that she could spend with David and Anthony and knew that she was just right for this job. Five years old, her little hands ideally suited to pull the teats of their much-loved wartime animal, she would fill up the pail with wholesome milk.

She ran straight through the stable door and flew over David's foot, landing in a pile of straw with a shriek. David and Anthony grinned at each other and laughed out loud at their little sister, not surprised that she had ended up in a heap; she usually did.

They got her up and settled her at the milking stool and soon the pail was filled up.

'Good work, sis', encouraged Anthony whilst David busied himself with the chickens.

'Can I collect the eggs too today?' asked Mandi, excited.

'We will have to ask Mother what she wants, as you know', replied David. 'Let's just do as we are told and take in the milk. We can do some races with Pyramus and Thisbe before we go back'.

Pyramus and Thisbe were Jane the goat's kids, and having just had them, Jane was milking really well. Mandi, as the youngest, always went along with her brothers, but loved it if they let her join in. She did not want to go back in just yet to the silent, still endlessness of inside, but even at that early age, she knew that it was best to get things right and keep quiet. Her brothers would not let her carry the pail, so after racing the goats, she entertained herself picking wild flowers as she walked more sedately this time back up the path.

You could just see Noel, the children's father, feeding off this imagined scene in his mind from his home in Whitehall.

Frederick Noel Hornsby, aged twenty-nine, was responsible for the running of Whitehall Court, a stylish range of clubs in the centre of the capital; he was also a captain in the artillery, his role during the war effort. He was a quiet, modest and retiring person that had learned the hotel business from his very successful entrepreneurial father, who had died too young at fifty-seven and forced the running of Whitehall Court onto him well before he was ready. He hadn't the character for this challenging role and the strength and forthright nature of his wife provided the fortitude for him to cope with the complexities and challenges of running such a business.

Before the war Noel, as he was known, liked nothing better than to ride his horse 'Skewbald' in Rotten Row; he would look forward to his annual ski trip to Davos with his brother Jack, find any time he could to play his violin or indeed escape to the law courts. He would return home from the latter with many a juicy life story that he would enact, recount or reduce to a short ditty or poem, which he could create with consummate ease and ready wit. He was quietly funny and, when permitted, entertained many, including his dear wife.

Now, times were different. He had to keep working and doing his part whilst his family was keeping as safe as possible in the country. He missed them very much.

The Hornsby children, their mother Enid, and their grandmother Rosa had been living at Firway Cottage in leafy, rural Grayshott in what is now known as Hampshire, but was Surrey back then. They had been there for about a year now, having moved away from Whitehall in Central London in 1940 when they had to evacuate. The family was living a simple life, eking out their wartime rations, but also supplementing them with their supplies of fresh milk and eggs and freshly harvested seasonal asparagus, which grew beautifully, but somewhat bizarrely, next to the cesspit.

Enid, Noel's wife and the children's mother, had tuberculosis; one lung had been collapsed and she needed to use her petrol ration as often as it would permit to go up to London to see her doctor. The doctor was known affectionately in the family as Seaweed, and he would draw off any fluid from her only lung so that she could breathe. She would return from these visits and collapse into bed. There was no doubt that she needed to look after herself very carefully. In truth, Enid had often been unwell and everyone knew and understood that her needs were paramount. She frequently reminisced about her very successful work as a physiotherapist and the difference she had made to so many. She, like so many post-WWI women, had enjoyed the freedom to study and have a career. She was certainly a very talented woman in a number of ways. Luckily, she still had her beloved piano and, relishing her own talent, would play it for hours when she felt up to it.

Throughout the family's evacuation, Enid did not feel well and was extremely concerned about her health. She was particularly comforted by her two darling boys, less so by her daughter Mandi. In reality she was terribly disappointed that she had not had the much planned for William to complete her trio of chaps and it was to her great surprise that she found herself mother to a girl. She was not fond of girls. Fortunately, she had been to see Noel Coward's 'Private Lives' the night before her third caesarian and both she and her dear husband Noel had appreciated the name Amanda, if not the character in the story, so the naming issue was solved easily enough. Now it seemed that not only was she a girl, but she was also clumsy, left-handed, rather loud, slow on the uptake and generally gawky with big feet. Just Enid's luck!

Resting was difficult with three children, Tony the Labrador, Kalo the peke, Tabitha Twitchet the cat, the goats and half a dozen chickens, but soon, dear old Mrs Jacklin 'Jackie' came to help, having been bombed out of her London home. One afternoon, when Enid was resting, she asked Jackie for 'a cup that cheers'. To her surprise, Jackie returned with a 'coupla chairs!' It settled into a comfortable relationship after that; Jackie just laughed off her mistakes in a way that Mandi was not old enough or confident enough to do.

The Anderson shelter, with its semi-circle of corrugated iron buried into the earth, was set up in the garden ready for them when the air raid siren went off and they would all shelter in there when necessary and play in there when not. They sometimes heard the drone of the German bombers on their way home after carrying out air raids on London and when the sirens sounded to warn them, they would rush out to the air raid shelter. On one occasion, Anthony was missing, but eventually he came running up, carrying a chicken in his arms. It was his favourite, Speckley, which just had to be saved from the German bombs.

Enid was a very expressive reader and at bedtime, she used to read *Treasure Island* to her three children in a remarkably dramatic way. The description of Blind Pew's stick tap-tapping along the road towards the Admiral Benbow Inn had the children cowering under the bedclothes. They never forgot it.

Mandi was naturally an energetic and enthusiastic little girl and it took a lot to deflate her easy happiness, but over time her mother and grandmother chipped away at what she might have readily become. 'Little hussy', her grandmother Rosa Roberts would hiss at her, 'you caused your mother to be ill. If she had not had that third caesarian, we would not be where we are today'.

Mandi was constantly reminded by her grandmother to think of her mother, not herself, to not be 'sinistre', a French word which her grandmother used and which eventually Mandi came to understand as both gauche and left-handed. Enid's father had been beaten into right-handedness as a child and ultimately became ambidextrous which he claimed served him very well as a dentist and also served to explain this attitude to left-handedness. Mandi also had to pick her feet up, sit properly at table, be quiet, be seen and not heard, listen to quotes from the Bible, know that Sundays were for rest and that she was a girl.

After the First World War and the death of so many young men, Enid had picked up on celebrations every time a boy was born and understood the need to repopulate the country with young men. She had not rationalised this, however, when it came to her own daughter and simply regurgitated an understood belief, leaving Mandi feeling of little value. Having enjoyed the freedom to study and build a career herself, she unwittingly put her own daughter at a huge disadvantage when it came to making her own journey as a woman.

Mandi was reprimanded constantly for minor moments of forget-fulness, misdemeanors, displays of ill manners or leaving a door open. She came to know that margarine was awful food and only butter was good enough and it was a frightful thing to have curly hair or wear the colour blue. She knew never to eat ice cream for it had allegedly been made in a chamber pot under someone's bed and brought out to be sold in unhygienic places and she would certainly never eat in the street.

However much she was tested by her mother, lying in the garden hammock, she just could not spell 'thought, through, thorough and though'[1] and was sharply reprimanded each time she misspelled them;

---

1 I have kept Mum's misspellings throughout this book and marked them with a * rather than 'sic' to celebrate her persistence with the written word despite considerable challenge.

spelling was to challenge her all her life. Indeed, it was hard to get things right at all when it came to her mother and grandmother and no wonder moments of freedom outside with her brothers and the goats provided Mandi with times of joyous release and relief.

The days slipped by and it seemed sensible to send the children to boarding school so that Enid could make her health and recovery the key priority.

Amanda, as she was always known at school, arrived as a boarder at the nearby St Ursula's, aged just seven. It was all rather confusing for this little girl, with a lot more instructions to obey and routines to follow. She would write to her Mummy, Daddy and Granny and tell them about the teachers with their whistles. When the whistle was blown, she had to put on her blazer and sit with her legs straight on the floor. Mandi told them about what she did, the fact that she was in the choir, and asked them how they were, but mostly she lived in her own little world of rather confusing instructions, repetitive routines, moments of freedom outdoors (which she always loved), and encounters with lots of different girls but no particular friends. She ate the frugal but nourishing enough meals, slept in her little iron bed, prayed to win the war, thanked the soldiers for their valiant efforts and tried her best in one confusing lesson after another. Above all, Mandi longed just to be outside when she was allowed to play with another child or just wander about the grounds, looking for flowers, birds, twigs, pebbles or any other wildlife that caught her attention.

After a solid first year and soon after Amanda had turned eight, a teacher wrote positively of her effort, but noted her lack of self-belief in her progress and wondered if her self-confidence had been shaken at some time or other. That thought only arose once in her academic life there and over her four years at the school, Amanda did make slow but sure progress.

On leaving, her teachers reported that she had improved her written and spoken English, but encouraged her to aim higher in literature. Her arithmetic had advanced and she clearly had tried hard, although her efforts had not always shown themselves in her examination results. She had not learned her History, Geography, Science or French carefully enough, but again had made valiant efforts and had shown interest. Her artwork had shown real promise and her art teacher of 1945 had written, 'Amanda's work never fails to interest and show originality'. Her use of colour and composition had also been celebrated. She had been described as 'quite good' at PE, but 'rather wild'.

She was made to be tidy, although this was not natural to her and one report stated, 'Amanda is still losing property. The trouble she has given in this respect has spoiled an otherwise satisfactory term' (July 1946).

Her spirit had been observed as was her lack of capacity to be steady, but she had been deemed to be 'obedient and polite, prompt and punctual'. Whilst she had no particular friends, she had also been considered 'a friend to all' in her reports and this was a phrase that would lift her all her life.

The war ended on the 2nd September 1945 and gradually the Hornsbys made their way back to Central London and their home in Whitehall Court.

Little Miss Mandi, as she had been known to the staff before she was evacuated, was rarely at home now as school kept her away most of the time. When she was in her home, it remained vast, now unfamiliar and strange in a way, changed by the impact of wartime bombing, yet it was somehow reassuring and warming perhaps because it was where she had been born and belonged. She remembered stories of the twin pram in which she used to be pushed out with the dripping hood when it rained and the many excursions with the Masseys and their nannies in St James's Park.

The smart palatial buildings that had miraculously survived the war were over forty years old, imposing on the Victoria Embankment, and of such enormous proportions that they were at once sumptuous, powerful and artistic. Within the buildings were housed various clubs such as the Author's Club, the Junior Army and Navy Clubs and the Farmers' Club, which all had to be licensed by royal decree to serve alcohol and involved Noel making an annual trip to Buckingham Palace to collect this right. To the left were St Paul's and Waterloo Bridge. Nearer to Whitehall was Charing Cross Bridge where the trains would rattle by regularly over the Thames. The trams would similarly clatter on their rails along the Embankment past the imposing County Hall and Scotland Yard close by.

Around her, Mandi could not miss the devastation of the war-bombed capital and the toll of five years of grueling conflict. What a contrast this represented to the simple frugality of evacuation in the fresh and abundant countryside. The change to their lifestyle was not discussed as such and the business of getting on with the next stage of life was paramount.

Mandi picked up on that vital energy and her father's ongoing concerns about finance, but otherwise was removed from the realities of adult and political life. In the afternoons she would go out walking quite sedately in St James Park with her mother's Pekinese, Poo or Pookie as she nicknamed the little dog, or sometimes along Horseguards Avenue as she had done as a small child with her governess.

She remembered those pre-war days at Whitehall Court very warmly. Despite its imposing grandeur, it was more her home back then, but perhaps the war had rendered it more distant and daunting. The days of indulging Little Miss Mandi's favourite pastime of playing hide and seek with the porters were certainly over; back then they were able to welcome guests, but at the same time, still try and find little Miss Mandi hiding somewhere under tables or behind chairs in the big welcoming front hall of the establishment. She now greeted these friendly staff in a much more formal and ladylike way. They used to let her use the service lift and she loved pulling the ropes to get to the different floors. She would laugh, chat and giggle with them as they went up and down in the lift delivering trays, newspapers and mail to different apartments in the very luxurious residence. Now she was a little too grown up for that and the post-war mood was inevitably sombre with so much still to resolve. She spent more time alone if she was at home, collecting and arranging her stamps, doing her needlework and longing for her brothers' return from boarding school.

She had been enrolled at Queen's Club to play tennis, but spent her allotted two hours sitting in the cloakroom as she had no idea what to do when she got there and did not have the confidence to ask. No one asked about her tennis at home, so it went unnoticed. Fortunately this did not go on too long as she took up squash after being introduced to the sport at the Cumberland Club by Sally Arnott, a girl that she had met at school. Through Sally, Mandi got to know various people with whom she could enjoy the game. Regular coaching helped her improve and she played a very acceptable game over time.

When she was hungry at home, Miss Mandi would ring for service and a meal was brought up to her by Bert, the head waiter. She would tend to have salad or hors d'oeuvres as her mother kept a close eye, ensuring that she ate a sensible, balanced diet. Bert would also come into her room in the mornings, the very room that was used during the First World War by the Secret Service, to let her know that her breakfast was ready and waiting under the silver salver in the hall. Bert was steady, reliable and funny and Mandi enjoyed a relaxed and equal relationship with him. She came to rely on Bert and cared about him very much.

Mandi would come down to see her parents whilst they enjoyed their early evening cocktails. Her father, Noel, would go to the mahogany corner cupboard to pour the drinks and serve them on the silver salver, a gimlet of gin and lime for his wife and a Noilly Prat for himself. He would take the gimlet to Enid, poised in her small, compact chair, and settle himself down to enjoy his cocktail in his big comfortable armchair. She would answer their questions politely about her day and share a knowing glance with her beloved father as her mother explained the complications of the day's ailments. It seemed to Mandi that if her mother did not get her own way then she would immediately become ill and her dear father would return home laden with magazines and flowers to make her feel better.

George Bernard Shaw, the playwright and one of the residents, became a good friend of Noel's and sometimes he would be there and from time to time, Mandi would listen to the various adults chatting and discussing how the world was changing, their drinks in hand, full of plans now that the war was at last over. Her mother would express her views as always and would direct Noel on what he needed to do to run Whitehall Court effectively. A product of her time, Enid would make clear that 'we do not want any coloured people in England or people with accents' for she could tolerate neither. Enid had heard that people were lending money which was appalling. Giving was fine, but lending was to be abhorred. Apparently women were going to church in trousers and some without a hat. This was utterly intolerable and certainly did not happen when they went off to St Martin's in the Fields or St Margaret's, Westminster to worship. Why would anyone need to spring clean? Surely their house should always be immaculate. To reference a 'toilet' rather than 'a lavatory' was common and any decent girl would sit with her knees close together, such that Enid would be regularly seen clapping her hands towards Mandi and giving her the directive eye. Anywhere north of St Alban's was of no possible interest to her. She could not bear the idea of the north.

Mandi was never part of these debates, if you could call them that, though her brothers were when they came home. Somehow they had a role to play, as the next generation was going to have to step up and take a lead now. To Enid's mind, it was a good job that they were at Westminster School, full boarding, receiving the vital education to lead them and the country forward. Enid did not believe that anyone with a state education had anything to offer at all.

The boys' achievements and accomplishments were constantly discussed and praised and it seemed to Mandi that they could do no wrong. She was uncritical of her wonderful brothers and came to understand that she was just the more inadequate of the three for a range of repeated reasons which she accepted through a process of relentless osmosis. Sometimes her mother would wonder out loud, as though she were not present in the room, what on earth they were going to do with her and a conversation of possibilities would ensue which invariably ended in the hope that someone rich enough and suitable enough would fall for her and marry her.

'We will have to get her teeth straightened before anyone will fall for her', they would joke.

'How will we disguise her enormous feet?'

'She still can't spell thought, through, thorough and though'.

The hope that she might be more attractive and more accomplished to increase options generated mighty family mirth; Mandi learned early on that teasing is only bullying if you cannot take it, so she laughed along, the butt of much family humour. Her father wrote a poem about her that Mandi can recite fluently to this day and which they would regularly enjoy at her expense during those early evening drinks.

Twelve-year-old Amanda Mary,
No matter how she strives and strains,
Has really no scholastic brains.
Her brothers both are sympathetic,
And help her with her arithmetic.
Elle save en français presque rien,

In fact she calls the cat "le chien",
And yet how prospective grooms will rally,
She's always willing, kind and sweet,
Although she has enormous feet!

The only conclusion ever reached from this family banter was that Mother was right: marriage was surely her best hope.

This harsh humour was countered with music, which was to always fill Mandi's life as a source of joy and solace. In those early days, it was her father playing his violin that gave her the most pleasure, despite his occasionally throwing it onto the sofa in artistic petulance. His rendering of the Thais meditations brings tears to her eyes to this day and she pictures her father's sister on the cello accompanying Noel on violin and Enid on piano, entertaining them all for many an evening with their family concerts and love of music. Her mother's beloved Brahms piano concerto No 2 in B Flat Major Op 83 or Schumann's cello concerto, brought alive by her aunt on her Stradivarius, were frequent fillers.

Mandi was not only uncritical of her brothers, but she adored them and loved it when they introduced her to their friends. During one favourite holiday, Ant, as he was then known, taught her golf with one of his girlfriends. Mandi was a natural and picked up the game very easily, even beating this girlfriend who went on to represent England in later years as a scratch golfer. The opportunity to play golf quickly faded as Ant moved on to other friends and interests, though Mandi would pick it up infrequently a few years later with her father.

A constant visitor to the family from when Mandi was fourteen onwards was Peter. Peter, rather shockingly, came from the north, from Liverpool in fact, and had curly hair to boot. He was introduced to the family by their shared piano teacher, known as Holly, actually Miss Hollis. Peter was a fine pianist and enjoyed music and sports very much. In this regard, he fitted in with the family and was welcomed, especially since he had had such a venerable introduction. He liked the Hornsbys and came to visit from time to time, always asking first if it would not inconvenience them too much, which they thought was hilarious and therefore never refused him. Peter took quite an interest in Mandi and she enjoyed him and the attention, even if she felt as though he was trying to impress her parents through his interest in her.

Firway Cottage had been sold long ago as it turned out that the mist would not lift there and it was ultimately not good for Enid's health. Her parents now owned Mandavant, a fine house on the seafront at Margate which they had bought just before the end of the war and which they had named after their three children, Mandi, David, and Anthony. It had been built in 1939 and not completely finished; there had been a lot of difficulty equipping it and finding appropriate supplies, owing to the wartime shortages. Rationing remained in place for quite a while after the war. Mandi described frequent weekend visits and parties there in her diaries, but she would spend the weekdays in town and understood herself to be a Londoner. The sea air was vital for her mother's health, but her father loved his garden too. This included his beloved begonias, which dominated many a neighbourly conversation, and his pitch and putt course, which he had installed and provided many happy hours of fun over the coming years.

In 1948, the family spent Christmas at Grindelwald, in Switzerland. The Hotel Adler had a fancy dress ball and Enid insisted that her boys go in Mandi's dresses and Mandi in one of their dinner jackets. They remembered it as a night of teenage embarrassment and shame in front of a staid audience. They recalled the hockey match between Cambridge University and the local team and Cambridge being defeated 0–1. They also had a clear memory of their mother playing the harmonium in church on Christmas Day of that year, conscious of both her talent and her social confidence.

The family had lovely holidays in Jersey. The insurance payout from the stolen family silver after Mandavant was burgled even paid for one of them. The redoubtable Rosie—the fearless, indomitable and more than eccentric grandmother—was often present with her dear and softer sister, Auntie Flo. They were familiarly known as 'Arsenic and Old Lace'. Guess which was which! Such were family times back then!

'Judge not that ye be not judged;
condemn not and ye shall not be condemned'.
— JESUS. LUKE VI, 37 —

A TIME TO SCATTER STONES
AND A TIME TO GATHER THEM

Mandi, still always Amanda at school, was at Bartram Gables now, a boarding school in Broadstairs founded in 1872. She joined when she was just eleven in September 1946. It only took a limited number of girls and Amanda remained there until she had to leave at the age of fifteen.

Perched on cliffs one hundred and fifty feet above sea level, the girls were expected to enjoy the expansive view of the Channel as they were invigorated on their daily run along the grass-covered cliffs. The days of running down to the beaches were long gone, with barbed wire preventing any visitors during wartime and for some time after.

The chapel, classrooms, open-air swimming pool, single hard tennis court and studio provided the facilities for a fine all-round education at the cost of sixty guineas per annum while the kitchens, vegetable gardens, poultry farm, comfortable sitting room and dormitories provided the environment for easy living. There were plenty of extras at the cost of about six guineas a year and at various times, Amanda enjoyed supplementary lessons in riding, tennis, Greek dancing and ballet. There were eighty girls at the school and the school was seeking to establish 'each girl's personality' on 'a foundation of reliability, good sense and self-discipline in each one' as well as 'spare no pains and sympathetic care' in 'the formation of good character'. Enid and Noel were hopeful for Mandi's development.

Amanda was to make her first real friend at Bartram Gables. Jennifer Jones returned as a vital confidante at different times over the years and has always been the very friend she was in those days at school. Jen was an excellent horsewoman and loved everything to do with horses. It was a passion that Mandi came to share, as she too learned to become a competent rider.

So the two bonded and Mandi looked forward to the times that she was invited to Jen's home in Amersham in Buckinghamshire. It meant the chance to ride Gunner and Brownie and be pulled round in the riding carriage by little Kitty. There was the occasional gymkhana and pony club and that freedom outside that Mandi so loved. Jen's father was in the cavalry and her mother was very involved with the Women's Institute and was an avid watercolour painter and jam maker. It suited them well that the girls were so well occupied together and they fully supported the friendship. At school they became known as the 'terrible twins', glued to each other as they were, and always out and about on their horses.

Academically, Amanda continued much as she had done at St Ursula's. Her progress was constant in a very cautious kind of way and no one complained. She was invited to extra art as she clearly had talent, but her parents declined the opportunity on her behalf, feeling that there were only so many extras they could afford. Riding was deemed so much better for Amanda, so much healthier, and surely the curriculum should accommodate talent in art at the price they were paying for her education, which was more than they were paying at Westminster. She was never going to be an artist anyway. Miss Beijal was so disappointed in this response and so excited by Amanda's talent that she invited her to attend anyway and Amanda spent many colourful hours drawing and painting with her beloved art teacher.

It was good to know that she was increasingly dexterous at needlework and she went on to impress her especially hard-to-please granny with her love of embroidery. Her French knots and lazy daisy stitch were ultimately enviable. Her parents were confused by her lack of progress in tennis and questioned it after twenty-six private lessons, but accepted ultimately that, whilst it was not a strength, she enjoyed it, and liked to join in with her brothers on holiday, so it was worth persisting. Greek dancing had to be abandoned in the end in favour of ballet. Amanda was uprightly proud to receive the school badge for deportment.

Over time, she became more accomplished and developed some skills and knowledge in a number of areas that were to stand in her in good stead in the years to come.

Suddenly at the age of fifteen, she became very unwell, experiencing difficulty with her breathing from nasal catarrh and spells of giddiness. The school matron was wholly unsympathetic and encouraged her to get on with things, but on one of her rare Sunday visits home during the term, her parents realised that she was too unwell to go back to school. She was having considerable difficulty breathing and suffering some kind of sinus complication.

Her father took her to a doctor the next day in London because he needed to have a boil in his ear examined, but the doctor took one look at Mandi and realised that she was the real concern. The rising sepsis was dangerously close to her brain and action was imperative.

On the 1st of January 1950, Mandi went into Gray's Inn Road Hospital for emergency surgery to have a cyst and polypus removed from her nose, but in fact the now banned Caldwell Luc procedure had to be performed, which required the surgeon to scrape clear areas precipitously close to her brain. Unfortunately, she had a secondary hemorrhage post-operation and did not recover at all easily. She stayed in hospital for quite some while and was kindly cared for. It was then that the seed of becoming a nurse germinated and began to grow.

She was withdrawn from Bartram Gables, unable to study further for the time being and certainly not able to sit for her General Certificate in Education. Her parents were very angry at the lack of care from Bartram Gables and engaged in a battle as to whether the school deserved to have the fees paid or not.

Alone in Whitehall Court with mainly the care of hotel staff to rebuild her health as well as the well-meaning, but infrequent attention from her parents, Miss Mandi gradually returned to full health, a quiet, rather unsure young lady now and mostly very alone. The occasional visit from Peter, now doing his National Service in Greenwich, or her brothers sustained her during that very difficult time.

What to do with her now? Her parents did not feel that they could send her back to Bartram Gables.

Firstly they had read a dreadful report in the Evening News that the two Crittall sisters who ran it were thinking of selling it and there were plans to turn it into a women's open prison.

Secondly, they did not feel that they could trust their daughter into the care of the school that had overlooked serious health issues and put her life at risk.

Thirdly, she had missed a whole year and would be even more out of step with her peers.

Eventually they settled on a London based crammer in Victoria

Street with a view to completing and taking the General Certificate in as long as it took, but hopefully as fast as possible. Mandi renewed her education and headed off to Miss Dixon and Miss Wolfe Tutors on the bus where she paid tuppence for each journey. She would have walked back, but the unpredictable, occasional and frightening pea soupers as they were known, heavy fogs which descended on London in the early '50s, prevented her from being able to find her way. Consequently, the bus seemed the safest means to get to home; even then, she would have to feel her way along the railings to return to the welcome relief of Curtis, one of the hall porters at Whitehall Court.

At Dixon and Wolfe, she studied English, Elocution, French, History, Mathematics, Geography, Art and Scripture. Her reports demonstrated the same effort and the acquisition of basic knowledge and skills, but noted ongoing challenges with interpretation, analysis, application and concentration over a prolonged period and in examinations. In the autumn of 1951, Amanda had succeeded in passing her General Certificate of Education in Religious Knowledge and Art; by the summer of 1952, in English Literature, British History and Geography; and by the autumn of 1952, her French. She had six subjects under her belt and had no real desire to pursue her academic education further and no real qualification to do so.

Live to learn, learn to live
— UNKNOWN —

A TIME TO WEEP
AND A TIME TO LAUGH

With French as one of Mandi's stronger subjects, her parents felt that a spell in France and an opportunity to learn French would be a suitable finishing education. The fact that her father had had to learn French for the hotel trade and hated every second of his time across the Channel was quickly forgotten and Mandi was dispatched on her own to M. and Mme. Pazery, a connaissance of Aunty Flo. Les Pazery lived in 5, rue de Mademoiselle, Versailles. It took some time to get her there as the flight had to be cancelled four times due to the weather. Eventually Mandi gave up on flying and set off by boat and train, ultimately arriving at her unfamiliar and rather unwelcoming destination.

This was an enormous adventure for this unseasoned traveller at seventeen and she was utterly bewildered by the whole experience. She found herself abroad for the first time in post-war France, living with an old couple in their seventies and their nervously disposed and rather anti-social daughter Christiane in her mid-thirties. They lived in a dilapidated house with imposing front doors, but very little money to match the size of those doors and on which to get by, and very little interest in living after a difficult and tiring war.

Religion played a key part in their lives, and Mandi was quickly taught the Lord's Prayer in French; they considered her philosophical views naïve and ill-thought out, especially when she suggested that one day in the future in heaven she would meet her little dog, Poo, once they had both died. They laughed at her and Mandi often felt very low during this time, and was forced to conclude that the young could not live with the old.

Christiane's unexplained nervous trouble involved frequent visits to the doctor; Mandi often went along to these as there was little else to do. She had nothing in common with the family at all and her French was very basic. They took her to the Palace of Versailles once and corrected her hard-learned French so that she did gain some fluency, but with very tentative confidence in the language. Fundamentally, a long and tedious three months ensued, but she adapted to it and got on with it, making the very best of what was supposed to be an opportunity.

Mandi returned to writing a diary and letters at this point. She had kept a diary before, but her grandmother, Rosa, had found them and mocked their content and their spelling, so Mandi had burned all the stories about her early life. Despite that, she now found expression again in her writing, often factual, with the odd punctuated expression of feeling. Perhaps it was the only way she could be heard.

Her 1953 diary recorded that it was her daily job to fetch *'une baguette, une ficelle* (types of long French loaves) and *un demi-litre de lait'. February 1953.*[1] Once this task was done, she would do some light house duties, go to church and sketch. One of her sketches showed the mice hiding in the kitchen, near the bread bin, and in the bathroom, which she found abhorrent, but about which she could do nothing. She learned how difficult the war had been for them, that money was still very tight and was the reason why they were so thin and lived on so little. One day when she was delivering church magazines, she was shocked to see a family through a window eating fish-heads off newspaper on the bare floorboards. There was soup for lunch every day and Mandi would often make this thin gruel of potato, carrot, onion, salt, pepper and water.

Mandi filled her diary with half-broken French, indicating her growing dexterity with the language, but she was still clearly quite at sea in any fluent conversation. She would also write to Tudor, her boyfriend at the time.

Tudor was Ant's greatest friend and Junior Welsh golf champion. His mother did not want him to have a girlfriend, in order that he could concentrate on his sport, so it was an infrequent and rather stealthy relationship. Mandi had been with him to the Westminster School Dance, courtesy of Ant and had a brilliant time. On the way back, Tudor dared her to knock on the 10 Downing Street front door which she did, then took off her shoes to *'run like the wind'* to escape any consequence. It was hugely exciting and recorded as such. Tudor thought that she was great fun and asked her to be his girlfriend. They barely knew each other, but thoughts of him and a repetition of

1 Mandi's diary and letter entries are recorded henceforth in italics

that first kiss and fun back in London made her laugh and sustained
her during the long and lonely stay in France.

The amount of bread and starch she ate meant that she felt tired
and unwell and her periods at this time were very irregular and
confusing to her. She had started her first one on the golf course with
her brother and he had come to the rescue with his hanky. Her mother
had been good to talk to about them, but communication was so
difficult from abroad in those days and she was alone trying to work
out why she felt so awful. Diary entries on this were frequent and
expressed her anxiety and lack of ease with her own body.

31 MARCH 1953

Haven't been to the aunt for two days and where is Jane? Jane
still hasn't arrived. She is a pest! Jane still isn't here. What the hell
is she doing? (On and off throughout the French visit Jan 19)

'Going to the aunt' was clearly a euphemism for emptying her
bowels and 'Jane' one for her period. Mandi had no one to turn to
for help about these feminine and body issues and her diary left her
questions asked but unanswered at that juncture of her life.

On her return, things picked up for the late teenager and she found
herself being invited out by her brothers' friends and meeting their
various girlfriends. She was still friends with Tudor, but he became
one of a few boyfriends.

David was at Cambridge now studying architecture and Ant went
into the RAF, signed up for four years, and returned from Winnipeg
as a night navigator with the air force. His Westminster friends
were very much around in London and a fair number of their friends
enjoyed taking her out to events and dances.

Over the holidays, Mandi had been sent to ballroom dancing
lessons with her brothers and her waltz, foxtrot, quickstep and tango
were really quite passable. At one dance which took place at the home
of her dance school, Eve Tynegate Smith on Baker Street, Mandi
danced with her dance school partners whose nicknames she diarised;
Ears, who was short and his ears would keep brushing her face as they
danced, and Slinky, Blondie and Bighead, whose names all speak for
themselves. Bighead was clearly not quite the master of the tango that
he thought himself to be; the real master was her father.

On one occasion, she danced the exhibition tango to the Carroll
Gibbons orchestra with her father at the Savoy with her plaits piled

high upon her head. Spied by one of his friends, they all laughed heartily when the friend commented, 'By Jove old boy, you take them young!' Mandi still hums happily along to the tango medley, 'Jealousy, adiós muchachos', to this day.

Around that time, Mandi noticed that she seemed to have gone up rather in her mother's estimation and their relationship appeared to have improved now that they could discuss her social life, her growing array of admirers and what she should wear to balls and parties. Perhaps her big feet were not going to be such a problem after all!

She and Jen, her great friend, had not forgotten each other and met up often and wrote to each other when they were apart. Jen went to Cheltenham Ladies College, whilst Mandi worked through her education.

On September 12th 1953, they gathered for a Bartram Gables reunion. Whilst this afforded an opportunity to catch up with other girls, it was really a chance for them to laugh together in a rowing boat on the Serpentine and hatch an adventure for the future. They dearly wanted to go cycling somewhere together sometime and planned and plotted to try and make this idea happen. They reminisced about the talk they had been to on reincarnation and had a massive chat about religion.

13 SEPTEMBER 1953
Jen has been confirmed. I have been contemplating it for a long
time and I MUST make a move.

Mandi was still only seventeen on her return from France and her plan to become a nurse was now somewhere on her parents' agenda, though certainly not her mother's first choice for her. In the meantime, a grounding at the Triangle Secretarial College in London seemed like a good idea to them.

Mandi began the course on the Ist September 1953, aged just eighteen, and set about learning shorthand, copywriting and dictation, seeking to improve her speeds every day. She became skillful at card indexing and filing, letter writing, duplicating, bookkeeping, committee procedure, the rudiments of banking, income tax and company work. By the time she left, she could claim skills in all these and ninety words-per-minute in a five-minute test in shorthand, fifty in copywriting over ten minutes and forty-two in dictation over five minutes. She knew she was not the fastest, but she had completed it whilst having a lot of fun with her many suitors and it was done. These skills would always prove useful to her and even without knowing that, characteristically she had given the course her all.

Once she had passed her driving test, which she did easily enough, she would drive her father's car, 'William' (named in honour of the third son her parents never had), to Mandavant. Dear 'William' was shared with her brothers and provided the carriage for many a local event and parties.

Mandi loved speed, and drinking and driving was not taboo in those days. She often went with one of her brothers or of course one of their many friends. Her relationship with her mother continued to improve and she too was equally sociable, inviting scores of people to stay at Mandavant. Mandi focused on her socialite life and worked hard on dieting and exercising whenever she could. Her behaviour did not meet with maternal approval exactly, but there was certainly less opposition. She always found time to visit her dear friend Jen and go riding together.

Now that she knew she could be great fun at a party, Mandi rather enjoyed the attention of the various men she met, leading them on, without ever going too far. Her mother had instilled in her from her early teens that if she ever got things wrong in this regard, she would be thrown out of the house and left to fend for herself. Whilst Mandi never understood herself to be attractive, she came to realise that being a party girl meant that she seemed to go up in her family's esteem and was not short of admirers, which fed her fragile confidence. She enjoyed having this string of admirers and this much busier social life.

One day Ant picked her up in his Austin with Anthea, his then girlfriend. The plan was to drive to Kingston to visit Julian, another of Ant's friends. Mandi had a wonderful day flirting with Julian and enjoyed a short dalliance with him. Peter loved to take her out too when he came to London from Liverpool, and saved hard to be able to take her to dance. Mike, whom she found *rather spotty and smelly, but rather a poppet'*, was always wanting to take her out. He was in the Navy at Dartmouth and she had met him at the Wards' party that David had taken her to. She had worn her yellow gown and he had flattered her, called her *'darling'* and kissed her the evening of the party in the garden. Thereafter he seemed unable to leave her alone, but she did not really bother after that, for there was one late night after another with Greg and then Robin and the New Year's Eve with Alastair to enjoy.

Unfortunately, Alastair got held up and she fell for disabled Jim that night. Jim had been wounded in military service and would never walk again, but Mandi found him quite charming and his need to be cared for really moved her; she took a long time to forget Jim. However, their paths did not readily cross and John was already keen to take her out, not to mention the overly amorous squash coach. Mandi had actually got her own squash racquet by now and was playing various other girls every Thursday after her fixed lesson in which she fended off both the ball and the coach.

She still had time to fit in Greg and Allan, and Tudor and Robin were still around. In February 1954, Mandi mused:

> Gosh, I have quite a list of boyfriends at the moment. I hope I'm not
> going to turn into that sort of rather fast girl. I suppose they are all
> the boys' friends really.

She was enjoying the theatre too and her range of London activities was definitely beginning to broaden. She was even invited to become a debutante and come out in high society, but Mandi flatly refused this opportunity, sure that this life was not for her, and her parents were inclined to agree.

Mandi undoubtedly knew how much she enjoyed mixing with people now, relishing the different characters:

> 18 FEBRUARY, 1954
> Go dancing at 1 o'clock with Bill at Eve Tynegate Smith. Denise is
> there, a pro at Latin American. She has got some venereal disease
> and has treatment at Guy's. I promise to take her home one day,
> but don't quite think she is the family's cup of tea.

She never did take her home! One 3.00 am night after another in mid–1954 left her feeling pretty tired and the constant phone calls and dating requirements of these different men were obviously rather exhausting and unsustainable.

> 24 FEBRUARY 1954
> I can't get over the way Jim kissed me the other day. It felt ergent*
> and frustrated and to tell the truth I was a bit frightened. The
> sooner I am safe in Guy's the better.

Fortunately that time was coming...

You make a living by what you can get;
you make a life by what you can give.
— WINSTON CHURCHILL —

A TIME TO TEAR DOWN
AND A TIME TO BUILD

So Mandi was to become a nurse. Her parents had agreed, but there was only one possible training hospital and it had to be Guy's Hospital, London. That was of course her mother's decision, since she had been there. Mandi was extremely intimidated by this and anxious that she would not be good enough, but her mother was not having any of that nonsense and the enrolment procedures were completed.

She was to start on Wednesday, March 24th 1954. She had previously been introduced to Jelly, a schoolfriend of her friend Jen, who was also to become a nurse at Guy's. They had discussed their pay, £7 per month as probationers. Mandi reflected on this and wrote in her diary after that meeting:

MARCH 24, 1954
To think that I could earn at least £5 per week as a secretary, but
what's money if your heart is in nursing?

On that day, she met Jelly and her parents for a pub lunch before heading to Holmesdale, the nurses' home in Redhill, to settle in together. This was where they were to stay for the first three months of their preliminary training. Mandi was in Room 23 with one other trained nurse and Jelly down the corridor in Room 20 with three other girls. Mandi wished she could have shared a room with the three other girls for the fun and companionship. Holmesdale was run by Sister Janet, a middle-aged spinster who seemed quite inhuman.

The first job was to get into uniform and ensure that the cap fitted. Bread, butter, jam and ginger cake provided a reviving tea and a chance to get to know each other before Sister Janet gave a lecture on general nursing. Mandi quickly belonged amongst the nurses, created relationships with them comfortably and felt happy and at ease. Jelly, Jill and more were to become lifelong friends.

Once tea was over, the afternoon bed making class ensued. Hospital corners confirmed straight and uncreased sheets which would not slip about; this would be something to practise until it became a honed and speedy skill.

A tour of the premises before supper.

After a mostly healthy meal of soup, cauliflower au gratin, potatoes, custard and a cigarette, Mandi collapsed into bed at 10.00 pm.

There were very few diary entries over the coming weeks, but enough to glean a picture of the kind of routine that Mandi experienced to pass her lengthy probationary period of nursing. A 6.15am start to the day and a bus ride to Guy's for breakfast and an 8.45am service. Then on to the ward to do the beds and the flowers, then perhaps a fracture bed, rub a patient's knees with spirit and powder, do the bed pans, attend a lecture or learn how to cook steamed fish and steamed pudding.

So the early days went on, merging into each other with their hard work, high expectations, endless learning, constant emptying of bedpans and serving of meals, until six weeks in Mandi was once again taken extremely ill with appendicitis this time and found herself unable to continue. Mandi was one of the first ever to have keyhole surgery by Mr Eckhof who rescued her from her poisoned appendix.

Once recovered, she was unable to return to her cohort as she had missed too much, so she was placed on the Dorkus ward to gain some experience as an assistant to the nurses until July 1954 when she was able to join the next set of forty trainees and begin again; this time she noticed her boosted confidence as she repeated those first six weeks. It also brought her fabulous new friends. Dear Sue Mace was to be a lifetime confidante and friend among many others.

The time came for Mandi to take her examinations at the end of the three months of preliminary training. She had to prepare for an abdominal examination in her practical, explain systemic veins in her written paper and respond to Professor Verdulio's questions in the oral exam. She did extremely well and for the first time in her academic life surprised herself with her success, although there is nothing to evidence that she even mentioned it back home.

She went on to write a letter of welcome to the new occupants of Room 20 at Holmesdale, advising them that the feeling of strangeness would pass, just as it had with her and that once their uniforms had been laundered a few times, they would come to fit better.

16 OCTOBER 1954

The sisters are really very sweet, their barks are worse than their bites. There are two disadvantages to this place;

1) *Incessant work*
2) *No men except Pip the dog*
3) *Sister Janet's eagle eye*
4) *Cookery with Mrs Copper at Redhill technical college.*

Man is as happy as he makes up his mind to be
— UNKNOWN —

A TIME TO KILL
AND A TIME TO HEAL

And with that probationary period behind her and with the right to complete her training for state registered nurse, the journey continued.

On Astley Cooper ward, Mandi discovered all manner of things. Bobbi Bodwell, 37 years, was recovering from the removal of his rectal polyp, but was not too keen to eat after his operation.

> JANUARY 17 1955
> What don't come in nurse, can't come out

In this way, he took his own control of the situation. Hernias, splenectomies, esophagoscopies, arterial disease, amputations, ruptured patellar tendons, carcinomas of the stomach, bladder and rectum, and fractured skulls were just some of the experiences on men's surgical, with plenty of banter and bedpans to go with it. 'I saw a dead person for the first time in my life', wrote Mandi, in a matter-of-fact accepting sort of way.

> 19 JANUARY 1955
> Arthur. 79 years, died at 11.15am yesterday. I had to dash around to find Sister to tell her that his pulse was imperseptable* and his respiration had ceased. Sister told me to ring the House Officer which I did. When I actually saw the body though, I wasn't frightened though it wasn't altogether an attractive sight.

One of her patients Bernard in bed 8 was so impressed with her dedication to duty that he nicknamed her 'Puffpuff' for her ceaseless efforts and was sure that even if an earthquake were to blow them up, she would still go on doing her duty relentlessly round the ward. She would nip here and there responding to a beep, delivering a bottle, a sputum mug, a vomit bowl, doing a rectal saline. She would joke,

> 7 FEBRUARY 1955
> The motion was moved by Mr Summer and carried by Nurse Hornsby.

Mandi would still go out, but this was greatly curtailed by long hours nursing, nights on duty and her study. She missed one staff ball as she had to work, sluicing apparently. Her May Ball with Greg was obviously a happy event. She realized that her life was rewarding and fulfilling when she decided to stay in at Holmesdale for the weekend and enjoy her new nursing friends, rather than go home.

On the Saturday of this weekend, the would-be nurses headed off in Mandi's car *'Dodgy'* to Boxhill to picnic. Her father had decided to give her a car for her twenty-first birthday, but he could not resist giving it to her early, on the 26th August just after her twentieth birthday, in fact. It was a Morris Minor saloon and she had named it Dodgy. It was not unusual for her to fit five nurses in it as she did on this day to Boxhill. With Merrydown cider, lemonade, and sandwiches of every type, she had the best day and revelled in the fun of her girlfriends out enjoying the sunshine and the drive. The stories that they could share together of their various patients and experiences had them giggling all day long. Mandi was always shockingly vulgar, never held back and was loved and known for it.

She spent another weekend off with Jelly's parents in Manchester. Jelly was now known by her actual name, Lilah. Mandy was so tired that she just arrived at Lilah's house and fell asleep. Luckily, Lilah and her parents understood and a weekend of backgammon, good food and gentle walking restored her for further demanding shifts. She was also in very frequent contact with Peter as well as John and Greg who would regularly write and invite her to events. She did not receive any Valentines on the 14 February of that year 1954 though and noted to herself in her diary, *No Valentines Hornsby! You're slipping!* She also liked just to go home occasionally and would go to the theatre or just relax.

17 FEBRUARY 1955
Take Pookie to Green Park and walk along Piccadilly. Buy a hot water bottle and some chemist requisites. Return to salad round the fire with 'Cheshire VC', a superb book. Write to John, Peter, Chris and Mr Kennedy. Dad settles down to his tapestry and Mum is making net curtains for Blenkarne.

She would occasionally play golf with her Dad in Margate and lots of cards with the family. There was always a cocktail party or few to go to. Rare visits from dear Jen were also very sustaining.

24 FEBRUARY 1954
Tea house of an August Moon. Most unusual—needless to say

> *Jen and I enjoyed ourselves completely and talked about*
> *reincarnation until after 2.00am again.*

Peter visited the family when he could and often missed catching up with Mandi as she was nursing. However, he took her out on April 7 1955 to the Berkeley to dance. They returned back to the flat to get a drink when Peter started becoming *'somewhat pationate'**.

> *APRIL 7 1955*
> *I told him I looked upon him as a brother. I slapped his face once*
> *or twice when he deserved it. He said he wished he hadn't got*
> *a conscience. I thought it was a jolly good thing he had. I didn't*
> *respond very much to his amorous advances, but I must say, I*
> *spent a most enjoyable evening.*

She struggled a bit with the way that evening left her feeling though and her brothers thought it was huge fun to call her *'Frusty'*. Teasing Mandi continued to be huge sport for them, but they loved her dearly in their fraternal, jocular sort of way. Mandi used to discuss Peter with them and the whole family would dismiss him as a possible suitor. He came from the north to begin with; he had curly hair and was inclined to podginess with possible man boobs!

Peter continued to be in touch and wrote a while later, inviting her to his Cambridge May Ball and Glyndebourne, but then similar invitations came in from Greg and John shortly afterwards. They were all to be disappointed as Mandi was working too hard to go to any of these events. She loved being so popular though and it made her feel confident.

Mandi laughed a great deal on the men's surgical ward. Apart from building her capacity to prepare a patient before and after anaesthesia; cleanse and sterilise instruments, catheters, bowls and syringes; dilute various lotions; prepare trollies; and dress wounds and dispose of soiled dressings, she found that she was very popular with the men. Taking a temperature often meant her hand being taken and placed where the men felt really hot and she would have to admonish them and advise them that this was not the way to take a temperature, but she could always do it lightheartedly and make them laugh.

She got on really well with the very down to earth cockneys and was grateful to her brothers for training her in their laddish sense of humour. No vulgarity shocked her and she could tell a joke or rhyme with the best of them as well as share in the jellied eels, a favourite cockney snack brought in by many a visitor. She was clearly a tonic on that ward, but her time was up and she was onto the women's ward, called Sarah, in mid-April of 1955.

She moved every three months to another ward for learning, appreciating the wonder of healing and the brutality of killing illness, making happy connections on the way. She made new friends among the nurses too, and Anne, another junior nurse, was to be one whom she would take home and know all her life.

As she moved from ward to ward, she learned about new special-isms and built her skills through doing enemas, swabs, bandages, bloods, stitch and clip removal, shaving, catheterisations, insertion of pessaries and vaginal douches. Bed making, delivering and emptying bedpans, blanket bathing, positioning patients, taking temperatures, serving meals, filling up hot water bottles, cleaning up vomit and diarrhoea, and nail and toe cutting were just some of many mundane other jobs that were familiar now and were part of the role.

Chatting and connecting to her patients, making them feel loved and cared for, as well as getting them to laugh if it did not hurt, rewarded her hugely. Her sense of humour developed further, perhaps lurking from her father, and she could recite and invent short and rather vulgar limericks and quip merrily. She was also brilliant at reciting poetry and there is no doubt that most patients would have left a lot more familiar with Hilaire Belloc and the plight of the unfortunate Jim who 'slipped his nurse's hand when he was able' and got eaten by a lion or Matilda 'who told such dreadful lies' that when there really was a fire, they only shouted 'little liar' and she burned alive. Then there was Sonia Snell who got stuck to the newly painted lavatory seat until someone came to saw it off her rear end, not to mention the more serious Highwayman of Alfred Noyes who came 'riding, riding up to the old inn door' and the adventure began. Mandi loved to keep her patients' spirits up and she was building experience.

In May 1955, Mandi was taking care of Mrs Reynolds who was only just alive. That same day, a certain Mrs Day had been admitted and Mandi wrote about her as a lastingly significant patient. She recorded the following exchange:

9 MAY 1955
She said: 'I want the toilet'. I gave her a bedpan and she then said, 'I've come over awful queer'. On removal of the bedpan, there

was a baby in it, about 6 inches long and the placenta was lying
on the bed. I picked it up and then deposited it in the bedpan.

Mandi learned from Sister that this unmarried woman had used some knitting needles vaginally and by some miracle not hurt herself or the baby, and managed to expel her twenty-two-week-old baby into the bedpan. She went on to make a full recovery.

The next evening Mandi was off duty and returned home, shattered to find her parents having a rather smart dinner party at Whitehall Court. Without thinking, Mandi burst into the dining room:

'Mum, Dad, I've had an abortion', she blurted out, only to be met with a stunned and clearly horrified silence.

When she realised the shocked confusion that she had caused, Mandi explained that it was the first abortion of one of her patients that she was referring to and felt the tangible relief of all present. One simply did not talk about abortions or indeed acknowledge that they occurred in that era. She got drunk that night!

Mandi was then sent back to Sarah ward.

11 MAY 1955

Mrs Reynolds died at 1.45pm. She had not had anything to drink all day. I had a funny feeling inside me when I realised that she had left this earth. Nurse Hawkins asked me to get brown wool, forceps, six inches of bandage and a bowl of carbolic. Then we stripped her bed, leaving only the sheet. We covered her eyes with damp lint squares, placed brown wool under her jaw and on top of her head, cut a slit in the bandage and tied up her jaw after having put in the false teeth. We used the forceps to plug the rectum and vagina with brown wool dipped in carbolic. We straightened her knees, placed brown wool between her knees and ankles and tied them straight, placed her hands under her bottom and whilst rigor mortis set in, cleared everything out of the cubicle without washing things, parceled all her belongings in brown paper. I then went off duty and when I returned the cubicle was bear* Dear Lord take Mrs Reynolds into your keeping, she will live far happier with you now that her body no longer burdens her.

Mandi was 19 when she experienced this, confused by her relationship with God. She spoke to the Lord in her diary:

20 MAY 1955

I'm a selfish creature; what am I to this great universe, but dear
Lord, help me to lead a better life and with your help and speed
I will try (very hard) to carry you in my heart always.

She describes the joy and freedom she feels in her car when she is driving too fast with the windows down and the air rushing past. She asks the Lord to keep her safe and the fear she feels when going on to a ward and does not know what to expect and asks for protection there too.

On May 26 1955, Mandi was told to report to Luke ward. There she blanket bathed and fed innumerable patients and was so energetic in her duties that she threw away the urine of a recently operated-on diabetic patient who had lost a limb, urine that was vitally needed for testing. She resolved the problem by sucking up the leaked urine on his thighs and bedding with a pipette so there was enough for a sample. A dedicated and resourceful nurse she certainly was!

Mandi got lots of presents for her nursing efforts and particularly celebrated the many packets of cigarettes that came by way of reward. It definitely was the '50s.

Mandi received some very positive feedback for her efforts and commitment to her nursing and, despite her hectic social life, would usually be seen with her anatomy or circulation notes or whatever needed learning close by. She was keen to do well and attended all lectures, listening as attentively as she could, but tests and exams were still not easy for her and it was always a surprise to her when she passed.

She also had the challenge of her inner voice that would repeat those early messages that she was stupid. Many women of this era received this message, whether because of dysfunctional families or because of strong social and cultural factors that privileged boys and devalued girls. Mandi was no exception. At that stage of her life, she was incapable of unpacking these ideas, with no psychological understanding at the time of the damage that such messaging had done or how to reframe it.

June 8 1955
Describe 1) the thoracic duct 2) lymph 3) atrio ventricular valves
4) superficial veins of the lower limb.

Surgical, theatre, pharmacology, first aid and hygiene all provided lots more learning and tests and she did well enough to pass. This led to opportunities and on 1 June 1955, Mandi was asked to stand in as Head Nurse for an afternoon, but she would have to wait to the end of September of that year to be asked to stand in more regularly. Usually it was a role for a fully qualified nurse, so she felt lifted and encouraged, but never good enough.

Anyway, she did as Sister asked and completed the stomach wash out and dressed a penis and the stump of a limb, but luckily Sister, who was keeping a close eye, stopped her giving eight rather than four pills to Bed 4 or it might have been a disaster. The mistake was almost the reinforcement Mandi needed to prove to herself and others that she was a fool, something she fell into so easily as a result of that early childhood messaging

Mandi loved her *'adorable'* patients and took time to write about their various ailments, families, characters, the stories she shared with them and the laughter that engulfed them as the various jobs got done. She would do any task, even when others refused.

> *3 AUGUST 1955*
>
> *Mr B is a repulsive man and no one wants to shave him, so I do it. He insists that I use sunlight soap, he coughs masses of sputum up in the most gruesome * fashion. He has six filthy teeth in his lower jaw and suffers from halitosis.*

She described how he would *'blow off wantonly as she washed his back'* and again how *'repulsive'* she found him. However repulsive, she would find some way to laugh and she certainly did not shirk the task.

Mandi was then moved onto another female ward, Bright Ward, where she learned about anaemia, septicemia, rheumatoid arthritis, osteoporosis, renal infection, brain abscess, tuberculosis and broncho-pneumonia, hypertension and much more.

She wrote about Mrs May:

> *2 SEPTEMBER 1955*
>
> *The garments she was wearing were: coat, hat, gloves, bag, three cardigans, two tee shirts, one bra, two petticoats and a corset, all held together by safety pins and stockings held up. Aren't I horrid! I've rarely seen such a vast abdomen and derriere and bosoms, like semi-deflated balloons. Poor woman, but she is the sort of woman who thinks she owns the place once she has arrived.*

Then there was Mrs Drysdale a day later, suffering from sub-acute bacterial endo carditis and *'an absolute scream'*. She would tell stories of dancing so tightly with a man that she had to ask him to remove his pipe from his trousers and the hotel cleaner who powdered her nose with the hotel guest's dead husband's ashes, thinking they were face powder.

Mandi recalled the time that she tried to do an Oxbile enema and removed the catheter really slowly, but it all went wrong and Mandi got spattered from head to toe with the very unsavoury contents. She described how they all cried laughing.

The round of practical and theoretical learning continued and the testing went on in between much socialising and scraping in just before the midnight curfew, narrowly avoiding Sister's eagle eye. She always had a good tale to tell, often of breaking the rules and just getting away with it.

Mandi went out with Greg in Cambridge on 11 June 1955. They went for dinner and to a film. She observed in her diary that day:

> Greg gripped my hand somewhat tight and I had to break free as
> he pressed on my ulna nerve and artery causing numbness. I had
> visions of Raynaud's disease. He was rather sweet, but somehow
> Peter affects me much more despite his wavy hair and irritating
> mannerisms.

Greg pursued her and Mandi noted that his pet word was 'capital'. That became irritating very quickly, but Greg persisted with more invitations, postcards and letters from wherever he went. A very keen admirer called Tony continually tried to win Mandi over, but she rarely had time or energy for him. Mandi found a note in her room around this time, June 1955, from Lilah who had come to visit her in Guy's:

> 'You are the end. You're just NEVER IN! Come and see me
> some time!'

Mandi, who still loved her dancing and went to dances whenever she could, with whomever invited her, though Peter and Greg were still waiting, noted in her diary that this was the year in which rock and roll was born and she loved listening and dancing to Bill Haley.

She also noted that Winston Churchill resigned as Prime Minister, Ruth Ellis was hanged causing public uproar, the new Queen televised her Christmas message for the first time and ITV was launched. Television was popularising and the entertainment industry booming. With war rations abolished, the modern supermarket was making its appearance. After WWII, women were, as in the case of WWI, expected to return to the home, and let the men have their jobs back. Many did, but, again, many did not and more and more women were enjoying the workplace. There was a dramatic increase in birth rates, and new housing was changing the landscape. A new home cost £2,000 and an office worker earned £14 a week. Mandi earned £8 a month, but received full board and lodging, and it was well worth it, even if she had to be in before midnight. Stirling Moss won the British Grand Prix. The development of better cars in the 50's led to the birth of the 'commuter age', with the first suburbs beginning to appear. New values appeared; there was pressure to 'maintain appearances' within towns, so more families attended church, community social functions, etc. The population stood at 51,199,000 while unemployment figures had reached a high of 181,000.

Much of this might appear to be random information, but little Miss Mandi was now away from the privileged Whitehall Court and earning her own living and contributing to and noticing the world about her. Mandi followed history, noting important events of the years and decades, not necessarily understanding that by marking these events alongside her personal milestones and tribulations, she was tracking the ways modern trends influenced and transformed her.

Meanwhile, she continued living everyday life as a nurse and young woman, struggling to survive on her meagre salary. Undoubtedly her tough nursing life was subsidised by some fine lifestyle supported by her parents, but Mandi was both coming alive and living at this time in her world of contrasts. She was growing and thriving and this period, the arduous, traditional nursing training and the gradual emergence of social confidence, was to shape the woman of the years to come significantly.

Peter, who by now had had at least five invitations refused as Mandi was working, was about to be rewarded for his patience. His chance was to come when Robin could not make the Dorchester Ball and Mandi phoned Peter to ask him to stand in. Mandi wrote out his whole letter the day after that event in her diary:

2 NOVEMBER 1955

My dear Mandi, It was wonderful to see my funny, little (?) Amanda again—thank you so much for asking me, I really loved every moment of it, that is until I had to leave you. I felt rather sad. I wish life could stand still and wait sometimes, but then it won't. Now I'm getting philosophical.

You are a darling, Mandi dear. I adore you, God knows why! You beat and kick me. I am sure no animal can be so bullied and bruised. I'm treated with no respect; I won't say as a chattel, but as a dog. People are wondering today why I find it difficult to walk. I shall never have to carry you again....I'm so looking forward to seeing you soon. Do come soon Mandi, and again, you silly old thing, PLEASE, PLEASE, look after that mortal frame of yours. There's not another like it!

With much love ma Cherie, votre Pedro, Don Juan, alias Earlam.

Mandi and Peter began to write to one another regularly, talking about all manner of matters. In fact, they talked quite a lot about their weight in the letters they share over the coming two years. Mandi regularly put her weight in her diary and it seemed to fluctuate between nine and a half and nearly eleven stones and she was very strict with Peter telling him not to get fat and not to weigh more than twelve stones.

She was clearly becoming very fond of him though as it wasn't long before she found herself knitting him a jumper and she went to visit him in Liverpool, warmly describing her first meeting with his family in the last week of November of 1955. Her letters to him were signed off with the phrase 'tons of love', and developed a relaxed, teasing tone and familiarity, telling him, for example, to fold his letters properly so they opened at the greeting line. He had definitely stepped ahead of the many other admirers. Greg was also writing to her at this time, but his letters did not get copied into the diary.

Towards the end of 1955 and early 1956, Mandi was Head Nurse on surgical. She paid the price of burning the candle at both ends and really struggled with sore throats, swollen glands and general ill health. She found it difficult to sustain her lifestyle and she was under pressure on the wards. After one tough night, Sister would not let her go off duty until she had named all the patients and their updates. She could do all the ones she had supported in the night, but not the others, and was not allowed to go until she had learned them. By this time, she had missed the bus back to the nurses' home and was not allowed out in her nurses' uniform. It took her the rest of the morning to find clothes to borrow to get back for some much-needed sleep.

However, Mandi persisted, still learning, building experience and taking her tests. She wrote to *'Pedro'*, a now familiar pet name for Peter, of a warmer mentor:

4 JANUARY 1956

Sister paid me a rather splendid compliment the other night by saying that they were so short of Head Nurses (you officially have to have been training for three years before you're classed as such) that she was taking me on as I was a reliable Junior Stripe and putting me on as Relief Head Nurse on Nuffield C. This is where the aristocracy of England lie when ill. Say a little prayer as I'm utterly nerve-racked at the moment. I should go wizardly thin with the responsibility and worry.

She wrote to him on the 16 January 1956 after ten frantic nights of responsibility of being Head Nurse. Both of them had had near accidents in their respective cars, and had admitted their love of speed to each other:

Don't kill yourself my love, think of all the good food your mother's given you that will be wasted.

Mandi did not necessarily mean to be funny, but her diary entries were often naturally so. She told him of a fellow nurse still very much in training who was asked to go and insert suppositories. She set off with the two suppositories in a kidney tray and looked at her patient, unsure of where to insert them. In response to her training and the ferocious Sister in the background, the trainee nurse thought it best to show initiative. The next minute the patient had the two suppositories sticking out of his ears and nurse returned her empty kidney tray back to its rightful place with the job done, only facing the consequences later and giving all the other trainees a huge laugh.

In September 1956 Mandi wrote to Peter to tell him that she had finished her schedule of practical work. Her next experience was to take her to night duty in what she described as the *'Loony Bin'*.

3 NOVEMBER 1956

Last night was quite a night. A dear old senile lady suddenly coughed up 24 ounces of blood from her lungs and I had to lay up a trolley pretty smartish to replace some intravenously. 3 doctors came dashing up and all would have been well if the other patients hadn't started playing up, but first a Jewish boy of 25 years went off his rocker and started battering his bonce against the wall that nearly killed him. An old faggot woke up who is an hysteric and started catching imaginary mice, that were jumping up and down on the bed. A schizophrenic with huge staring eyes, would insist on parading up and down the corridor talking about economics and commerce one minute and wildly gesticulating the next in a bizarre manner. What with feeding three hungry doctors at the early hours of the morning, giving approximately 30 injections of every type of stuff, comforting the dying and crying, wrestling with the insane, trying to write a full report on every patient, it was quite a night.

Then at 5.20am the dear old soul started coughing up more blood and was too weak to cough it up. Though I half flung her over the side of the bed, she died in the proceeds at 5.30am. It was a good thing that she went to her maker, but to watch her go black and die in my arms was not too pleasant. Anyway, tonight is much quieter, so I am writing to my beloved. I've been practicing a love song that I am going to sing to you on your return. The piano piece is not going too well though.

Mandi partied hard throughout 1956 and 1957, although she had become committed to her relationship with Peter, a commitment they confirmed just before his departure for Nigeria in May of 1956 following their romantic sojourn in Jersey with her family. Mandi had invited Peter on this holiday and that had been the turning point in their relationship. He wrote in his letter of the 1st September 1956 that the Jersey holiday served to make sure of the thoughts he had been increasingly having during the previous months and in it, he was sure that Mandi would be the one to know how she felt and would declare her feelings when she was ready; he advised her to take her time about it.

He had asked her father for Mandi's hand in marriage in January 1956, and whilst her father was agreeable to the idea, thought as Peter was to be in Africa working for his shipping company for the next year or so, it would be better to wait until his return to confirm how everyone felt then. Peter clearly accepted this idea and saw no need to pressure Mandi, encouraging her to fulfil her commitment to Guys and her nursing training as well as being sure of her feelings for him.

In the meantime, Peter and Mandi corresponded sometimes passionately, sometimes quite matter-of-factly. Peter was far more romantic than Mandi who was inclined to be quite down to earth. In describing how much she missed Peter, she wrote:

21 MAY 1956

I'm missing something, as if, for example, I've forgotten to put my pants and stockings on. I most probably have, but that is not the point.

Mandi wrote to Peter after Greg's May Ball saying how disappointing it was that it had not been Peter:

12 JUNE 1956

Greg's a splendid chap, you know, and incredibly kind, but lacking in so many of your little ways. He does breathe through his nose though.

She went to another dance too and wrote in the same letter of her frustration not to have her Peter to dance with her. Life was suddenly very different.

Mandi addressed her letters to Peter in her own style:

VARIOUS LETTERS of 1956

Hello you ridiculous one, Hello Mr Tiddley, My dear old Pedro, Hello you dear old thing, Cooeee my dearest old Pedro, My darling one, Oh Mr Wonderful, My widdley bear, Mr Crews Manager, You dear old ridiculous lump of a muggins, You silly old sausage, Dear Sir Pedro, My darling Squiffy.

She wrote in a letter of 9 May 1957:

Do you realise what you are taking on? I'm crackers, wispyish, ridiculous and moody, my darling old poppety, scrumptious, huggable, heffalump you!

She often referred to her own craziness and mood swings, but whatever she said or did, there is no doubt that it was met with devotion. They had all sorts of names for inanimate objects and had great fun together laughing about their lives.

13 JULY 1956.

What grand news about your new car, though I adored Edward.

Later she added,

14 FEBRUARY 1957

Doesn't the TRIII look simply wizard, wizz-bang, you won't see me for dust when I nip off in it!

She remained quite forthright with him:

20 JULY 1956

*Work hard, read, mark and inwardly digest and don't give much
thought to your sylph like girlfriend at home in case, like one
of Somerset Maughan's characters, who thought so much about
his loved one when he was in prison, that when he was released,
he's grown sick of the thought of her.*

*You are FAT! Remember you are to weigh no more than 12
stones 6 pounds when you return. It is unhealthy. How are your
teeth? Are you going bald? Do you still have bouts of diarrhoea?*

In September 1956, she gave some very clear advice about his not
becoming *'a pompous old sausage'* in a number of letters.

Mandi debated in the letters what her life would be like if they
married and moved to Africa and whether or not to continue her
nursing career in Africa, but it is obvious that it was not going to
be possible. She wondered what she would do and imagined having
a baby quickly and being a housewife. She lamented the loss of her
hard-earned and much-adored career, but proclaimed that love had
won the day and she was ready.

All of Mandi's experiences and decisions have to be considered
against the subliminal backdrop of women of the '50s. She had grown
up hearing that her only hope was to meet someone and marry, and
suggested that she should feel uncertain about her capacity to do well
in her chosen career. Despite all the praise she was receiving to the
contrary, Mandi did not know how to receive a compliment or express
herself with any real confidence. She was also quite genuinely in love.
She made the only choice she knew how to make, the only choice many
women of her generation could make—indeed, the same choice that
many women make today, because love and the demands of family
require it.

In her letter to Peter on 18 October 1956, she confirmed her total
passion and commitment. During Christmas 1956, Mandi wrote of how
much she was missing Peter and his love, of her connection with his
sisters, of Christmas fun and love on the wards and the importance of
her family to her at home. She congratulated him on his twenty-fifth
birthday on the 16th December; he was four years older than Mandi.
She asked Peter never to leave her again as she loved him so much.
On 4th January 1957, Mandi went to visit his family in their Liverpool
home, Quendale, and once again confirmed that she was sure that she
loved Peter more than nursing and felt a very real affection for his

very warm family already.

On 1st November 1956, in one of his many typical letters, Peter wrote to his darling *Wispy*, sharing his love and passion, the challenges of his work, and his distance from the African people, but explained how he managed to find solace in his love for her, at the club and through his sailing. He would often make plans for them, their wedding and their future together. He spoke of how he was a romantic and a dreamer and how she brought him down to earth with her practical, matter-of-fact approach.

Mandi, to be fair, had her moments when she did not give orders or was less forthright and became rather *'soppy'*, as she put it.

16 JANUARY 1957

Never, never, never have I ever wanted anyone as I want you now. I yearn to experience the sensation to be, as yet unknown to me, to be intoxicated by it, lifted into another world, our world, to use the feelings which at present lie dormant within me. When you left me way back last year, I adored to tickle, tease and torment you; indeed I still would I know, but gradually, very gradually, a love, a deep love has stepped in and I have grown, more and still more crazy about you.

She goes on to long for his arms about her and the fulfilment of that passion. High society and various hit songs at the times were definitely fueling the romance. Mandi was totally in love with Peter and just a bit crazy with it, absence certainly making those hearts grow fonder.

11 FEBRUARY 1957

I could just do with another Jersey holiday with you darling and being just as evil as we were—I don't really feel in the least guilty now you know. I know for certain that if we holidayed again in the near future, I could not be responsible for my actions. Oh my love, it seems so silly writing a lot of lovey dovey stuff on a stupid, flimsy pad of paper, so different from my vast hunk of male in Africa. Oh, there's a horrid daddy long legs buzzing about, I'll have to swat him. That's better. You see poppet, I am capable of being thoroughly soppy. For goodness sake, let me be Mrs PFE soon. All my love, Mandi.

Mandi also raised the issue of family planning in this letter and Jane, which was now known as *'the curse'*. This still plagued Mandi with its irregularity, stomach pains and tendency to moodiness. Peter responded in his next letter lightly and referred to it all as unromantic, but he did not shirk it. They seemed comfortable to talk about anything in their letters.

On 20 February 1957, their engagement was announced in London in *The Telegraph*, the *Times* and *The Liverpool Post*. Mandi's next letter to Peter told about a book she had bought to further her knowledge about her conjugal duties and described herself as 'quite worried' after reading it with a fellow nurse. Apparently it had left the fellow nurse *'in a state of frenzied frustration'. 26 February 57*

When John heard about her relationship with Peter, he was overwhelmed by how fast things had moved and wrote to tell her about how disappointed he was and the hopes that he had nurtured over the years about her. Mandi responded kindly, but somehow one just would not have wanted to be John!

31 JANUARY 1957

Now John dear, I have always enjoyed your friendship and the very quiet and pleasant way that we have trundled about together, and above all respected the unemotional and thus platonic friendship we have had for one another. You can be quite sure though that, in the years to come, when I am a busy wife and housewife (diving in the sink every five minutes), and even perhaps a mum, Pete and I will always welcome your company in our house.

Mandi told Peter all about it in this letter, loving the fact that she could share anything or ask him anything; he was her best friend and like a brother to her, but the greatest story of all she hoped was going to be their growing love story.

2 APRIL 1957

I suppose our letters are a serial of our love story aren't they darling?

Finally a holiday with Jen and that cycle they had planned and plotted three years before. In February 1957, Mandi set off from Esbjerg to Copenhagen and then wrote all about it to Peter just after she had got engaged to him by post. On 26 February 1957, Mandi and Jen cycled 262 miles in all, which Mandi carefully measured on the cyclometer that Peter had given her. Her most challenging day was fifty-eight miles.

We are both now in rude health and horribly muscular, but it
was all tremendous fun and very memorable. We had hundreds
of adventures, met masses of charming people, didn't bath for a
fortnight, but took the occasional cold shower.

Mandi described the *'inmates'* of the youth hostels as *'like our Teddy*
Boys' and said they wanted to paw at them, so they got ignored and
she found the food too awful for her own dog or cats.

Grey lumpy-looking meatballs, half-cooked mash and thick
whitish looking gravy with afters of sweetened brown water with
pips.

She much preferred the food she could get from the slot machines
outside the shops in Denmark. As was fast becoming her way, she
met all sorts of new people on the journey and later wrote to Peter
about the great fun she had with the Danes and also with two South
Africans, Steve and Brian, in Copenhagen. The budget for the whole
adventure was just £10.00 each and it was going to cost them £1 6d
per night to stay in youth hostels. In the end, the trip cost £12.00 and
the boat fare.

The jaunt was a great success. Mandi fed off Jen's easy confidence
and Jen off Mandi's growing sense of fun and they laughed and
laughed together. Even when Mandi caught her wheel in a tram rut
and wrecked it, she showed the initiative to carry it to a garage where
her forlorn expression and unfortunate plight won the heart of the
garage owner who repaired the wheel and replaced the tyre for nothing whilst the girls ate crumbling pastries, drank hot tea with his
kind and generous wife and laughed over the incident. They could not
believe their luck and laughed about that too.

It was clear that Mandi returned from this trip pumped up with
her own capacity, energy, sense of fun and resilience, genuinely a
much stronger girl than the one she had been when Jen first met her.

Her *'great pash'* for Peter did not stop Mandi from going out with
her nursing and other friends. One night at a nurses' party in
Blackheath, which Mandi considered rather vulgar, her dear friend
Gill overheard Patrick, a rather seedy Irishman comment,

28 APRIL 1957
I'm going to twiddle Mandi round my fingers, she's the one with
money and she should be easy bait if tackled properly.

He tried his hardest and got to hear all about Peter. So did John at

Jen's champagne party in the country. Mandi drank far too much and danced the night away, but refused to go into the garden with him.

8 MAY 1957

As he pecked me goodbye, he said: 'By golly that man of yours is a lucky fellow!', (—good job he didn't know about my moods wasn't it darling).

She recounts how she was chased in her car and had to drive like Sheila Van Dam to escape them.

12 MAY 1957

Aren't I awful! Thank goodness you will soon be back to protect me.

She referred a lot to music in the letters of 1956 and 1957 and clearly loved the top twenty and jazz to dance to which she and Peter greatly enjoyed together and did rather well.

In February of 1957, Mandi was loving her nursing on Outpatients, but was crazily busy from 8.00 am to 6.00 pm. She gained experience from various clinics and could not believe what she was finding out on some of the gynaecology clinics. A while later, she was sent back to the wards and here she developed a really meaningful relationship with one of her patients that she *'specialed i.e. looked after individually'*.

She rarely wrote in detail about her patients to Peter, but she did about Jessie. In February of 1957, Mandi had donned gown, cap and mask to watch two renowned ear, nose and throat surgeons operate on Jessie's malignant facial tumour. She observed the way in which the surgeons just lifted her rotten nose off her face, took away her left eye and indeed most of the left side of her face, filled up the space with a kind of wax and put in a rubber drain to constitute a nose. Mandi took note of the way in which they made a skin graft from her left leg to reconstruct her face. Nurse Hornsby then had to feed her glucose and check her *'pulse and resps'* every fifteen minutes. Mandi wondered if it would be better if she were to die, but then again, she had a fifteen-year-old son and no husband. She was clearly very moved by Jessie, inspired by her bravery and was to get to know her very well over a short period of time.

On receiving Peter's letter in January 1957, planning how they would enjoy their engagement for a month in June and their marriage and honeymoon for a month in July, a very confident and happy Mandi wrote to Peter telling him that she would finish at Guy's on June 22nd,

1957 when she took her final examination. The honeymoon turned out
to be six weeks and they were to spend most of August in England,
before heading for Africa. Mandi would become a state registered
nurse by the time she left, though not receive her Guy's badge until
she arrived in Africa.

17 FEBRUARY 1957

*Providing you're not too interfering, I can't see why I can't get
organised for Africa then. I'm not like you, you know with regard
to taking hours to pack and as Mum says, all my things can stay in
my room until I return from Africa. It's farcical wasting time, do
you hear? The sailing sounds colossal fun. I'm sure I'm going to
adore it. The brand new flat sounds just the job and the plans for
our honeymoon seem to be taking shape. Isn't it all terrific fun!*

Peter flew back to London on West African Airways on 9 June
1957 and Mandi finished her exams around the same time. They had
proven their constancy to her parents and whilst there was still huge
uncertainty over Peter's provenance, hair follicles and girth, he did
provide the longed for suitor that had been so discussed over the
years. Mandi had developed enough confidence to take on her parents,
hold out to marry the man she wanted and complete her demanding
nursing training. It was time to move on. Mandi and Peter were at last
together to make the final preparations and to really get to know one
another as man and wife.

*'You remember what someone said for a day,
what they did for a week, but you always remember
how they made you feel'.*

— MANDI —

A TIME TO KEEP
AND A TIME TO THROW AWAY

So their wedding day came on the 20th of July 1957 and Mandi set off in her pure silk, classical white dress, her arms covered by the dress and arm gloves, her long hair high in a chignon with not a scrap of makeup on her lovely, fresh and eager face. Slim and fit from the Denmark cycling, the exertions of final examinations at Guy's along-side ward life, and final wedding preparations, she looked happy and radiant and people still comment on that striking young bride that shines out from many photo frames today.

She set off for the 10.30 am service in the pelting rain in a London taxi with her father from Whitehall Court; as they rounded Trafalgar Square, he invited her to reflect for a moment, obviously considering the marriage he had given his blessing to still impulsive. 'It's not too late to change your mind darling', he said half-jokingly, conscious of the expensive reception ordered for their return.

Mandi was adamant and committed wholeheartedly to her vows that day as did Peter in front of their one hundred and fifty guests. They married in St Martin's in the Fields, Central London, singing hymns including a family favourite, 'Praise my soul the king of heaven', listening to three pieces of Peter's beloved Bach around making their vows and the formal address before leaving to the triumphant tones of Mendelssohn's Wedding March. Her adored patient Jessie was with her for the service and for the last time, her face masked, something that Mandi would always remember and always share with others.

Then came a fine celebration with friends and family. Mandi's cluster of bridesmaids included her dear friend Jen; Hazel, her cousin, one of her best friends today; and Peter's sisters, Mary and Ruthie, with whom she is still close. Her other bridesmaid was Ingrid Seward, 'Seaweed', the doctor's daughter, only eight at the time. She was only allowed to invite six of her own specific friends and these were of course her dear fellow nurses.

The reception was held at the King Charles Suite, number 4

Whitehall Court, from 12.00 pm to 4.00 pm. Peter had agonised over his best man, wondering whether to invite Mandi's much loved brother David, or Freddie, as he was often known. With Mandi's advice, he had settled on his own brother who made a memorable and extremely short speech.

20 JULY 1957

Peter has an enormous appetite. He once ate a whole box of Kellogg's cornflakes at one sitting.

With that said, he sat down. Neither of the mothers were best pleased, and it was never forgotten! Richard went on to become a renowned and eminent surgeon and redeemed himself, but the marriage took place before such competence. The reception was a fabulous and simple celebration. Mandi and Peter were lavished with gifts and everyone wished nothing but the very best for them. Mandi's childhood and adolescence were well and truly behind her and a new era of young adulthood had been launched.

Mr and Mrs Peter Earlam spent the first night of their marriage at the Mermaid Inn at Rye in a magical and memorable double bed and set off the very next day on their unforgettable honeymoon in the TRIII. Over the Channel to Le Touquet, stopping for the night in the Hotel du Sud before going onwards to Lake Lausanne and the next night in the Hotel de l'Hermitage. They did not remember much about those places. It was finally time for each other. Then to Lake Maggiore through the stunning Italian pass to the Beau Rivage, their hotel bedroom and balcony with its breathtaking views of the lake, and more vital time together. Lazy, idyllic days in the blazing sun, bathing in the mountain streams and rivers, with the occasional walk to the nearby Baveno.

Mandi heard that she had passed her State Finals on the 30 July 1957 and celebrated this and her twenty-second birthday with Peter on the 1st August 1957; her career definitely took second place to love at this point, but passing those exams was a defining moment. Peter gave her a blue towelly wrap and beach shoes and her parents had sent her letters and money. She felt loved and spoiled.

They left Lake Maggiore that day at 10.30 am and drove the 270 miles towards the Adriatic, the roof lowered, the TRIII speeding along under the clear blue sky of that beautiful day.

1 AUGUST 1957

Find Club Hotel on the Front and have a glorious swim. Wizard
grub! Drink a whole bottle of chianti and retire to bed in the best
form event.

Mandi always reported quite openly that love-making with Peter could be ecstatic, wonderful, blissful and she always wanted more. She described them as *'both sublimely happy and brown as berries'* on their honeymoon. It was obviously evident that they were just married as they were asked by one nosey Italian on 3 August 1957, *'Is you on your moonlight?'*

They bought a ball to play with on the beach and enjoyed the new people they met, noting the hairy armpits of the women and the fact that the men wore bathing caps and necklaces. They danced, swam for hours, relaxed and relished exploring their honeymoon destinations and each other. Things boded very well indeed for this young couple who had launched so confidently into marriage as virgins and so unknown to each other in real life.

They had shared so much about each other in their eighty or more letters to each other over two years and had known each other in their early teens from Peter's regular visits to the Hornsbys. This undoubtedly helped bring them close as friends that somehow becoming lovers was the natural step for them, the icing on the cake. They relished each other as they were. Peter had already indicated in his letters that he knew Mandi well. He understood that she could be loving and tender, but equally prone to pre-menstrual tension, uncertainty and moods.

27 AUGUST 1956
Just a minute whilst I remove my rose-tinted spectacles. Oh yes!
But why? You are still my darling girl who I want to take in my
arms and love for ever and ever. But then I suppose I can also
see the other side with my glasses off. You know full well I have
always tolerated that side, although I can't say I've adored it!!!!
Well, well, I must put my glasses back on!

Through their letters, who he was had emerged strongly too. Mandi wrote to her *'silly old sentimental banger'* as she called him.

3 AUGUST 1956
From your letter you appear to be becoming a pompous old
businessman, incapable of enjoying the simple things in life and
criticising everybody and everything—it must cease.

She would always tease him, invoking and beginning the questioning of her mother's ingrained distastes, by loving her man with curly hair.

3 AUGUST 1956

Your photos show that you are cultivating your curly hair again.

Nasty!

She was totally open with him about her many social engagements with different men and they clearly trusted one another totally and said as much. Peter wrote,

Peter's letter 6 June 1956

'You always do as you like and always will. I have no illusions about that, I expect it is one of your fascinations'.

During his time away, Peter had really shared his love of the sea, sailing, music, playing the piano particularly Bach, dancing, tennis and his intolerance of those that were not very good at it. He talked of squash, TRIIIs, Jaguars, Bentleys, Mercedes, cars that he could not afford, and speed, fun, reading, theatre, cards and board games, cine film and his camera, food, including sweets and a whole cup of brown sugar that he ate at a sitting, drinks at the Club in Lagos and wine and beer. He was not very fond of the Club and complained about it, saying it was full of selfish people and he was all in favour of a return to class distinction rather than the democratic socialism that seemed to exist there. He was a strong character and knew his mind.

Peter clearly worried about his weight; Mandi regularly exclaimed about it and had told him not to return from Africa to marry her unless he reduced it, expecting him to be no more than 12 and a half stones, a frightening target for the tall, but well-rounded Peter. In the August before they married things seemed to be going in the wrong direction as he reached over 14 stones, but he did not take total responsibility for it.

Peter's letter 19 August 1956

'I had not seen these people for three weeks and when they saw me they expressed great horror at the size of my tummy, I've stopped eating sweets, potatoes and I don't have much beer or spirits. I'm also stopping eating ice creams in quantity. I shall never forgive the company for sending me here if I grow so fat that you will have nothing to do with me when I get home'.

She married him a little over the target weight! He referred on occasion to loneliness and depression overcoming him. He would chastise himself for self-centred letters, but recount that he was living in a self-centred place. The job was about making your mark and he was sharing with three other bachelors, so the atmosphere was competitive, challenging and often lonely. Peter had an idea about the role of the wife. He described himself in one of his letters to Mandi on the 21 October 1956 sewing his pants, explaining that his boy had ruined them and felt that he would do well in the future to have a wife to do this sort of thing for him. He also knew that he was not thrifty.

Peter's letter 31 October 1955

'I have rather overspent recently! A bowler hat, a model railway engine (my second childhood you know) etc, all so unnecessary, but I'm so weak. I will never be rich'.

Peter outlined the nature of his austere father, giving everyone money round the table on Christmas Day 1956 to put into their savings. He was not actually there, but he painted the scene for Mandi, including the monetary gifts to his siblings—Richard, Mary and Ruth—and then to his mother, whose birthday was also that day. With his bachelor friends in Africa, it was not his family that he was missing in that moment, but rather Mandi. His letters of that time are full of hopes and dreams; she had become everything to him.

Peter also had to take on his family on occasion about money:

29 April 1957

'With regard to buying the TR III, I have met with quite a lot of opposition. Father has never been a believer in making hay, being mad and living for today. I've told him we really must be allowed to make our own decisions'.

He made it clear in this letter to Mandi that he had very little money for extras and would always be too proud to ask his father for any.

Peter came through Paris sometimes and spoke bad French, but he liked to use it and hear himself speak it. He often signed off his love letters, 'au revoir, je vous aime, Chérie' and, like Mandi, had a string of names for her, but perhaps of a slightly more conventional nature: 'Honey bee, sweetheart, beloved, you maddening woman, poppet, my dear old fish, my sweet'.

He was very loving and tender towards Mandi, but knew that he

would often get told off for being a *'sentimental old sausage'*. In his
letters, he would get very emotional and would have to stop himself
as she would not want to hear it and then he would continue anyway,
especially if he had had a glass or two of wine.

Peter's letter 29 July 1956.

'I listened to Ian Stewart playing from the Savoy—it brought
back all the lovely times we had had together. I danced all
round my bedroom, getting hotter and hotter—it was just
like being in a trance, until I came to life because my arms
were getting tired, holding the only girl in the world (who
wasn't there)'.

In this letter, Peter acknowledged Mandi's plans for giving up her
nursing at Guy's and was clearly humbled by her sacrifice for him.

Peter's letter 9 January 1957.

'I pray God that I shall not disappoint you as a husband.
I long to be yours, but sometimes tremble and wonder
whether I shall be good enough for you'.

Peter's letter 3 December 1956.

'You are as precious and necessary to me as my heart. The only
difference is that I live for you, but my heart lives for me,
the former is the thing that matters'.

In his letter of 10th October 1956, Peter gave considerable time to
describing the contemporary house of his dreams, with modern kitchen
and bathrooms that are easy to clean, as one has to do most of the
cleaning oneself these days, one that has the bedrooms decorated
in his favourite colour, red and grey and cream and green, but the
sitting room should have old-fashioned furniture. He was definitely
a romantic and a dreamer and had plans for their life together and
the family they would build. They had even decided on the Christian
names of their first two children, Nicholas and Lucy.

Peter's work involved overseeing the victualling, supplies of food
and drink, into Lagos, Nigeria for their customers, and understanding
the inward and outward freight arrangements of the Elder Dempster
Line ships, the Accra, the Apapa and the Aureol, amidst the heat
and dust. There was an office where Peter would spend time doing
administrative tasks when the ships were at sea and there were twelve
passengers to organise for each voyage of the Aureol. He would describe nights watching the ships load and unload. These experiences

were to provide the foundations of his career and there was no doubt that he was eager and ambitious to be noticed and promoted fast.

Mandi was to describe the Peter she wed twenty years after they married as part of her musings in 1977. She wrote:

He was far more mature at 25 than I was at 22 when we married. He had been my best friend for many months and I could write or say anything to him. He was the eldest of four, his father a private family doctor, authoritarian and austere, but with a warm, kind, caring side that endeared. His mother was games crazy, decisive, bossy, definitely a lot to give to her family, but with a selfish streak. Peter was good-natured to a fault with baby soft skin and a gorgeous smile. On first acquaintance, he had a noisy, nervous laugh, that later completely disappeared. Educated at public school and university, he is full of common sense, more than academic ability, though he has a definite flair for Maths. He has remarkable practical skills and physical energy and has to be 'doing' all the time. His sense of humour has come a long way since the early days of marriage when he needed teasing and was inclined to be pompous and bossy; he liked to be seen doing the right thing. This ceased to be the case after a while. He is thoughtful and kind to a fault. He has a flair for organizing and loves trains and timetables. Loves himself, women and me?, dancing, gardening, being admired, hates disorder, loves mending things, looking after his possessions and has a thing about socks. He is a romantic, sentimental, always loaded with ideas and new projects; he has drive, initiative and is gorgeously cuddly and can be a really fabulous lover.

During those first months together, they were to find most of that out about each other, talking, laughing, playing, making love and getting the most out of life together. They were young, in love and life was a big adventure.

*'Love gives, forgives, outlives, for this is love's prerogative —
to give, give and give again'.*
— Unknown —

A TIME TO LOVE
AND A TIME TO HATE

Mandi and Peter returned to Lagos, Nigeria via the R.M.V. Apapa, arriving on 22nd August 1957.

14 APRIL 1957

I'm told twelve cotton dresses, 12 bras and panties and some sandals are all you need out here. You certainly mustn't bring anything too good or beautiful out sweetheart; it just isn't worth it.

Mandi packed as Peter had instructed her earlier in the year and quickly found that the only entertainment she was to have in her new home, apart from Peter, was the record of that Brahms second piano concerto that reminded her of childhood musical evenings in Whitehall Court and two penguin books that Peter had. They moved into a company flat straightaway, Mandi applied for work at the hospital at once but was told that she would have to do a minimum of three months night duty. Neither she nor Peter wanted this, having spent so much time apart. When she wavered for a moment in favour of protecting her career, Peter was adamant that this was a wrong choice for them and her safety in Africa and won the day. Mandi then found herself home alone with the Brahms concerto and the penguin titles to read.

Whilst she was still very much in love with Peter, she was not happy in her life and Peter again consulted his colleagues. There was a housekeeping role going for all of the Apapa company flats, but this was not something Mandi wished to do, so in the early days of their stay in Africa, she had to accept that she could not work.

28 SEPTEMBER 1957

Felix, my black boy is getting quite good. He washes sheets, Peter's shorts, shirts and my dresses very well and very quickly.

Only ten days later she had sacked him as he had stolen butter, a lot of food and packets of cigarettes and she had to get the police to physically remove him.

The days were long and she was grateful for another family she got to know who were tenants of the same block of flats, a couple with three children. Mandi became very friendly with the mother of the family, Angie, and that friendship kept her occupied a little. Mandi wrote briefly in a very small diary that year. A few entries about the rains from June to October, the swamps and markets she went to visit, the fruits she bought and ate, the nits crawling over the plaited hair of the woman who served her fruit at Igeghi Market, the conditions in which some people lived, the floral dress she sewed and the people she met. Mandi recalled going sailing round the jetty, past the barracudas, dangerously close to her beloved helmsman's overhanging bottom, their making it to the beach with a huge sense of relief, and then getting back into that uncertain water to swim. The houseboys then made them a tasty curry on the beach before they made the return trip. An eventful, yet uneventful day, in that unfamiliar land.

On another occasion at the same beach, Mandi was swimming near to the shore, but got caught in a cross current that she could not manage. Her feet were constantly pulled off the bottom and under the water. She was really struggling to stay above the water line and yelled for help. At first, Peter, who was with their friend David, just waved jovially, until he realised that she really was in grave difficulty. It took both those 14-stone strong men and what seemed like several minutes to pull her to safety and she never forgot the fear of that incident.

Mandi's feelings were mixed in those early days. She loved the thrill of adventure, but at the same time felt a little scared and somewhat alone as Peter was often at work and she was very conscious of the alien nature of her surroundings and the very unfamiliar West African culture. She was growing as a woman—as a wife, as a soon-to-be-mother, as a woman whose career was on hold for the foreseeable future. And it all took place in a foreign country, in a cultural context that was far different from that of home. It was both a time to love and a time to hate, so wonderful to be together, but so very far away from anything and everything familiar and easy.

They were moved to a different dwelling in Lagos very soon after arriving and living in the new cockroach infested home was horrible. Telecommunications at this time were severely limited and she continued to communicate with her family and friends by letter. This was a slow and unwieldy process, leaving her disconnected from her London life. She had worked so hard to qualify as a nurse and in Guy's Hospital, where she felt needed, wanted and rewarded, and there was always a story to tell. In Africa, she was much more isolated and there was a lot less going on.

One day, Mandi felt that she had to break the rules and took the TRIII out to Lagos to do some shopping, promising to dash or tip some boys if they looked after the car whilst it was parked. She got away with it and came back in one piece with the car, though it was stained with deep red dust from the laterite, the Nigerian equivalent of tarmac back then. Peter expressed his displeasure but was firmly told in response that her love for him was going out of the window.

He took her to the Coi Club and there she met a judge's daughter who was going to do an interview as a copy typist and thought that Mandi could try for that too. Tragically, her lovely new friend and neighbour Angie's husband had contracted polio and died within a few days, necessitating the bereaved family to return to England. This was a real loss for Mandi and she needed this job more than ever. She hadn't typed for several years now and on the day of the test, her typing was accurate but slower than the other candidates. Nonetheless, her application was successful, but she refused to take the job unless the judge's daughter got taken on too. She managed to persuade her new boss that this was a good plan! *Typical Nigeria*, she thought! The boss had just taken to her regardless of her performance, but she was pleased to be on the lucky end of things or so she thought until she started.

31 MARCH 1958
Yours truly bashes away at the keys on her own with one other very smelly clerk in the office, who wafts a revolting odour all over me every time he swishes back his typewriter carriage.

Mandi did at least earn the money to pay for her twin tub washing machine when they got back to England from these efforts! Fortunately, before too long she fell pregnant as she had predicted she would and wrote all about her life in Africa to 'Freddy', as she often called her brother David.

31 MARCH 1958
Pedro and I are both very fit. Nicholas kicks me perpetually. We

have got another cook, this time called Peter to complicate mat-
ters. Damion had a colossal row with me, refusing to wash the
kitchen floor more than once per week and saying he couldn't
make bread as he was kept too busy by me. As I work from 8-2,
it was absurd, so when Master came home, he was told to make
a hasty exit.

Life appeared, unsurprisingly, to have quite a number of cultural challenges, but she persisted, making the best of the situation and looking forward to her first born.

Peter and Mandi were then moved to Takoradi, Ghana, just before Nick was born. It was much better accommodation this time: a house, complete with houseboy, cook and night watchman, who would sleep on the concrete front doorstep to guard them.

On 20th June 1958, Nicholas Peter Francis Earlam was born to Mandi and Peter in Takoradi Hospital, if you could call it that. It was a rather haphazard affair. No such thing as antenatal classes and scans existed in Ghana back then and Mandi sat up all night on the lavatory thinking she had an upset stomach, when in fact she had gone into labour. When she returned to bed none the wiser in the early hours, Peter questioned her absence and it was he that put the idea that she might be in labour into her head. When the realisation dawned, Peter had to get the roof off the TRIII to get Mandi in as she could not move easily with the very frequent pains at this stage. By the time they reached Takoradi, Mandi made it to the operating slab, covered with a well-washed but still very stained sheet, and gave birth to Nicholas within forty minutes.

Once Mandi had delivered her first baby, she immediately seized on the midwife's offer of breakfast and was given bread and jam before heading home again. Having been involved with twenty-seven safely delivered babies and a number of complicated births as a nurse in London, Mandi confidently embarked on motherhood—feeding, bathing, changing and loving her precious Nicky with wonderful and unsupervised confidence.

Nevertheless there were some very difficult moments at home in those early weeks. Mandi had been pregnant at the same time as the houseboy Denny's wife, but sadly her baby girl had died and Denny just could not cope with seeing Mandi with her adored Nicky. He kept appearing at the window, frightening Mandi with his glaring faces and threatening gestures, to the extent that Peter had to have the family removed. Two men came with a lorry from the docks and rehoused the unfortunate couple.

Mandi felt badly for Denny and his wife, but did not feel sure of what he might have done next. The lioness with her cub had been awoken. The following months were spent being utterly in love with both her husband and new baby, though Mandi sometimes rued the life she had given up and missed the professional buzz, finding herself alone with Nicky for hours on end in the dust and heat with strict instruction from Peter and anyone who knew better not to go out. However, she was not afraid of challenge and busied herself with her new roles purposefully and positively.

'The great man is the one that has never lost the heart of the child'.
— MENCIUS IV, 2, 12 —

A TIME TO BE BORN
AND A TIME TO DIE

It was mid-1959 when the family learned that they were to be posted back to Liverpool.

On arriving in Liverpool, Mandi and Peter moved in with Mandi's in-laws and she found herself pregnant again. It was one thing visiting your husband's family for a weekend or two before marriage and quite another turning up to live with them with a baby and pregnant.

Mandi adored her father-in-law, Francis, and was very much on the same wavelength as him, loving his stories about his GP life and genuinely interested in medicine and him. He had honoured her before she married Peter by taking her on a GP round with him, introducing her to his patients, which he had apparently never done with anyone else previously, and he and Mandi were close. However, she found her mother-in-law extremely critical. Elsie always knew how things might be done better and did not hold back.

As Elsie was one of the first two women to graduate in Chemistry from Liverpool University and was also an accomplished county tennis player, Mandi had yet another formidable mother figure in her life, which brought back familiar and threatening childhood memories. This undermined her fragile new independence and confidence considerably.

In truth, Elsie was a born leader, a capacity which had really emerged during the war when Francis had been determined to make his contribution and went to West Africa from 1943-1945, leaving Elsie and baby Mary sleeping under a great steel table in the cellar every night for protection from the bombs. When the bomb did come, it hit the house opposite in 1943 and blew out the windows and doors of Quendale. She had neither for the remaining two years of the war, but carried on, driving ambulances at night after Francis disallowed her from flying cargo planes from Speke to Dublin. Her boys, Peter and Richard, were evacuated to school in Penmaenmawr during the war, but came back for holidays, and she held the fort with her three children during that time.

When Francis returned from war, just walking in one day, he was clearly unwell, and Elsie was under a great deal of pressure to help him rebuild his practice after the war. She did this by socialising, visiting patients, leading committees and running the detail of the practice, allowing her husband to get on with the medical side. She was a very busy woman. Elsie was also very aware of the role of the mother-in-law and clearly both she and Mandi recognised the challenge of the relationship.

However, Elsie became known to Nicky and his siblings as MumMum and because she lived in Quendale, in Liverpool, Mandi often referred to her in-laws as the '*Quendalites*'. Arrangements in Quendale did not make for easy living and Mandi felt that she had to do as she was told, though she was also very eager to please in those early days. She could not stay there long and removed to her parents' home in Whitehall Court, until they found their own home to live in. It was Mandi's great relief when they moved into their own flat in Aigburth Drive, Liverpool, a few months before delivering me in a straightforward home birth and she set about managing life with two very small children.

In the end, they did not name me Lucy at all. A cousin of Mandi had recently lost her only daughter, Jennifer, in a tragic accident. Jennifer had been picking blackberries in a field at the foot of a very steep hill when the brakes of a car at the top of the hill gave way. The freewheeling vehicle gathered speed and momentum as it hurtled down. Jennifer had had no time to save herself and the least Mandi and Peter could do was name their little girl after her.

Equally tragically, Mandi's beloved father-in-law Francis was to climb the stairs to their flat only once more after my birth in November of 1959. He admired me, congratulated Peter and Mandi and told them that he would not see them again. He became ill and died just six weeks later.

Life was hectic for Mandi then, helping her mother-in-law to adapt to a different life as a widow and sorting out Quendale and also, it turned out, Whitehall Court. Mandi always managed to give of herself generously to Elsie and Peter's two sisters and indeed her own parents, never mind her immediate family.

It may have been a hectic time, but it was equally fulfilling for this loving and energetic young mum and even more so when Lucy joined her two siblings, just eighteen months after that. Mandi actually gave birth to Lucy with Peter fast asleep beside her, oblivious to the unfolding drama when the umbilical cord wrapped around Lucy's neck. It was obviously all becoming very exhausting for Peter at this point, but Mandi would go on to liken birthing to *'shelling peas'* for the rest of her life.

Indeed at the same time that Lucy was born, her dear friend Mickey had a stillborn child as her first experience. Mandi remembered the overwhelming feeling of guilt at her good fortune, two healthy children and her beautiful new baby and even wondered if she should give her baby away. Lucy, who has often been told this story, has remained grateful that she did not!

Three babies in three years and the '60s well underway. Mandi did not do much diary writing around this time given the pace of life, but her snippets in her blue book gave a real flavour of contemporary life, its colourful popular culture and breakout from convention. In 1960, Peter and Mandi were given £600 by Peter's godmother, beloved Aunt Eva, who was always in the background as an invaluable support and who regularly came to Sunday lunch with one of her homemade jigsaws. Jigsaw making was to become a popular family skill because of Aunt Eva, beginning with wholesome family scenes and moving on to the careful cutting of attractive pinups in the teenage years, but that is for later. Mandi and Peter used their windfall to buy a plot of land and build a holiday house at Ravenspoint, overlooking Trearddur Bay, Anglesey.

By October 1961, the roof was on. Peter was twenty-nine-years-old at this point and working hard with Elder Dempster, still travelling to places such as Hamburg as well as occasional trips to West Africa and returning from these trips with presents for all the family. They now had a pale blue Morris Oxford car called *Hunka Munca*. Mandi was extremely busy with their three children, three-year-old Nicholas, twenty-three-month-old me, known as *'Pins'*, and baby Lucy of four months. They lived forty-four stairs up on 23 Aigburth Drive, Liverpool 17, and Mandi was constantly occupied feeding, cooking, shopping and cleaning. She relished the open love that her children lavished on her at that time, in a way that young children can. Those snuggles in her arms, those bedtime stories and prayers, brought her great love and joy.

Helga, the first of two not very successful au pairs, was around at the time of Lucy's birth and accompanied Nick to his grandparents in Margate whilst most of the action was taking place in Liverpool. Helga only lasted six months before Mandi lost patience with her tendency to preen herself and contribute nothing and when this was pointed out to her, she returned home! Otherwise Nicholas was child-minded by Mrs Patterson three times a week. Mandi described him as *'difficult'* at this time and is sure that she loved him too much. If left alone with me, his sister Jen, he was usually sweet, but if an adult was present, he would show off and hurt me.

> 5 OCTOBER 1961
>
> *Lose my temper with Nick as every single toy in the pen is broken or chewed and all his cars ripped to pieces—he gets a pretty hearty smacking and I remove all his toys into the dining room or turret until such time as he learns to respect them.*

The day that he actually urinated into the toy box, Peter had to remove Mandi from him for his own safety as so many of the toys had to be thrown away. The colour had just run everywhere and little teddies and other soft toys were ruined. Neither the toys nor the funds were very durable and Mandi was furious with her eldest! He wound Mandi up a few times, but her exasperation never lasted long as he also made her laugh and of course she loved him to bits.

> 29 NOVEMBER 1961
>
> *Go to Mossley Hill Village Church Fete. Nick gives the flowers to Mrs Leece of Dale Hall and bows to me instead of her!*

I was painted as an adorable podgy person with a fair wispy horsey tail and the sweetest nature, who could twiddle her father round her finger. That ponytail did not last too long. Nick cut it off as a prank and I loved him so much that I would just say, *'I love my little hair!'* Lucy had hardly ever cried in her life apparently. Mandi made some good local friends, Peter's sisters and mother were frequent visitors and dear Jen Jones came to visit from time to time.

Mandi ran her home very much in the style of many '50s and '60s wives. She got dinner ready for Peter every evening and welcomed him home, trying not to appear frazzled by putting the children to bed early. By five o'clock the children and she would have cleared away the clutter of the day, gathering up the books, toys and paper so that Daddy could return to a sense of peace and order. Mandi believed in structure and routine and we were in bed by six, after baths and stories, and just dropping off to sleep as he arrived home; they received their paternal kiss goodnight, before he unwound in the drawing room as Mandi poured an aperitif in the style which she had seen her parents enjoy for many years. Mandi and Peter would sit opposite one another by the fire and discuss the day, Mandi always doing the listening first and then trying to make light of any issues in her day. She always reported that she had coped, told of traumatic moments with humour as this was in fact what got her through those long, demanding and *'hairy'* times, as she described them.

As was common at the time, there was no doubt that she made his life the more important of the two. By doing so, she fell back into becoming self-effacing, finding ways to cope with the challenges of such small infants independently for the most part and making light of the enormous challenge that they undoubtedly presented. Peter's career and life was allowed to have more importance than hers and without realising it, she was echoing a familiar pattern of her child-hood, of so many women before her and of the day, giving herself little value, or voice, despite doing a truly sterling job. She naturally rejected the same forthright role that her mother had played in her marriage as it had never sat easily with her, so an easy pattern of male dominance existed without there being a need to question it.

It did not matter at that point because, for the most part, Mandi truly loved being a wife and mother and was in her element, even if it was extremely tough. She had learned resilience well before and was drawn positively to the challenges she faced.

22 OCTOBER 1961

The children are beastly and cry all day.

She clearly had very normal but demanding children. She seemed to be forever getting us up, dressed, fed, breastfed in Lucy's case, in and out of the flat, taking us to and from pre-school and play activities, feeding us some more, telling us stories, trying to keep Nick from biting me too badly and destroying the toys and dealing with our colds, high temperatures, bodily functions and minor ailments, before bathing us and getting us back into bed. She kept to her strict routine and tolerated little nonsense and generally impressed those she knew and met with the way that she ran her little team. Nicholas would let her down from time to time with his headstrong determination to do things his way, but Mandi was inventive and found ways to make it quite clear who was in charge, even spending time sitting outside a large, imposing mansion, which for the purposes of the exercise doubled up as a home for naughty boys; Nick had to make his choice! Throughout these years, Mandi confirmed and deepened her very genuine love of and commitment to us, her children and husband.

Nick wrote recently of his Mum:

'Mum was the one that had all the emotions. When I look back on it now, I was the recipient of a huge amount of love, but Mum also had me when she was 22 and there is no way you are emotionally mature at 22. She then went on to have two more children in quick succession, so I feel looking back on it now that I was the recipient as the eldest child of the whole range of Mum's emotions, which probably contributed to an immense amount of passion, but possibly less objectivity; she put significant responsibility on me, which I liked.

I think being a Nurse from Guys gave Mum a practicality that few other mothers had. She had seen terrible things in hospital so she had zero tolerance of self-pity. I am pretty sure every school report I ever had stated zero absences for illness, something I have always appreciated.

She knew that to manage a family and everything around that required an immense amount of love, self-discipline, hard work, hygiene and common sense, all of which she had in spades. She also came from a family that had status and responsibility as an employer and as opposed to Dad at the time of our growing up, she flouted society's class rules, which I absolutely loved. However, I'm not always sure she stepped back enough to realise the huge influence she was having on us and perhaps re-direct it occasionally. We got the full range of who she was, raw and unedited, most of which was pretty positive'.

As part of her daily life, Mandi would transport Peter to and from various engagements in Hunca Munca, to the station and the airport, often after a passionate and loving night or a crazy party, and get on with the daily demands of cooking, baking, washing when the washing machine worked, shopping, cleaning, cocktail parties, dinner parties, occasional theatre and concerts, tea or lunch with friends or Peter's family, and dear Aunt Eva, whom she adored.

She also visited the hairdresser about every ten days. She had her long hair cut off for practical reasons. Very regular visits to Trearddur Bay were also essential to see how the building was coming along. She would do these activities repeatedly. Peter would give her £25 housekeeping per month, which she eked out incredibly carefully and was so grateful to her now more generous mother who would come to the rescue with new shoes and outfits when they were needed.

Siegrid, the second au pair, lasted longer than the hapless Helga, six months in total; she was mute for most of her visit as her boyfriend had died just before she arrived and her stay was on balance more trouble than it was worth, but naturally there had to be some understanding and sympathy. Peter and Mandi gave up on having any further help after her six-month stint ended.

Ruth would come over to help as often as she could during her holidays. Mandi was still moody pre-menstrually and often tired, which was barely surprising given her schedule, but she had exceptional and very renewable energy and persisted with the relentless tasks and ceaseless demand for love from her 'tribe', as she came to call us.

Peter's career was something of a battle. He had fairly regular meetings with the Company Chairman who was not very sympathetic to the costs of having a young family and told Peter to get on with his job and use his £750 annual pay wisely. He began to look around to see what his options were, especially when they considered sending him back to Africa for a longer stretch, and had a promising interview just before Christmas of 1961. There was certainly no doubting his energy, drive and determination, but making it happen was the challenge. He was handy around the house, mending and fixing the fuses when they blew and sorting out blocked drains and, despite the demands of his career, still found time for squash and tennis and to play with his trains.

Christmas that year was with Peter's family in Mandi and Peter's flat. Peter dressed up as Father Christmas and I guessed at once:

24 December 1961

What a funny hat Daddy has got on!

Christmas Day 1961

Children adore their stockings – a great thrill. Pete and I both have stockings and even Lucy a little something. Breakfast— after feeding Lucy at 10am, we go into the drawing room and open all our presents under the tree. Siegrid is with Lucy and enjoys opening hers, so much so that she does not want to go to her friend for lunch and stays with us. Lots of presents for the babies, a wee umbrella for Pins. The main fuse blows just as I start lunch and P mends it. All P's family come round. MumMum brings a half-cooked 23lb turkey round in foil and I've done all the frills.

Eat in the dining room which P and I decorated at midnight last night. Great success! Mary, Ruth and Elsie and Aunt Eva, Sieta the dog and Siegrid and our family. Finish having presents. Listen to the Queen's speech. Ruth loved playing with the trains laid out in the drawing room round the tree. Have a cup of tea. Feed midgets. Talk to Mum and Dad and GG in Margate. The Quendalites return. Mary has been very miserable all day. Her ex still tugs at her heart. Siegrid in good form. Peter did a good job talking to her. Have hot punch made from wine and sing all the carols round the piano. Buffet supper of everything cold, cider cup and choc mousse and then play 20 questions, (a sort of family version of Scattergories) and they go at 11.00pm. We wash up and retire.

In the late December snow, the whole family was to be seen having great fun, making snowmen and throwing snowballs. Peter did not get that job, but continued to work hard and with ambition.

1962 began and the daily routine was sustained. We grew with all that good food and daily exercise and Mandi became very slim and toned with climbing the forty-four stairs and the demands of three very small children.

As the time came for Nick to go to school, they decided to move across the Mersey to the Wirral peninsula to Pinhey, 29 Croome Drive, a four-bedroomed detached house in the village of West Kirby, and subscribed to the small, but well-reputed education of Dormie House School. Both Mandi and Peter came from privately educated backgrounds and it was a must to prioritise this. The mortgage and education left them struggling financially, but it did not stop their enthusiasm for life and soon Mingo, the black Labrador, was added to the family, given to me for my fifth birthday. Mingo was deeply loved by all, but added mightily to Mandi's workload.

She was a glutton for punishment however, and her fourth and final baby, Joey, arrived on the 27th July 1965. All of us, the children waited excitedly with our grandparents in Margate and pushed Joey excitedly up the road to show him to all the neighbours when he arrived.

Peter and Mandi's family was complete, but there was much daily living ahead.

Mandi often described herself as poor during the upbringing of her family and it is important to understand her perspective. She never sought any sympathy, but had to work hard to have what she had. She had had a privileged upbringing and had not been short materially, although emotionally she could certainly have received more of value. Peter was not earning a great deal of money, yet they had two houses, a sensible family car by this stage and private education for their children. Having made these choices, there was not much left over. Most of their money went towards bills, so it meant that Mandi had to be very careful with housekeeping. She constantly felt under pressure financially and had to learn to manage her budget very effectively. Meals were judiciously chosen and bulk cooked for the freezer to make for better value and simpler delivery.

Joey just fitted in, feeding at the breast, and was much loved as one of my dollies whenever I was allowed to role play. I was just about the right age to help with him and Mandi encouraged it. Once we children were at school, Mandi would put Joey in the large play pen where he would occupy himself for hours as there were loads of washing that needed to be done, the ironing, the putting away, the tidying, cleaning and hoovering, the scrubbing of floors and bathrooms, the polishing of the silver and brass, the beds that needed stripping and remaking weekly, shopping, the cooking of a range of favourite meals. Mandi produced constant dishes, shepherd's pies, cottage pies, fish pies, risottos, stews, casseroles, curries, a range of mousses, soups, salads, Sunday roasts, lamb chops with a selection of vegetables, pavlovas, jellies and fruit salads. She noted down the meals on the majority of days that she kept a diary. Out of school, she would shop for our clothes and school uniform at the Beanstalk, a second hand clothes shop, saving money where she could. Even so, she was proud of her smart and well-turned out family when required and equally determined for them to wear old clothes when out in the garden or just mucking about at home.

Mandi was a great believer in the regular constitutional, so would lead the daily march in the fresh air on the beach or on one of the many nearby commons or hills. Hours were spent kicking and throwing balls as well as acquiring key educational skills and we all had lots of fun. Weekends and holidays always afforded time to play and the outside playroom was a godsend. Hours were spent with the dollies and schoolrooms. We loved our dolls and the best break that Mandi got was when we all removed to the outside playroom to play schools. This space had a big chalk blackboard and Nick was headmaster to all the dolls in the school. Perhaps it was a sign of the environment we understood around us that Raymond, who was the naughty African doll, was regularly sent to the Headmaster to be disciplined, and Rosie and Susie, the big, blonde dolls, won everything.

Lamare, our bungalow in Trearddur Bay, was where we, the Earlams, spent our holidays. It was to strengthen the foundations of our family and friendships over the years as well as provide a permanent symbol of the growth of the family relationship. The name 'Lamare' was created by Mandi's father Noel as an anagram of Earlam and a homonym of the French for the sea. Lamare funded itself through a detailed holiday let programme which Mandi oversaw and ran, often dropping us off at school and then driving the 180-mile round trip to Lamare, cleaning it, getting it ready for the next tenants and returning in time for school pick up.

Packing for the long six-week summer holiday became quite a ritual. The lists and their good value and bulk buy shopping before departure allowed the holidays to be affordable and the shopping whilst away was then limited to the buying of fresh food only. Fitting it all into the car was a military operation which was undoubtedly Peter's specialism.

Once the methodical packing was done, the familiar journey took them past various landmarks on the way. We would admire the beautiful marble church in Bodelwyddan, Conwy and its long stretches of beach along the A55 and around Conwy Castle. Penmaenmawr was always appreciated as the place of Peter's wartime evacuation and we would hear the stories again and again. The Britannia Bridge eventually came to be used instead of the original Menai Suspension Bridge and then through to the town with the unpronounceable name, *Llanfairpwllgwyngyllgogerychwyrndrobwllllantysiliogogogoch*, to the moment of greeting, *'Salaam Sir'*, the greeting which was always made to the Marquess of Anglesey as he sat proudly on his column, the Y Fali Valley sign with its bright orange wind sock signifying the airport, and 'Main Beach' which we, the children, would customarily yell out as the first large beach was sighted in Trearddur Bay before passing Boat Beach and Little Beach. Later we would come to find out that all these beaches had their own Welsh names, Porth Trearddur, Porth Diana and Porth Y Castell respectively, but that is how it was back then.

Finally the huge excitement of arriving at Lamare, our bungalow. Set on the rugged cliffs and just fifty metres from a rocky climb down to Little Beach, the house was a haven. Family holidays were five or six weeks long with Peter joining for at least two and this time together was vital and happy bonding time. Beach time, swimming, building sandcastles, collecting shells, looking for sea life with buckets and nets, picnics, barbeques, walks, time spent with other families, supper parties and dancing for parents. The simple suppers took place around the formica kitchen table with the double bed pushed up into the wall in their bedroom and the double doors opened to reveal a decent expanse of wooden floor for dancing. All those favourite 45s would be put on the record player as they smooched to the likes of Peter Sarstedt's 'Where do you go to, my lovely?', Petula Clark, Cliff Richard, the New Seekers and more. Peter would also spend hours perfecting Lamare, doing lots of DIY jobs which were much needed in this exposed bungalow on the cliff edge. The sailing and boating slowly took off as a family activity and Hebe, the fourteen-foot wooden clinker built boat, was acquired to facilitate this.

One breezy summer's day, Peter asked Nick, aged ten, and me aged eight, to bring our fourteen-foot-boat in from the mooring to the beach for everyone to go fishing. We set off, but the engine just died and Nick could not start it again. I was not much use except that my screams were heard from the headland and Mandi and Peter were fetched only to see their children floating out to sea. Peter dropped his trousers, preparing to take his first swim ever in the Irish Sea, but before this futile effort occurred, the persistent Nick got the engine started again and brought the boat home. I will never forget Dad taking us round the bay a couple more times just to eradicate any fear; I am equally never quite sure that this was successful!

Our exchanges abroad signified growing up and it was particularly Nick and I who did the first ones with the De Monteynards, very dear family friends based just outside Paris. They had five children and Nick was matched with Bruno, aged just eight, and I with Anne and Veronique. Nick disliked his trip abroad with Bruno so much that he sought revenge during the reciprocal exchange in the Trearddur Bay Swimming Sports. The well-toned and well-honed Nick sped home with his French counterpart having to be rescued out in the bay, unable to put his feeble crawl together in the ice-cold Irish waters. I fared better after a three-week sojourn in the Alps with them. I learned to ski and loved the *'poisson d'avril'*, the French equivalent of April Fool's, and went on to pursue those opportunities in the years to come.

Alone with her four children for several weeks in Trearddur Bay, Mandi really built the capacity to lead and manage her family and deal with situations as they arose. Both she and Jo remember this one that he wrote about:

> 'I nearly lost my hearing in my early years. Raging tem-
> peratures and terrible nightmares plagued my early years
> and Mum was always there for me. She would never let us
> be wimps so one would truly have to be half-dead before
> a visit to the doctor was warranted! My earache was so
> terrible one day that she had to beg the next-door neighbour
> to take me to hospital which he kindly did and to Mum's
> credit was the reason I have my hearing to this day'.

Mandi begged a man she did not know up the road to take them in his car to the nearest doctor whom he helped her find and she left us, her other three relatively young children, to care for each other at Lamare, an act of desperation in itself. The doctor was shocked at the state of Jo, his ear infection and high temperature, and came to visit every day for a week after that, only letting Mandi keep him at home on the basis that she was a nurse. Apparently the sea, a lot less clean than it is today, was responsible for the hearing problems. If one of her children were seriously ill, as Jo often was as a child, Mandi would move heaven and earth to care for them.

Mandi was introduced to the idea of marriage guidance counselling on Boat Beach in Trearddur Bay in 1968 by a counsellor who thought Mandi would be perfect for the role. Her empathy, capacity to listen, nurse training and ready connection with others were ideal starting points so the counsellor recommended her.

The selection was very thorough and demanding. Firstly she had to apply and then attend an afternoon of activities. She was observed throughout that time alongside other candidates, including a lawyer and a vet, and it always amazed her that she was chosen and not they. It took her a very long time to appreciate that the very qualities that she was recommended for might be the ones that they did not have, such was her own view of herself.

It was through counselling that Mandi began to see herself through others' eyes. Her sessions as a counsellor reflected back to her that she was both an active and empathetic listener. Those long childhood hours spent in silence being seen and not heard had taught her to listen actively, process and rarely comment. Perhaps the empathy and ready connection came through her nursing training and learning to love that range of patients as she did. She came to understand that her focus on physical health as a nurse could be developed through this new focus on mental and emotional wellbeing and she learned well before it became popularised that emotional and mental stress impacts very negatively on physical health and sorting out the former is often the solution to the latter. Again, her sessions showed her that others found and appreciated those qualities in her and wished they could find them in themselves. Mandi heard that her humour, which often manifested itself rather vulgarly, worked for some and not for others. No surprise there!

Mandi also spent part of the summer holidays in Mandavant, her parents' house in Margate. Her parents now resided at 60A, Northgate, St John's Wood, having sold Whitehall Court for a million pounds in 1960, leaving Noel with two hotels as part of the group and the money to acquire three more, which he did. Mandi had helped them move out despite her pregnancies. What a job that had been. She had found 144 pairs of skis in the turret and given those and the other contents of it to the staff. They were delighted with the skis, all

manner of furniture, cigarette card albums and more, which they sold
to supplement their meagre salaries.

'No man is an island, entire of itself,
every man is a piece of the continent, a part of the main'.
— JOHN DONNE 1573–1631 —

A TIME TO GET
AND A TIME TO LOSE

The '60s marked a new era for Mandi's family.

The famous '60s slipped easily by in a frenzy of family and career activity, for both Mandi and Peter. Mandi's brothers, David and Ant, were both married by this time and established in their careers. Life was very busy indeed.

Whilst Peter and Mandi's family was growing, 1961 saw the construction of the Berlin Wall, the first man in space and the founding of Private Eye. In the next few years, the Cuban Missile Crisis and the 'Big Freeze' occurred and the Telstar satellite was launched. The Great Train Robbery took place, Kennedy was assassinated and Beatlemania took off. By 1964, the Wilson Government came to power, Vietnam was causing all manner of moral dilemmas and the Nobel Peace Price had been awarded to Martin Luther King. Winston Churchill died the following year, UDI was established in Rhodesia and the first female High Court Judge was invested. By 1966, England had won the World Cup, the Aberfan disaster had occurred and the London Tower Centre Point was completed. The next couple of years saw the Torrey Canyon oil tanker run aground on the southwest coast, the first heart transplant in South Africa and the Six-Day War as well as the Paris riots and the Ulster civil rights disturbance. London Bridge was sold and shipped to America. As the decade came to a close, Woodstock, Concorde, man walking on the moon, the Equal Pay Act and the first Earth Day were all celebrated.

So much of all that passed Mandi by in the flurry of every day, but she recorded them all in her diaries more than ever before, noting a changing world about her, but caught in the small story of her own family life. This family life that she described in her diary in 1968 was mundane, demanding, but clearly loving and fulfilling. She talked of Joey collecting his toys that were broken and putting them on Peter's chair for him to mend on return from a trip; she described her social engagements, what she was cooking, the plants she was growing, how she was looking after her mother-in-law, her mother's impending visits and what she had given up for the various Lents, how she dressed the children and how they behaved with each other, the rather unpleasant habits of the next door neighbour Mr Corner and weekly Sunday lunch with him, how Joe had chopped his own hair off and was now called Baldy, countless parties with friends and their small children, music, how they loved the Beatles, Jane Birkin, Serge Gainsbourg, Nana Mouskouri, Sandy Shaw, Sacha Distel and others. Music, dancing and partying, as for so many at this time, provided a sense of freedom from the responsibilities of life. However, by committing to a career in emotional intelligence, Mandi contributed to a time of change without even realising it.

As they approached Christmas Day in the late '60s, the difference in us, the children was noticeable, the entourage no smaller and the pace just as hectic.

1 JANUARY 1970

Nick wore long greys and sports jacket. The girls wore lovely green velvet dresses with lace ties and cuffs made by June Sixsmith. Joe wore a lovely green corduroy suit given by Gran with brass buttons and a shirt made from one of Grumpy's [her husband's] and a red bow tie. Peter gave me super Carmen curlers for Christmas; had Elsie, Mary and boyfriend, William, Aunt Eva and Dick Corner for lunch. Boxing Day party for 10. Gave them prawn curry and lots of different sweets.

30 DECEMBER 1969

Arrived to hotel in Llandudno. Thought we were late, but apparently early. No one there. No booking for us, so Peter had to complain. Did so vigorously. Got us a room. Room was dirty, so Peter set off again complaining. New room. Changed, fresh and showered, and down to the party. No party! Wrong hotel! Awkward moment! Moved to right hotel! Hotel Llandudno. Marvellous riotous New Year Party—ten of us in right place. Too much booze. Got tight. Can't remember the end of the party. Peter on great form. Mum held the fort.

The 1970 diary describes a whirlwind of activity largely in note form, often a couple of days after the day had passed by. Peter was thirty-eight by this time, Mandi thirty-four, Nick eleven, me ten, Lucy eight, Joey five and Mingo six.

When Peter was home, it was hectic socially. Otherwise, Mandi was still very busy with us. Peter was away a great deal now, often in Africa, and Mandi spent weeks alone, with these times often leaving her feeling less loved and more distant from him. In her diary of 1971, she cited Joe's prayers:

10 MARCH 1971

Dear Daddy, come home soon. I want you, Mummy does too. I hope your tooth is better.

All of us were at school by this time and there was a real sense of school routine and activities dominating daily life. Mandi was ambitious for her tribe and wanted them to do well, so she supported them as best she could. Nick was aiming for the 11+ and the local grammar school; I was Head Girl at Dormie House, the same local prep school, repeating a year to get to the right age; Lucy was in the year below her now; and Joey was six and there too.

Mandi drove herself to keep up with them all, her extended family, the children's friends, her friends, Peter's and her friends, the dog and her ongoing counselling training. It was piano practice first thing which was pretty hard work in itself, then exercising Mingo, their trusty and well-trained black Labrador running beside the car. Once round the block at quite a speed, Mingo would run alongside and largely be calm for the rest of the day. Any mornings with a fraction of space in them and she would get a run on the beach, but this was all too infrequent due to the endless domestic tasks.

Once the children were at school, there was that same round of home activity to be completed; it never went away and there was no budget to get any help with it. In went the loads of washing, once dried, the ironing, the putting away, the tidying, cleaning and hoovering, the scrubbing of floors and bathrooms, the polishing of the silver and brass, the beds that had to be stripped and remade weekly, the lists and the shopping, the cooking of a range of now very familiar but still favourite meals. There might be counselling, a lunch, coffee with friends, a charity or business function, children's friends to tea, homework to get done, the various activities, the garden to keep on top of, the church knockers to polish, letters to write, phone calls to make and so the round continued.

Trying to save money was always on the agenda and one plan that she cooked up with her friend Penny blew up on her. Bulk buying of honey required it to be shared into jars between the two of them, which Mandi agreed to take on. When she tried to heat it on the stove to be able to pour it into jam jars in a more liquid form, an air lock created undue pressure and the drum of honey exploded across the kitchen, spraying the sticky substance everywhere. Months of sticking to the floor and indeed every surface imaginable followed this unfortunate moment. 'For God's sake, why the hell am I sticking to the floor?' shouted Peter on his return, even though Mandi had cleaned it as often as the days he had been away had allowed.

It took months to return to normal and just as long for her dear husband to see the funny side of her cost-saving efforts. The fact that she had to repay the friend £50 was kept quiet just to keep the peace. The early attempts to use a pressure cooker had much the same result as the boiling rhubarb when it hit the wrong pressure point and blew up, shattering its sugary, fruity way over the kitchen walls and ceiling and never quite reaching the planned destination of hungry mouths. Ultimately Mandi mastered these various domestic appliances and became very proficient with them.

Out of school, she would still shop for our clothes and school uniforms at the Beanstalk, never able to exchange any items as the children always wore them out. Nick recalled:

'I remember going in to see Penny Baines at the Beanstalk and Mum buying my second hand rugby boots and second hand shirt when I got to grammar school and her saying: 'I'll buy you a new rugby shirt when you are captain of the first team'.

She certainly had expectations for us all and set high standards, but always with love and support and the undiluted belief that we could deliver. She would take us to our round of activities, sailing and rugger for Nick, Brownies and then guides and their various badge demands, dancing and later ballroom dancing and cross bearers for us girls, tennis for all. At home, lots of reading occurred, Enid Blyton in favour one year, Arthur Ransome the next, and Joey doing his daily reading practice in his parents' bed as well as cycling and playing for hours with Mingo and me outdoors whenever he could.

Mandi cut a striking figure on the School Sports Day on 12 July 1971. Asked to present the prizes, she borrowed an outfit to keep her costs down and spend her tight budget on the necessities. She arrived in the shortest of hot pants with a fitted white blouse and a flowing sleeveless coat with a broad-brimmed navy blue hat. The deep red and white outfit matched her long high heeled boots perfectly; she did not realise the statement she made as she stood patiently waiting for her introduction as the Guest of Honour. Far more eyes were on her than the worthy trophy winners as they came up one by one to shake her hand, including Lucy for the Project Prize and Joey for winning the flat race and the potato race. Mandi had done an enormous amount of work on that bird project, including taking Lucy to visit aviaries and finding relevant poems, and was particularly delighted to present her daughter with her prize!

That outfit and her fine and very shapely legs were discussed for some time to come and certainly at the drinks party at the school in the evening, which Mandi and Peter could not attend due to another party in their busy social calendar. Home after Sports Day, a quick supper, bath, film on, change of outfit, babysitter fetched and briefed and off again into the night. A tasty dinner, lots of booze, dancing into the early hours and the blessed relief of the slightly slower Sunday with only a few sets of tennis in it, homework catch up, gardening, washing, ironing and family time in the early evening.

The four children's birthdays followed a standard pattern with sandwiches, shortbread, flapjack, mother's cookies, biscuits, meringues, strawberries and cream, jellies, cornets and ice cream, homemade lemonade and orange as standard food and drink with fifteen or so friends to devour it. No great concerns about health back then, not sugar content or ADHD, and there were plenty of carbohydrates and few chopped vegetables in evidence for birthday teas. Standard games included pass the parcel, musical bumps, chairs and statues, a football match, guess the drawing on the blackboard, and racing with glasses of coloured water in teams and all of this marked Joey's sixth birthday party that year. It is easy to skip over the games, but Mandi's version of the coloured water race was always incredibly competitive and exciting and somehow she made 'Pass the Parcel' into a game you just could not wait for! A homemade birthday cake every time and this year, Joey had soldiers on his.

4 JULY 1970

Survived, but they were very lively.

Of course the children went to lots of other parties and the round of presents and to-ing and fro-ing was constant.

The outside playroom was now more of a hide-out, a place to play games, make dens, take time out, invite friends. Hours were still spent out there. Aunt Eva had given the family their own jigsaw and this was a popular hobby, particularly of Nick's. Mandi frequently had the children's friends to stay and the Earlams were a favourite household to go to. It was open and friendly and everyone felt so welcome. There was a madness about it all, with crazy games round the table. Twenty questions remained a favourite and Mandi would always join in and loved playing with everyone, hooting with laughter and never minding if she lost.

Dinner parties happened as often as they could afford and Mandi's diaries are full of various menus that she conjured up. Veal Marengo and a good curry were favourites and she even did a beans on toast supper when she was broke and to make a statement about not keeping up with the Joneses. She made every effort to notice what others served too and was either impressed or not. She would also often note down the cocktails she enjoyed or a decent wine.

4 JULY 1970
Prawns, 2 fresh chickens, bread sauce, cauliflower, sausages and bacon, strawberries and cream, pots, Blue Nun wine. Cost a fortune.

Their social life was extraordinarily busy whenever Peter was around: rounds of drinks and dinner parties, either given by them or by others; coffee and lunches given by friends; all manner of family picnics; the Grand National where everyone took their cars, piled in and set up for the day at the Canal Turn, TVs wired into the battery so something of the racing could be seen, picnics and entertainment for the day, walking the course, drinking too much and betting. Wimbledon was an annual must and so much more.

It was at one of those dinner parties in the very early '70s that Mandi remembers her dear friend Stuart Errington discussing sayings that represented their values with her. For him, it was 'I felt for a man who had no shoes and then I saw a man who had no feet'. For Mandi it was 'Judge not that ye be not judged'. From then on, the loo door was to gather sayings that would leave people sitting on the throne for ages contemplating their lives, states of mind or thoughts. Consistent with this ethos of provoking some self-reflection, the sayings that have come to express her values in life are set out at the end of the chapters to illustrate what drives Mandi's values, but also perhaps to prompt the reader. Undoubtedly her counselling training and practice was playing a role in causing her to think and question and it added both interest and challenge to the family dynamic as well as her own development.

'When you are through changing, you are through'.
— UNKNOWN —

Mandi became the consummate multi-tasker, mostly just getting on with the ceaseless round of challenges that beset her, but just occasionally *'blowing her top'*, as she would put it, before jumping back on her hamster wheel. When you follow the pattern of her diary entries, she herself notes that it was when she and Peter were both really tired that it became dangerous. One or both could lose control and Mandi would be likely to hurl whatever came to hand. At one point, and it lasted for some years, they set a control by only allowing the word *'cabbage'* to be uttered when a potential row was imminent. This word could be delivered with as much feeling and passion as necessary to make a point, but it could not be developed into a thought. One can only imagine!

Making up was sweet, but there was always regret and frustration with the self at this behaviour, particularly on Mandi's part.

Mandi makes regular entries in her diary about how much she loves her Peter.

22 OCTOBER 1970
How I adore him, curling around me. What joy to share such closeness with another person. If I ever lost Pete, how ghastly it would be. He is v.v. precious to me.

There are many entries about love-making in her reflections; these are slightly coded perhaps for reasons of discretion, although discretion is not an obvious part of Mandi's valour and her diaries were for her eyes and ears only or so she thought at the time! In typical Mandi fashion, Peter's penis was called *'George'* and George's activity is regularly if obliquely referred to. Such expressions as *'such heaven'*, *'a sublime moment'*, *'bliss'*, or *'a blissful moment'* confirmed that all was very well with their sex life despite an extremely busy time.

Nick and I were in the habit of bringing up breakfast in bed at the weekend and thought that their parents' closed door was for them to enjoy their boiled eggs, but the diary later revealed that this was private time and many of those ecstatic moments are recorded on Saturday and Sunday mornings.

The boil over of anger during those moments of blowing her top did not really occur until Mandi started doing her Marriage Guidance training. Certainly she was aware that she had an enormous load to carry and could become overtired. She really struggled with pre-menstrual tension, bloating and moods, as well as really heavy periods when they came, and she regularly notes the frustration and interference of this aspect of her life and body in her diaries. Indeed, her diaries reveal that she could be very hard on herself, but gradually, instead of slaving to please everyone or blaming herself for whatever had gone wrong and working hard to put it right, she started to stand her ground when criticised.

As her training freed her self-confidence, so her more forthright self emerged, and it was as though a different woman had been released. As Mandi became more confident professionally, so her voice became stronger. This new woman could express herself more freely, but had yet to make sense of the complexities and labels her childhood had left her with. Growth is never a completely upward trajectory. There are always ups and downs, losses and deals one must make with one's family, friends, and conscience.

Towards the end of November 1970, when her mother-in-law started with her customary pointed remarks, Mandi gave her a piece of her mind, letting her know just how unappreciative and ungrateful she was and hurling an ashtray at her to make the point. Lucy recalls MumMum coming upstairs and telling her that her mother was trying to kill her, but even at a young age, Lucy knew it was just frustration that she could not be heard.

Mandi, dealing with the expectations of being a wife, daughter-in-law, and mother, during a time period in which each role was undervalued, recorded half a page of vehement feelings:

> 30 NOVEMBER 1970
>
> *Silly old mean bitch. She can take a running jump. She is the last person I want around when Peter is away. I wonder what tale she will hatch to tell...*

At this time, Mandi had yet to understand that part of it was out of her control hormonally, part of her response was reaction to so many years of control and part of it was reaction to overload. Furthermore, she had yet to really make the space to reprogramme her habitual responses in order to make her own choices and say what she really wanted to, although her counselling training was teaching her that route for the future.

Seven development weekends for marriage guidance during the early '70s afforded the opportunity for detailed discussions about different techniques to draw out clients. These included free discussion and silence as well as gentle or provocative questioning. Listening was honed as a key skill. One might think 'active listening' is a modern term, but it is used back in that diary of 1970. There were sessions on how to question for different types of response. Perhaps a psychiatrist would come and give a talk on behaviour, looking at how depression might manifest itself for example. The early stages of marriage, later stages, individual behaviours that affect emotional relationships and everyday living such as manic depression were discussed and related to particular cases that people were working with.

Mandi would find herself with complete strangers and opening up about her hidden feelings as a child and adolescent, recognising how alone and neglected emotionally she felt in those early years by her mother and 'uneasy' about what to do with it or where to go with it.

27 JUNE 1970

Mental exercise and no physical exercise are no good. Must have both.

Learning about group dynamics and the effect that we all have on one another provided Mandi an interesting study of the various types of fellow students learning to be counsellors. Mandi noted who they all were in her diary, their different professions, observing those that talked too much, those that chipped in with just the occasional gem and those that said virtually nothing. She clocked the way people interacted together and was interested in that. She was able to relate much to her tutor and discuss her individual cases. Equally Mandi received feedback about the way she interacted in the training group and was encouraged to look at the way she used her sex amongst everyone, possibly as an attracting or diverting tactic.

Mandi would gain a great deal from these weekends, but get back both drained and exhilarated and with a desire to share and find answers to the questions that this time away had raised. She would find Peter rather uninterested in what she had learned and described him as distant and offhand.

29 JUNE 1970

We talked about being oneself and my need to have something
tangible to talk about and how I occasionally hurl things. P rather
quiet, unresponsive and a bit aggressive. Is it me?

Mandi was so excited to have something to challenge her that she
struggled to see that she had upset the status quo for taking whole
weekends out to do this training. Despite her careful arrangements
to make things go smoothly, her absence inevitably had an impact on
the way things usually were.

28 JUNE 1970

Caught 3.10 from Birmingham New Street. Big delay. Home
by 7.00pm. Big welcome. Jen had given P breakfast in bed and
cleaned everywhere, bless her. Nick reacted badly to P telling him
to do this and that instead of suggesting.

On another occasion, Peter's sister, Ruth came and helped Peter
with the children and they got through yet one more unfamiliar
weekend with the help of Mandi's many instructional notes.

Mandi's cases consisted of all manner of marriage difficulties.
Quite standard ones such as overdominance of one partner, lack of
communication, waning appreciation of one another, sexual intimacy
and its challenges, infidelity, selfishness, anger issues or other emotions such as jealousy, loss of trust, the stress of financial difficulty
or children on relationships, career ambitions, the role of gender
in society as understood by the self and others and their resultant
expectations, the intrusion of childhood patterns on everyday lives
and the pressures of work. More dangerous situations, such as wives
who were beaten up, but who were inextricably bound into the
complexities of the relationship and so could not leave their families,
would come up too. This kind of fear in relationships was very
complex to explore and solve.

Some of the most rewarding cases were the ones when Mandi
thought her clients would not return. One notable example was a very
highly-strung mother of three who had been married for fourteen
years and who had been brought up by a mother whose husband had
left her to look after five children alone. The client was the eldest
and at eight years old had been left to tend to her siblings whilst her
mother went out to work. The youngest of the children had been run

over whilst in her charge and then she and her siblings had been taken from their mother and put in a boarding school in Wales. She had enjoyed the five years there and met her husband just after that at seventeen. He was kind and reliable, but she did not love him and the more he loved her, the more she resented it, which she could not understand. She had come to counselling at the time of falling in love with her husband's friend, which was not helping matters at all. Mandi worked through all sorts of feelings and choices with her and the client constantly fed back how useful she found it. All very rewarding and a slow, but awakening time for Mandi to understand her own choices and responsibilities.

As Mandi established herself as a counsellor, she also was asked to go into the local convalescent home as it was known and offer relationship and sex education to children from very challenging backgrounds. This home provided foster care and the children had limited contact with their parents for various reasons. Mandi would discuss themes such as identity, development of friendship, and adolescence in terms of emerging physical and emotional change and how this impacted their relationships.

This was group work and confidential to those involved and 'Mrs E' became key for these children as an emotional crutch more than anything else. She had various recordings she used to play to her own children that explained the physical changes to the body, the growth of pubic hair and the transformation of various bodily features, which would cause a mixture of mortifying embarrassment or hoots of laughter at home, depending on the audience. They were of course intended for her students.

She became known as the sex teacher amongst her children's friends, which was certainly different and, in its difference, something to be proud of. All kinds of conversations used to take place around the table when friends came to supper if Mandi or the guests were given the chance to initiate it. She always found time to lead chats about all manner of aspects of life and most of the young visitors loved this. Caroline, a friend of mine who had no idea where babies came from, soon found out! Peter missed a lot of this activity as his work took him away so often.

Mandi saw three cases each week, and with the travel and writing up, this amounted to a full day's work. However, there was no doubt that the kind of cases that she was resolving often left her very churned up with unanswered questions of her own regarding her own needs, value, identity and relationships. She would write up her cases for a regular monthly tutorial where she had the opportunity to discuss specific characters, their behaviours and their impact on her. The idea was to ensure that she was not carrying too much emotionally that she could not deal with. She obviously needed this and wrote several entries in her diaries about it.

One example concerned three complex cases in the early '70s, that of a social worker who had been beaten and bashed by her policeman husband for almost two years, a Belgian Jewish lady in her early thirties who was very immature and angry and a desperate forty-year-old husband who had told his wife that he was in love with another woman, which had left her feeling suicidal. They had two children and no outside interests. These cases had hung over Mandi all the time that she was dealing with them, preying on her mind; there were no easy solutions, only weekly sessions for their support and monthly tutorials for her support and a sense that she was carrying the lives of these individuals in her hands during this very inexperienced stage of counselling.

The days of safeguarding were still a long way into the future and Mandi would try to help these very unhappy and desperate people see how they behaved and begin to understand why they did as they did, but with none of the support of the different services and agencies that exist today.

The training and the knowledge were not advanced enough to deal with the fact that Mandi's experiences were constantly having an impact on her own marriage in ways that she did not have the means to deal with. She would return from her weekly sessions in those early years and write diary entries regularly during the week about how she could not stop thinking about various clients, how she would like to talk to Peter about them, but how he did not want to. She indicated that he closed down when she would raise issues of MG, as they called Marriage Guidance. At times, she referred to his becoming irritated.

Mandi was clearly engrossed, but MG became the elephant in the room. Peter was too busy to spend time on working out what was getting in his way. Perhaps subconsciously, in his masculine role, he wanted to provide for Mandi and the children and constantly reminded her that she did not need to work and that her work was voluntary. The fact that it was marriage guidance that she was involved in seemed to make him feel scrutinised in his every move; it was threatening and he did not identify with it at all. Consequently, he showed only perfunctory interest and Mandi was silenced again, feeling devalued, something that was now very familiar to her. It intensely echoed her childhood patterns of inferiority.

The added burden of the work on top of four children and a hectic social life led to more frequent mentions of tiredness in her diaries and being close to the edge. Everyone knew the danger of that tiredness and it was eroding for the family. The sad irony of this time was that Mandi's generous efforts and learning on behalf of others were rendering her very vulnerable in terms of her own marriage and family life. Equally, she wanted something that recognised her capacity; she could see and hear around her that society was changing and women were emerging more strongly, speaking up for themselves and being valued, and she knew that she had something to offer.

Nick later wrote:

> 'We were all the recipient of her training as a Marriage
> Guidance Counsellor, which I think encouraged an openness
> and a communication skill set that would not have been
> there with just Dad. She would throw outrageous bomb-
> shells into the middle of a discussion and it was usually
> about sex'.

Peter and Mandi's marriage suffered a near crisis in 1971, nearly fourteen years in, when Peter found himself very attracted to another woman. Jane probably appealed to Peter at this point because his life was on full throttle and a lot of the fun had gone out of it in favour of these rather heavy conversations about Marriage Guidance that he constantly tried to avoid and the demands of a very busy family life on a very tight budget. Two teenagers added to the pressures of family life and, whilst work was a constant pressure, Peter was beginning to appreciate himself as a successful businessman. Perhaps he just could not help himself, but it was a measure of their deep friendship that he told Mandi all about the attraction before things got out of control. It hurt her very badly, making her extremely jealous, angry and frustrated. Perhaps the sharing of the responsibility for the distraction, Peter being away so much and Mandi moody at times and crazily busy, together with their very real love for each other, allowed the moment to pass and the marriage to get back on to its even keel again.

However, Mandi's life did not change and Peter was to remain very busy with his career in the '70s and away a great deal. He apologised for leaving Mandi for the whole of Christmas to prepare as he wrote to her from his trip to Paris, Hamburg and then Japan in late 1972. He had stayed with his good friends the de Monteynards in Paris and promised to take Mandi in May.

12/13 DECEMBER 1972

We've been on board the huge Jumbo 747 for 7.5 hours. There are only 7 in first class and it is like our drawing room, very spacious and far better than smaller aircraft.

A couple of annual business trips for Mandi also kept the pressure up, but the interest in their relationship alive. She met all manner of people and Peter was proud of the way she connected so easily with his various clients. He loved her to come along on trips because of the wonderful way she could draw people in and make a social situation flow. She was always willing to organise the household, leaving copious notes for the godly souls she found in *The Lady* magazine, and come along, borrowing smart outfits from girlfriends, and playing the part to the full.

1974 was one such highlight for Mandi when Peter passed on the invitation to launch a ship in Stettin, Poland on 15 December of that year. She immediately set to learning Polish with one of the girls' Guiding connections and with a tremendous amount of effort was able to deliver a fluent and very competent speech of welcome and gratitude in Polish, one which she can still recite to this day as can her children as she practised it so often!

'Jest mi bardzo przyjemnie byc tutaj razem z wami...'

She went down a storm in her striking fur hat, taking the interpreters by surprise with her competent use of their language and the good ship 'Sherbro' was duly launched, complete with champagne over her bows and cut ribbon. The little axe with which she cut the ribbon is displayed proudly in her home today and the story is relayed to any passing Pole, complete with the speech. It always makes for an unusual and very surprising encounter!

Trearddur Bay holidays continued to provide a vital getaway and treasured family time. Mandi sailed with Peter and completed her usual round of jobs, but in simpler fashion. The children still lived in swim gear and washed it out in the bath at night, so life was easier. Her rickety twin tub washing machine had a spin dryer that shook the whole kitchen and Mandi became famous for laughing with everyone about how the corner of that washing machine on full spin provided the best vibrator of all time, especially after Peter had just returned to work. Goodness knows how many imagined her in her tiny red bikini that Peter had bought her enjoying that unusual stimulator. Her marriage guidance counselling training following her nursing training had left her capable of addressing any often taboo subject with light-hearted directness, which more often than not deepened her connection with those that she met.

There is a real sense of the sensual in Mandi's diaries in these holidays: stunning views of sailboats, motor launches, big yachts, the imposing Holyhead mountain always in the background; the sun, the rushing wind, the flapping sails, the heat, the cold, the salt spray on faces and its taste on the tongue on wild, windy days; the waves splashing or crashing depending on the day; running towards and jumping into that inviting but always perishingly cold sea; the scrunchy sand everywhere in hair, under fingernails, on floors and carpets; the stones and pebbles that hurt under your feet. Long hours in boats or on rocks fishing for mackerel, letting the line slip through your fingers and unhooking their slippery and elusive selves from the hook, marching over springy heather and scrambling over rocks. These were activity holidays; Peter taught Nick to sail and he did DIY jobs. Nick taught me to crew for him in our red cadet, Red Fox. The day started with a swim in that ice cold sea; each of us coloured our box on the family chart by the back door to indicate that the swim was done and that they deserved their breakfast. Hours were spent on the beach making sandcastles, picnicking, relaxing, swimming, playing ball games and hooting with laughter. We all played tennis with friends and family.

The garden was also a space for countless games of French cricket and ball games with Mingo the dog. If the weather was right, meeting with other families on Main Bay for surfing and jumping the waves in the angry sea was a must, closely followed by baths and hot chocolate. If the weather was calmer, then a rowing boat and fishing and prawning were much more suitable activities. Over time everyone acquired a bike there and this became a key way of getting around or running the odd errand.

The evenings in the height of August were great fun as couples got together and the annual Trearddur Bay Dance was always a fabulous night out as the family became established in the sailing club. Mandi and Peter would continue to hold several of their own such nights, but the music was more '70s now and those Top of the Pops favourites provided the dance beat.

As the early days of September came closer, blackberry picking was a much loved pastime and purple fingers, stained mouths and clothes were inevitable. Pounds of blackberry jelly were made and stored each year, the blackberries being strained through muslin sieves. It was another of those holiday rituals that only ended when the autumn term was brought forward and the blackberry season no longer fitted in.

The only restaurant meal of the year for the children was always with Mr Venables on the very last day of the summer holiday after the big clean up. This was the reward for everyone's cleaning contribution, after which no one was allowed to set foot inside the immaculate Lamare again. It was always both a joyous and a poignant moment. Those holidays were a very happy time in the early years. There was always an adventure to be had. There are days that are indeliby etched on the children's minds for one reason or another.

Mandi records the one when they all went down to the water and she and Peter tried to save the boats that were crashing about in the waves. The children could only watch as it was too dangerous and Mandi's fear for Peter grew as he went fearlessly into the surf to try to secure the loose boats. She described it as *'a day that we will never forget'* in her 1973 diary.

> *14 AUGUST 1973*
> *I will never forget the day in Treaddur Bay when we lost Hebe—at that point in my life having not lost anybody close to me it was probably one of my saddest days. I remember Dad immediately buying Argo, another Trearddur Bay one design, from the Westons to focus on something new.*

The shocking event that Nick remembered was experienced by our whole family at the time and we all have a version of the story. He, Mandi, Peter and I had headed off to race on a rough day and the weather had really blown up fast. Nick and I, both of quite sturdy build, had survived a lap of the race on the relatively inshore course quite well, but were called to shore because of the storm and had to head for the beach. Mandi and Peter, meanwhile, were further out to sea and failed to get round the buoy as they went about, their boat capsizing and leaving them both struggling with the huge seas, heavy clothing, lifejackets and boat equipment. The lifeboat arrived quickly and picked Mandi up, but getting Peter to leave his boat was a tougher matter and in the end, he reluctantly obeyed the order. He did not want to leave his boat because he was trying to release the anchor in the hope that it would stay until after the storm. The boat held its position quite well for a while because the anchor did drop with Peter's initial help, but the ferocity of the storm and currents pushed it onto the rocks overnight and it was smashed to smithereens by the next morning. The silence, the shock and the sadness of that reality is what we all most remember.

By the mid-70s, Mandi was to tire of Trearddur somewhat and long for some more of the travel and excitement that she felt that Peter was getting from his work and which she occasionally got to enjoy on their trips. Nonetheless, the family holidays prevailed with the same commitment and gusto with the children beginning to go out much more with their friends and spending less family time together.

At least one annual trip to Mandavant, Mandi's parents' house in Margate, continued to take place. A three-hundred mile, six-and-a-half hour drive, with the children in the back. A picnic and a quiz about London on the way to keep it interesting and a chance for Mandi to reconnect with her birthplace and for the children to be impressed by her knowledge.

16 JULY 1971

They thought I was a walking encyclopaedia.

These days at Mandavant were always more relaxing for Mandi, fewer chores and a moment to breathe and catch up on her parents' lives. She would sew, a jumpsuit for me in 1972, and plans for an evening dress for herself, having bought the material for a pound. The pink dress Mandi really wanted was nine pounds and far too expensive. Enid really spoiled Mandi these days, buying her things very generously. This time, a rotary iron for her birthday to make sheet ironing so much easier; her standards were extraordinarily high and needed to be with Peter at her side; a sheet would never be put back on the bed creased. Enid also bought her two new pairs of shoes and other necessary items for the children. It all helped so much with the limited cash flow, a source of constant worry.

The children always enjoyed their time there, happily playing, but also connecting to their grandparents who would include them in the day-to-day activities. Writing, reading, cooking, turning out drawers to discover their family history, and pitch and putt were all favourites. Time to admire her father's beautiful garden. His colourful blooms in mid-July welcomed them and the children loved the expanse of garden to play in and pick the raspberries in there as well as be by the sea. Mandi adored that time in the garden with her father and taking cuttings for her own garden was always a treat; she writes enthusiastically of her geraniums, pelagonia and hydrangea cuttings in 1974. Nick reiterated this relationship with her father and how it impacted him:

'I loved the relationship she had with Grumps; she wor-
shipped him and it is largely through her and him that my
love of things such as Jerusalem, Land of Hope and Glory as
well as Religion and History, came'.

Mandi equally writes of her mother:

21 JULY 1972

*Mum has to be top dog, has to blow her trumpet and be the best.
She is so contradictory. No two statements tally. I have hardly
seen any of you during your stay. You are out all the time playing
games and the next second she is telling you to get out of the garden and go out and enjoy the beautiful day. You just cannot win.*

At home, life was always full on. Although the home computer was of the mid 70's, it did not find relevance in this family. For Mandi, it was all about discipline and routine, plenty of fresh air, good food, loads of fun and laughter and exercise. She found the energy for it de-spite any setbacks such as Nick's injuries on the sports pitch. I chopped off the hems of the new dresses to make them shorter and trendier, despite my mother having just turned them up. Lucy's love traumas and Jo's many accidents and the sad death of dear Aunt Eva in 1973 were just a few examples of the setbacks that Mandi constantly overcame. Peter had worked a long way up the corporate ladder by then and the external demands on him were constant. Mandi had a fair number of godchildren by then too and it was and would always be great joy to her to have them and her brothers' children in her life.

Nick recalled:

> 'I remember at School in 2B when I fluffed my exams on
> account of not having been able to see the blackboard all
> year because of my eyesight and her going in to plead my
> case with Mr Brown, my music teacher, although largely
> we were left to our own devices at school'.

She was game for everything; I remember winning the Handicap Mixed Doubles at Hoylake with her on a few occasions and the Ladies' Race on a few occasions at Trearrdur Bay. She always had bags of enthusiasm for whatever she did and that is a huge positive for whatever one does in life. I remember winning the school poetry prize with 'Mrs Reece has laughed' and her saying you have to say it with passion which I did and even though I missed off a few lines, the adjudicators said that it was the passion and feeling that had made me win, which came from practising with Mum.

The dinner party scene was still full on with the children old enough to be helpers in the mid–70s. A lot of business entertaining and *beef chasseur* and *carré d'agneau* followed by hazelnut meringue became specialties which the children loved finishing up afterwards.

6 MAY 1974

The party jelled from the start and P was so proud of me and thrilled with me as a hostess.

This meant the world to Mandi. She had come to need Peter's frequent reassurance that he valued her.

The transistor radio was well and truly part of bringing the outside in and it was not until 1975 that TV was established in the home and then very rationed. Such programmes as *Ironside*, *Starsky and Hutch*, *Kojak*, *Doctor Who*, *Benny Hill*, *Steptoe and Son* and *Dallas* all became favourites. Paul Newman, Robert Redford, Clint Eastwood and John Wayne were all household names through their films.

Bringing the outside world into the house was an important development for Mandi. Until this point, it had had to be kept distant, but now she was beginning to have the time and space to see more. While she didn't make or want to make drastic or immediate changes, she couldn't help but move forward with the times. She was always a woman who accepted growth and change, and life for women in various parts of the world was changing enormously: abortion services, health centres, feminist magazines, militant theatre, day-care, shelters for battered women and rape crisis centres and increasing movement towards equal pay. Although she noted events and change in her diaries, these bigger picture stories were still not where Mandi focused her attention; she concentrated on the individual story, the physical, emotional and mental health of her clients and family. But she failed to notice her own story, and the necessary or helpful changes she needed to make!

Space hoppers and walkie talkie sets were toys of the decade that we played with. Next door to the playroom, with the jigsaw now producing those pin ups, was the greenhouse and this also was a sanctuary. Plants, salad vegetables, seasonal flowers were all grown here and it was the focus of great effort and a source of great pride. The lawn, the size of a tennis court, was often used as just that although it was not of the right quality. It was kept immaculately by Peter, if he was available, and Mandi, if Peter was away. Peter had a penchant for brown earth and took his life into his hands the weekend he dug up all Mandi's newly planted bedding plants to clear the bed and achieve tidy, brown earth in his beds. Mandi was always inspired by her father's beautifully tended and colourful Mandavant garden and sought to emulate it. So to see the seedlings she had so carefully grown in the greenhouse ready for planting be hoed up in favour of brown earth was a step too far and she took her anger out on a collection of jam jars innocently stored by the dustbins. One after the other, they felt the force of her wrath as they hit the brick wall and her language matched her fury! No one would ever forget that 'day of the jam jars' or the value of the colourful bedding plants!

On the path between the lawn and the house was a space for the dog kennel and a table tennis table. Gradually over the years, the quality of the practice and matches ensured that all children had table tennis as a key skill, a source of great fun and a keen sense of competition. Mandi was the genuine facilitator of this and would lose endless games to boost her children's belief that they could improve, always making them feel fabulous about their wins and sure that they could do better next time if they lost. They were a lot less kind to each other! Mandi was a surprisingly natural teacher, but she never seemed to be conscious of it.

Sunday was an important family day with a number of familiar rituals. Music played a significant part and would begin early on the Sunday morning with some Bach, Beethoven, Handel or other favourite composer, always a popular way to wake up for the emergent teenager! This was masterminded by Peter. There was never a Sunday without a delicious Sunday roast lunch accompanied by various aunts, Mr Corner, the next door neighbour and an assortment of other visitors, to enhance the conversation and family values. The evening was still very much family time. Top of the Pops and Abba songs and ghastly no 1 hits like *'Tie a yellow ribbon round the old oak tree'* by Dawn and *'My ding a ling'* by Chuck Berry that stayed at no. 1 for weeks and were sung from memory by the whole family. Guffaws of laughter broke out round the stereo player that was housed near the piano as dance moves or variations on lyrics were initiated and sometimes this would turn into a sing song as Peter played the piano for everyone or the children demonstrated new found skills on the piano.

The family, led by specific members, listened to and became fans of some emerging progressive rock bands including the now famous Genesis and Pink Floyd. Fans of The Rolling Stones, Led Zeppelin and Queen, they equally enjoyed the more glamorous Gary Glitter and David Bowie and bands like Slade and Wizard and possibly the most successful in the 70's being ABBA which provided hours of dancing and singing. I had David Cassidy posters plastered all over my half of the bedroom while Lucy plastered the other half with the Sweet. Nick loved Barbra Streisand and Jo longed to be in Gary Glitter's 'Gang', which was an acceptable ambition at the time! *Top of the Pops* was necessarily followed by a drama series, such as *Poldark* or *The Onedin Line*, which was equally a must for all the family over a simple supper of soup and sandwiches, and this vital together time came with endless laughs and banter.

Football on the TV brought the popularity of the game to new heights and Mandi's diaries often talk about Nick and Jo going crazy with excitement or frustration depending on how their adored Liverpool was doing. The home was not a safe place if they were losing, as furniture was hurled and waved at the TV, such is the passion of the supporting scouser! Mandi had supported Liverpool all her adult life and cared intensely about the team's performance. The girls were less keen, but there was not a member of the family that was not tennis mad. They all played it and were glued to Wimbledon fortnight, not to mention their total commitment to their local club where they all competed avidly.

In 1974, Mandi wrote about her children to Mrs Clark with whom she was going to leave them before heading off on a business trip to Africa with Peter. She described Nick as sports mad and preparing for his CSEs and O Levels and well–motivated, if under pressure, to deliver. She went to great length to describe my genetic makeup and how I absorbed food according to the dietician she had recently seen and whilst it was unfair, the bottom line was not to feed me much as I just did not need it, especially in readiness for my trip to Las Palmas to learn Spanish on Mandi's return. Lucy was growing up too fast, was very popular with the boys, was coping admirably with the demands of life and was generally very easy and Jo equally so, but needed to have his nose kept to the grindstone, be reminded to wash and put on a clean shirt. He was mostly good and rather a poppet and awfully good at cleaning windows by the way. Mingo was getting old by this time, but still had her demands.

The exchange opportunity took me away from those Trearddur summers and I went to spend my thirteenth summer with the very glamourous Frédérique of another family just outside Nice and also had a spell in Las Palmas aged fourteen in a Spanish speaking school, whilst living with some ageing colleagues of Peter. Peter organised for me to travel on the Aureol, one of his passenger ships, ten days each way, in the care of the purser and then stay with these colleagues, attending school, improving my language and having quite an experience, before shipping me back to England. Whilst Trearddur Bay was the chosen holiday destination for the family, both Peter and Mandi were supportive of any opportunity to see the world and never said no unless they were financially forced to. I quickly became keen on languages and had lots of exciting and challenging adventures. Lucy had wonderful times in Portugal with her friend Claire, chosen as this only child's special holiday friend.

Mandi and Peter themselves loved travel and Mandi described her trip to Africa in 1974 in her diary in detail. The trip was clearly marred by a major epileptic fit. However, she did not dwell on this and kept going on her busy travel schedule with a quick trip to a doctor for some appropriate medication, allowing her to relish her time with Peter, and as ever, not putting herself and her own needs at the top of the agenda.

Mandi needed this time out from her busy life back home, and there was no way she was going to let it to be interrupted by ill health and nor was Peter; he had so much on with work and so much to worry about with his career, so they brushed it under the carpet, hearing and wishing to believe the doctor's amateur diagnosis that it was probably just overload. Those business trips remained important for giving them time together and giving to each other, but Peter also had to work hard during them. At least Mandi had some time to relax and recharge, which she clearly needed. Right from the start, they had been in the habit of Peter and his career coming first and that had not changed, despite some pertinent warning signals.

23 MARCH 1974

Dancing at the top of the Reina Isabel together, P having smoked the most enormous cigar, given to him by the cigar factory, my feelings flooding me for his brown and handsome face, put-ting lacquer on his hair these days to keep it down. We talked last night about our relationship, my unaccountable swings of temperament and what it does to him. I promised I would show him what I am made of, His gorgeous tanned body, his glorious smile for me today....He buys me a beautiful gold ring with diamonds, really beautiful. Oh precious! I don't deserve you at times, but my jealousy springs from fear of the unknown.

There is no reference in the diary to Mandi's unmanageable workload, to her health and wellbeing, to the fact that she really did struggle with pre-menstrual tension and had little idea of how to manage the excessive mood swings and bleeding each month. She just knew that her challenge, as it had been all her life to date, was to do better. Interestingly one of her key lessons that undoubtedly served her as much as it served her clients, the students she taught and her children was the 'cutting of the cake' lesson which is still famous with a large number of my students to this day and Lucy used as a technique in a behaviour change project. Mandi summarised it for the purpose of this book:

4 APRIL 2020

Your life is a cake and it is up to you how you cut it up, but it is vital that you sit down and work out how to cut it up. Your values and principles sit firmly as the centre of the cake and direct your choices, and you then have your 24 hours in which to put your work, pleasure, exercise, sleep, eating, other which might need working out: the place of church, the role of money, time for yourself, others that you need to give to, and want to or perhaps do not want to, your possessions and whatever else matters in your life. You can use the cake to see the balance of your life and then make adjustments to greater control.

Mandi never pretended that it was easy. With renewed vigour after each small hiatus, she continued to do her best as she had always done, only letting out her feelings in those bursts of pre-menstrual anger or frustration that she had, or perhaps now through epileptic fits, but not making any changes to the pressures of her own life, which in truth was probably what was needed for her to be able to get some degree of control. It was so difficult to lead emotional and mental wellbeing when there was no understanding of it from those immediately surrounding her or in wider society.

A year later, she was off again, this time to Italy, a country which was to become very important to Mandi over the years.

Italy is the country where Peter and I first really took stock of what we'd done, spending our honeymoon round Lake Maggiore and the Adriatic Coast. Nearly 18 years later in 1975 and with a lot of water having passed under the bridge, we were off on a conference with my constitution at a very low ebb indeed and the Chief Executive, Peter, not far off the ground either.

Grand National day – The Tooseys had organised a big do and the Brunswick Boys dance were missed. Too much going on. Too many things to get to.

Having collected the deep based voiced Coinwein from Lime St today before and still harbouring uncertainties regarding leaving her with my darling Nick, Jen and Lucy, we set off early Saturday for the rendez vous at Wolverhampton to drop of Jo and redeliver the hired car at Heathrow which left not even 5 minutes to spare on either occasion.

They had dropped Jo off with his godmother whilst they went away as it would have been too much for the well-meaning help that Mandi had found in the *Lady* magazine to look after all the children.

The DC8 transported two rather weary individuals lacking sparkle to Rome Airport. Even here among the crazy, jossling, giggling mixture of hundreds of bodies trying to pass the Passport Control, enthusiasm wasn't in our veins.

After an hour we were finally sitting strapped into our Avis Fiat, lira in our wallet, we set off in search of Rome and Hotel St Anselmo; only then did I pause for breath and realise what was happening, the River Tiber curving in and out spanned by many bridges, the overwhelming feeling of history, religion, its architecture, why of why hadn't I paid more attention in my history lessons?

Bless Margaret Hoyland, Peter's latest secretary, for she had too lived in Italy and armed us with Maps, dictionary and guide and above all had contacted her old friend Barbara Apostal who had lived there for 16 years and had found us our Pension – Room 82.

Once in, she wrote this rhyme as a reflection of where they were at the start of their trip.

My curse was flooding, I was beginning a stye,
It wouldn't have taken much to make me cry
Pedro's seering headache and neck glands like nuts
And the usual squitters were gurgling from his guts.
(Not really right!!! Well you know what I mean!!!)

She recorded the trip very carefully on loose leaf paper and these notes are to be found in the otherwise virtually empty 1975 diary in chronological order, but without dates.

Our bodies announced food was required as we strolled down the pleasant avenue lined with trees about to burst into leaf. The façade of the restaurant called Taverna Castia was brown and dingy, but fatigue and hunger propelled us to push open the door. How right we are! Pizzas were being made before our eyes and shoved into huge log ovens – the vino, minestrone verdura, sogliola and the cost was BELLISSIMO.

Nerves of steel are required to drive round Rome, but it was Sunday and, refreshed, we sallied forth in the car for a wizz around the Colosseum where gladiators and beasts in the far off days had fought to kill – Cast St Angelo, nestling in beside the Tiber, St Maria Maggiore, the biggest church in Rome.

We paused for a snack round the Piazza Venezia, the hideous whiteness of the Vittorio Emmanuelle, where Mussolini harangued his all too easily won mob. Toasted pizza with cheese and ham inside and cappuccino. First big mistake, we sat down and were charged twice the price for doing so!

The City stands on seven hills, the scenic material for an artist is endless, it is so much smaller than London. The narrow streets with gaudy washing hanging precariously from bits of string and lacking the 'persil' whiteness.

The Campaglio is the museum containing endless treasures. Peter had even gone to the trouble of obtaining special passes to enable us to enter free, but their opening times, like so much of what is Italian, were bizarre, we missed the views of the Bronze of Romulus and Remus.

We parked the car close to the Spanish Steps and drank in the scene. At the bottom, Benini's white marble fountain with a mottly collection of jean clad bodies idly sitting around; on closer inspection, the cigarette butts and garbage that were strewn around rather spoiled the beauty. A chubby little Italian selling onyx cigarette cases had a bewitching smile and an uncanny collection of English phrases. 'No judge a book by its cover'. Was he being personal or not? He told us he had learned his English during the war. We strolled back up the Steps— paintings, ceramics, leather goods, crucifixes, nick knacks and any amount of self-portrait painters only waiting for a suitably conceited person to offer themselves. On our left was Keats' home. We climbed into the Fiat and wended our way toward St Peter's Square. Time marched on and we were drunk with it all. With our minds full of roofs, monuments, domes, the crazy-loving laughter from the people of this country, we weaved our way back to the pension.

The Conference, there was nothing arranged for the ladies and Peter had committed me to drive Madame Naff, Frau Wassermanand Deidre McCormick round Rome in our hired Fiat. On the day in question, I took the wheel for the first time to deliver Peter to the meeting. It was rush hour and it took an hour to get to the Hotel Parco del Principi by the Villa Borghese. The night before we had just dropped by to establish its location. I thought

I could map read, but you have to drive in Rome to know that you are not infallible.

'Turn right' No way, you have to go over those lights. You have to turn left in the one-way system further and further from your destination. All the time lights are blinking and flashing. Traffic shreaks over passes, under passes, round roundabouts at about 70 km per hour. The aim seems to be speed and noise and to hell with where you are going. I leave my darling armed with briefcase and the fearful USA representative who said 'Hi Dave' to David on first introduction, ignoring us. He had seven children, a monotonous drawl, bored the pants off everyone and P. invited him to spend the evening with us the following night. He will never learn to curb his instinctive kindness, even when entirely unnecessary!

I had the Fiat and three female companions and off we set for the Vatican. Italian traffic is just crazy nonsense. It seems hysterical and follows no rules. You haven't a clue what the driver ahead or behind or beside you is going to do next and he usually does it. The hazards are innumerable. Motor scooters, thousands of cars weave in and out like flies, weeny cars hide in front of massive ones and leap from left to right without bothering with signals. There are gigantic trucks, tankers, even horses and carts, bicycles by the score and, to top it all, pedestrians walk blissfully about, oblivious to the fact that they are on the main highways. Trams lunge forward and jerk to a halt; the roads are not covered evenly with asphalt as that would be too much to ask! Pot holes the size of small craters with cobbles all around, the ruts of the tram carts, all add to the challenge of driving in Rome. Naturally Italians are Italians and when in Rome, do as the Romans do. This means driving around at 100km per hour, blowing the horn with gay abandon and screeching the brakes. Do not try it unless you have nerves of steel which miraculously I had this morning. (God must have been guiding me). I even held up a tram with a flat hand on the windscreen, a big grin and then topped it by blowing the driver a kiss and squeezing through a gap in the traffic without a centimetre on either side.

So we had no difficulty getting there or finding a parking space, but later learning that the area had been declared a

*forbidden area in the Italian newspapers. We all walked around
the wall, drank in the sunshine and surveyed the splendour
of St Peter's, its magnitude, the vast columns of marble,
Michelangelo's exquisite statue on entering, but to one who
likes simplicity, it was so overcrowded and I thought the high
altar, where the Pope takes Mass each Sunday, was a vast, black
monstrosity; its four high, black, twisting pillars with gilt to me
only needed curtains to turn the 'blessed' thing into a four poster
bed for Goliath. Far, far too much of everything. The paintings
were not a patch on the National Gallery and there wasn't a
stained-glass window anywhere.*

The ecoustics were excellent and a service conducted in
German by Bishops all clad in red. How I wished the organ would
spontaneously burst into 'Praise my soul the king of heaven',
then it might have come alive for me. There were hundreds of
sight-seers.*

*I need hardly say that I had read very little about St Peter's,
but my limited grey matter had absorbed a fair bit about the
beautiful Sistine Chapel and I was dying to lie on the floor and
gaze at the beauty of MIchelangelo's painted ceiling, but time
did not permit. So into the Fiat we settled and off to the hotel for
lunch with our menfolk, making it just before they rose from their
green baize table, having finished their business. Smoked ham,
veal, mash and broccoli, gateau and coffee. The men and our
Italian host all made desperately uninspired after lunch waffle
until we said our goodbyes. WE WERE FREE AT LAST!*

Mandi went on to recount the rest of that day and the next in
great detail, the time spent exploring and meeting new people, having
fun and ultimately conscious that they kept the USA representative
waiting, which made him cross, and he then ordered the most
expensive dishes from the menu and, unsurprisingly, bored the pants
off them.

She was not very interested in the entertaining aspect of this trip,
although always played her part, noticed each person she met and
picked out aspects of them in an almost cartoon-like manner. She
was amusing about Barbara, the manic depressive who popped round
to them for a drink, and consumed several drinks punctuated with
regular, 'I must go really' promises, recounting all manner of manic

depressive problems increasingly fluently as she drank.

Meeting such people and hearing their life story was something Mandi became very good at, though it was definitely not of huge interest to Peter. He was nonetheless always impressed when she could recall colleagues, their children's names and their family histories. She had of course recorded her various encounters very thoroughly in her diaries and a quick reread always meant that she was perfectly briefed to entertain on business trips or wherever required.

Mandi's great excitement on this trip was about her love for her husband, whom she was clearly worried about, his tension, his edginess with the slightest sign of pressure, his headaches; she relished having this time with him and revived quickly to care for him, but she also drank in the culture and loved the speed and the challenge of the driving in Italy. They went on towards Naples, past 'the double coned Vesuvius smoking gently like my old Pedro with his pipe beside me'. As they made their way down towards the Amalfi Coast and Positano:

> I had no time to peruse the scene, first left, then right, then lost for
> half an hour, then back on the autostrada and off we went again.
> Suddenly we were whirling into the mountains behind Sorrento
> and then we flashed onto the coast road, high, high above the
> Tyrrhanian Sea, which hooked, then corkscrewed on a knife edge,
> designed I am sure to be first too narrow for two cars side by side,
> naturally coaches, buses, trucks, livestock, scooters and ambling
> pedestrians were all to be found on it. The oranges and lemons
> hung in their millions from their trees on either side and we had
> to stop and buy some; they were delicious, juicy and refreshing.

Mandi and Peter were then to enjoy a real break in Positano, where they had honeymooned together seventeen years before. The strain of leading was telling on Peter and as they relaxed, he became ill. Mandi enjoyed nursing him and talked about the value of this time to get to know one another again. She noticed that just like her father, he had to have something to worry about, whereas she was really living in the moment, reviving her resilient self, and there are more vivid and animated descriptions in her diary of all the activity that she saw and enjoyed in Positano, the local crafts, the views, the nature. Yet again Mandi revealed herself as very sensual, very aware, very conscious of the gift of now and of love. As their break came to an end, there is a humour and lightness again that had been missing, lost in the craziness of their respective lives, and they both loved it.

> *Blissful blue sky. We paid our last visit to Chez Black where we were given the royal treatment. We consumed a couple of bottles of red wine and delicious gambari fried with lemon. My P's eyes were shining out of his newly tanned face and he was talking to me with sincerity and fun. What heaven! The next day, the bill paid, we set off to see Sorrento, laughing and joking. P's pipe empties and burns a hole in his trousers. He is getting like Dick Corner next door.*

She went on to describe their wonderful trip to Pompeii and the cultural treat it was for both of them. She adored the Italians and celebrated the way they charmed her into buying more ice cream than she needed or wanted. She fell for it whilst some voice in the back of her mind was asking her if they had made it in a chamber pot and kept it under the bed. Her mother had somehow come with her in that brief moment! Her final entry for this day was, *'So, so, so happy!'*

Once back from that memorable and sustaining trip, the home routines began again and both of their lives became time poor. Peter's work meant that he and Mandi barely had a moment to recreate that cherished togetherness and in the rush of every day, it was quickly lost and forgotten, or so it seemed. Peter was tense and anxious to prove himself, mostly away from home or bringing back a self that was unfamiliar to Mandi. She carried on holding the family home together and entertaining or being entertained as requested. Somehow, Peter slipped away from Mandi at this time, drawn to the life he was lead-ing and the people he was meeting elsewhere. Mandi, driven by the requirements of her children, marriage guidance and the ongoing unpredictability of those moods, knew he was slipping away from her, but they had neither the time nor means for them to focus on one another.

In the summer of that year, Nick was sixteen. He spent six weeks working at Margate Railway station living with his Gran and Grump, Enid and Noel. Jack the gardener and Mrs Henley were all part of that happy picture for him and he recalled the beautiful garden, the putting green, gin and tonics, test matches, Grapenuts for breakfast and the most wonderful tea in the morning served in Indian Tree teacups. He felt treated as an adult always. Gran and Grump would sometimes fight, but it was always with good humour and a twinkle in the eye. As the eldest grandson, they would giggle over their memories, him as 'a naughty little boy', burning his jumper and being unkind to his sisters, whilst staying with his grandparents, waiting for his baby brother to be born. Stealing sweeties from the cupboard next to the fireplace was another favourite. Gran saving his life as Nick saw it when he returned from the awful French exchange and there she was, offering him a luxurious tea at the Coburg after all the terrible French food he had had to endure. They laughed over Christmases together, the Earlam family's terrible green-eyed cat and the ghastly singing in church. His straightforward love for his grandparents carried none of the baggage that Mandi's did, but then he had not grown up with them and wasn't a girl. Mandi's children were growing up and beginning to disappear from home for quite lengthy periods.

Over the Christmas of 1975, Mandi was to undergo her biggest personal trial ever when it came to love and marriage. She didn't write anything in her diaries at this time as it was all too painful and this has been pieced together through conversations. She was going to take Peter's suit to the dry cleaner and she checked the pockets as ever. She found a loving note to him from another woman.

When confronted, he admitted all. A dreadful Christmas ensued with her parents present as Mandi went through anger, grief and then a process of acceptance and determination to fight. Lucy and I will never forget getting in the car with our mother around that time as she drove to Thurstaton Hill, a local site of natural beauty, smashed the car into the car park wall, declaring:

DECEMBER 1975
He cares far more about his precious possessions than me. This
will teach him!

Of course his love for his possessions was just part of the problem; she then shoved open the car door, got out, slammed the door, and, tearing a branch from a tree, swished the trees and bushes in anger as she marched, we two girls in hurried but tentative pursuit. Her hurt was palpable at this time and her parents were there to support her during that dreadful Christmas.

She confided in Nick a great deal and he was always there for her when she needed him, though he reflects at this point in his life that he was probably too young to be the confidant he was required to be. Initially Mandi could not cope and Jo was sent to stay with his godmother for several weeks. Here he had a nasty accident:

15 MARCH 1976

Jo had an accident. Taken off in an ambulance. Egg on head and twisted ankle. Bike with no brakes went headlong into a van. Thanks be to God. Jo knocked unconscious and came to in the man's arms. First thing he asked was if the van was OK. Arrived home at midnight v.v. bruised. Head, ankle, knee, shoulder, obviously in great pain and shock. Took him for X ray at hospital next day and he was loaned some crutches.

The children did a lot of growing up in that year of supporting their very distraught mother and rather absent father, but equally learned about their mother as a character as she steeled herself to get back under control. She knew what mattered to her and she had seen temporary breakdown of marriage; she knew that a marriage had the capacity to deal with sexual betrayal if the reasons could be understood and if the deeper love was strong enough to warrant fighting for it; she knew a marriage could be made all the stronger through persistence and resilience from the many cases she had seen in her counselling. She was not going to give up the values and marriage that she had been living for many years easily and, with the initial crisis under control, she hung on, though the strain was considerable and the performance inconsistent.

She hung on through the death of her father. Her mother called her back from Trearddur at the end of a happy family summer of 1976 in Trearddur Bay where she had felt that things had gone as well as they could have done. Her diary noted the efforts all the family made to pull together and housework and meals were shared and for once Mandi had more of a holiday. As soon as she was called, she drove in the Honda only to be greeted by her father worrying about where she had parked it. She had left it in Orme Square next to the Savoy and had to go and move it immediately for him to relax.

From the minute she arrived, Mandi nursed her father as his systems slowly collapsed and she had to change the sheets, keeping him clean and comfortable, but unable to feed him much due to the cancerous ulcer in his stomach. Enid could not cope with the situation and sat in the drawing room and spent the few days that Mandi was there with her brothers when they came. She did not want to see her husband, choosing to remember him as he was.

Her brothers came in to say their goodbyes and Noel quietly passed away on the 8 September 1975, sleeping most of the time in the last couple of days until he went. Mandi adored her father and felt that he was at peace when he went. It was only when those few days were over did she realise that she had lost a stone in weight. It was a time that she quietly stored away in her mind and struggles to bring out to this day. Perhaps she just had too much going on emotionally in her life at the time.

It was later in 1978 that Mandi wrote to the daughter of a great friend of hers who was getting divorced and really shared something of her own learning with her. Perhaps Mandi could write this with the benefit of the wisdom acquired on her course, through her experience and through the pain caused by Peter's choices. It was not that Mandi did not understand the attraction of another within marriage, she well and truly did, but she had resisted it. From the insights of this excerpt from her letter, it became clearer why Mandi chose to fight for her marriage and her husband.

5 NOVEMBER 1978

I wonder how you are. You were so amazingly honest on the telephone to me. Life can become very empty and meaningless at all ages due to some reason or another.

We often get disappointed while growing up. We hope that our family, friends and teachers will approve of us and give us a lot of praise and criticism in what we do—what happens? Criticism. I certainly tried and tried in all those all days to win my Mum and Dad's and Gran's approval, but the things I liked were not the things that they thought were important and I found it very difficult. I shut off trying. I was longing for them to say, 'Well done! We think you're great!', but what happened was that they saw all my faults and played on them and made me feel one big failure. They compared me to others; I was a big disappointment and was not very attractive physically to boot. A huge inferiority complex developed.

I had lots of boyfriends who appeared to approve of me initially, but due to my inferiority complex, I always thought they'll see me as the big failure I was so almost willed them to keep their distance. Then when they became aloof, or the relationship lost its intensity and the boys became distant and unaffectionate and suddenly inhibited, I became a failure again.

Luckily Peter was incredibly tolerant to a fault, because in the early days of marriage I gave him a really hard time trying to find me, not my parents' views and expressions, or my friends, but what I felt.

I think often people go into a relationship or marriage thinking here surely we will find love and be accepted. The Church, the women's magazines, films, TV, couples around us, all says so, telling us that our fantasies will be realised, but is that what happens? All too often not and the divorce figures of 1 in 3 prove it. WHY NOT? Because most human beings can only think of WANTING love, they are not trained in GIVING it. We expect our partner to understand us and give, when half the time we are not taking the trouble to understand them and give to them. Love has a much better chance of survival if we talk TO each other, not AT each other (there is a huge difference) and if we try terribly hard to communicate our feelings to each other and not pretend. If we are jealous and possessive, it is usually due to our inferiority complex and feeling of insecurity and fear. If a person feels trapped in a relationship due to jealousy it will very rapidly die. For a relationship to last, it needs to be an extension of you, not trying to own your partner body and soul.

Even if your relationship is over, there are many positive bits that can never be taken away from you and you can learn so much from it for the future. Do not let the negative and failure bits destroy you. We all have to close the door on things in life which are irreversible. If we constantly rehearse 'if only...', we can destroy ourselves, wallow in self-pity and it is all very negative and unconstructive

Nick later wrote about the importance of those foundations in his own life:

'I think overall my Mum has been the major influence in my life especially in my early years and it is from those years that one establishes one's foundation'.

Peter was settled into his Chief Executive of UK/West Africa Lines role by this time and leading on the activity of the Group's thirteen new ships. This fleet of combo-multi-purpose vessels were being introduced to serve West Africa and, in particular, the boom country of Nigeria. Peter was delighted by the company's £75m investment in the ships and the opportunity to sell off some of the older ones. The company was now in a position to compete with other lines by fair commercial methods and he was well and truly there for the challenge.

It was his biggest job yet and he needed to take his young secretary, Lyndsay, everywhere with him in order to be able to execute it. Mandi was still at home with us, her children, who were growing up fast. Typically she gathered herself together and got on with getting the house organised, seeing the many people in her life, including her counselling clients and making a difference to other people's lives, putting her own personal life on the back burner in this time. Peter had got on with his. Her letter from Peter on this trip was in marked contrast to earlier ones in their relationship and shocked her with its distance. It was typed up by his secretary and was fundamentally a detailed account of his trip to West Africa including his short stay in Hamburg, with a fairly detailed description of the late night visit to the bars of Hamburg, which was in its way reassuring.

6 MARCH 1978

Turned out to be a lesbian bar and absolutely fascinating and fantastic in the dress and general performance. I thought I had seen it all, but clearly not.

It went on to describe his shambolic and constantly postponed meetings, his many cocktail parties, the life of vice of his African business counterparts in which they tried to involve him and his English colleagues without success, his lazy weekend afternoons by the pool and no reference to Mandi or the children, not a single question as to their wellbeing or activities. Moreover, it was signed off by both himself and his secretary.

Peter was clearly very ambitious and involved in his career at this point and distanced from the family and their very different life. Mandi did not know where things were with the other woman and if they were still having a relationship. She did not really want to ask as she was trying hard not to be jealous. She knew that it was a time of self-involvement for Peter and that she would lose him completely if she made it about her, so she did not. In truth, she had started to become very menopausal, so this was a really difficult challenge too, but Mandi did her utmost to keep calm and carry on, never voicing her own feelings and putting the others in her life as her top priority.

Back at home, Nick was attending the local technical college and under huge pressure to perform academically and find a career which suited, at the same time as emerging strongly from a two-year relationship with Tanya with whom he had had a lot of fun. He also played high level rugby and other sports and enjoyed having a few beers with his friends as well as carrying the cross in the local church. He was fairly independent, driving himself around in the small Honda that he and I were able to use for getting about, and he had taught me to drive, amazingly helping me to pass my driving test in one lesson. He and our father also took huge pleasure in leaving for school ten minutes late every day and sitting in traffic at the local town Upton so that I would have to explain myself to my teachers. This was family sport and I was the only one who did not find it funny!

Lucy and I were by this time well established in the well reputed local girls' private day school and had both thrived there. I was taking A Levels very much in my stride, loving school, apart from arriving late, and doing lots of drama and events, playing plenty of decent club tennis and really relishing club matches with my Dad when he was home. I enjoyed my friends and various brief and ultimately unrewarding relationships with boys. Lucy had just started her demanding A Level course, was elected Head girl towards the end of the year, was working at Littlewoods and had decided to end a two-year relationship with the much loved Charlie. The whole family was involved in this one, particularly Mandi.

22 FEBRUARY 1978

I feel drained, but manage to get Charlie into bed with a whisky and two mogadons. The next morning, take in porridge and try to persuade him to eat. Tears, tears, tears. I listen to his confusion. I tell him to get up and we go for a walk on the common and I listen some more. I cook him roast chicken and tell him to ring me when he is safe. He phones from the motorway and again from London when he arrives. I listen some more. I feel like a rung out dishcloth.

Mandi continued and has continued to listen and she and Charlie are great friends today. She has become like a foster Mum to him and he has become godfather to one of Lucy's children.

Joey gradually became Jo and he was a popular and easy-going boy, confidently attending the local grammar school. His hobbies included his paper round, biking and skateboarding; he spent hours happily sanding down his beloved board in the garage, reminding Mandi of her Peter in his love for DIY.

There is always a tremendous sense of pride in Mandi's diaries, pleased with the ground her children were making, quietly proud of who they were becoming, delighted to know that she had steered them when she had to, but encouraged too. Whilst there were worries about which career each might follow, my weight and some repetition of childhood labelling such as I was the brains and Lu was the beauty, it wasn't as dominant as it had been in her childhood. Mandi's natural positivity and the early hurt in her life meant that she instinctively looked for the best in her children and she never dwelt on problems and difficulties, but rather sorted them or rode the time and lived each day with the commitment, which was now very familiar to her children.

The house was crazily busy with endless friends coming and going and Mandi still reported daily on the round of household chores and the considerable amount of routine activity that dominated family life. She was often tired, but persisted valiantly with her relentless tasks. When Peter returned in April from his two month 1978 trip, he was exhausted and fell asleep immediately.

7 APRIL 1978

P. returns at 10.00 pm. Good job I never get excited these days. I have been let down too often. He had been out till the early hours and was overtired. Goodbye freedom, back to being a wife!

Mandi was preoccupied with our lives and so many other lives too.

She continued to work with many couples in need of marriage guidance and always felt rewarded by the ones that returned week after week. There was the very anxious mother of four who had married someone a lot older than herself for security and not for love and was trying to work it out. How could she want to leave someone who was so kind and good to her and yet the marriage was stale and boring and she yearned for some magic, some excitement? The husband who was having an affair, but felt guilty about his family and children and what he is doing to everything that he had built over the years, but he yearned for something fresh and passionate, perhaps only temporarily and perhaps just to prove himself before he settled down again to his older age. The wife whose husband seemed to have switched off her completely after only having been married a short while. They wanted it to work, but did not seem to be very attracted to one another anymore and could not understand why. The husband who wanted sex all the time and the wife who was repulsed by it, but with no understanding of why. The university graduate history teacher with the confusions about dominance, submissiveness and indecisiveness, all for discussion. There was the entrepreneur's wife, full of jealousy, pride, retaliation and self-pity and unable to stop thinking about her husband. She had known him all her life and he was obviously playing away and the wife was trying to work out how to play her cards. She had had everything as a child except love and was frightened that she might find herself in that position again. This one was a bit close to home.

All these and many more were issues that Mandi worked through carefully, helping each person or couple to work out their own answers through her guided questioning and listening. The irony of where her own marriage was at that time was not lost on her, but nor was the guidance to be patient, to believe in what you thought your marriage could be and to work towards it. In the meantime, she had stopped putting pressure on it and largely bided her time.

A fabulous business trip to France and Belgium was a huge success for Mandi and Peter and a real sense of togetherness was beginning to regrow.

17 APRIL 1978

My Pee-Tee is adorable and reads maps perfectly and looks after my every need. He is so kind and thoughtful. Truly there is no one to touch him.

In early May of that year, things were going really well for Peter and Mandi, but her own life was still very demanding.

4 May 1978

Mumpy, the cat, generously deposited a mouse on the kitchen floor, a dead one of course which had to be cleared away. My darling made love to me deliciously last night and yet I felt grumpy facing today. It was some day again. Jen and Lopsy went off in the Honda as it was the first night of 'The other Cinderella' produced by Lopsy. I filled up with petrol and off in the citroen after clear-

ing up. A morning of cases and case discussion about domestic violence and returned home to find Sprog (Jo) cooking pasta with friends, having come home early from school. I took him to golf. He wanted to beat 130. I rang Flea. Convalescent Home, Girls' Hostel. Good welcome. Thrashed out some useful topics. Felt shattered afterwards and went to bed. P to AGM of tennis club and then the girls came in jubilant as the play had been a huge success.

Mandi continued to support her mother who was very trying when she came to visit in Lamare, Trearddur Bay of 1978 and put extra pressure on her.

10 AUGUST 1978

Mum continued complaining about everything and everything became related to I, Mandavant, her home in Margate, which she had managed to find a buyer for, her own apartment in the Coburg Hotel across from Hyde Park which she could continue to use, her deceased brother or her own parents. 14 times she repeated herself saying: 'You do make me laugh' or 'oh, the left hand'. Peter was unbelievably patient. 'Mip' when she behaved and 'mother-in-law' when she started her dominating behaviour. She can't receive. She has to be the giver. I go silent, for any answer I give will be criticised. I bought her two new nighties and got: 'You know I never wear blue'.

These crazy days of the mid-to-late 1970s were punctuated with passed exams, failed exams, sorting out drains and household issues, visits from family members, bashes to the car, punctures, Jo getting a broken nose from a school bully, bouts of teenage drunkenness, lovely parties and not so lovely parties, Lu's ambitious sixteenth birthday party for one hundred teenagers, ten puppies, very smart trips to Ascot and more entertaining, more loud music, shrieks of support for sporting events, huge amounts of mess and fetching and carrying from various Saturday jobs. Dear Mr Corner died when the girls were doing their A Levels and as I said before bursting into tears: 'He was a filthy old bugger, but he was part of our lives'.

'Community is possible, but only through the commitment of one person to another'.
— UNKNOWN —

A TIME TO SEARCH
AND A TIME TO GIVE UP

Christmas 1980 was much more of a grownup party with the teenagers in full swing with their friends. No more early visits from Father Christmas now. Late night Christmas Eve drinking in the pub, over-loud carols in the midnight service and a massive lie in on Christmas morning. A family party was held to celebrate with games and dancing and everyone dressed in pyjamas. Food and drink abounded and there was a lot of rowdy fun.

By 1980, Mandi had her first night in their home alone when Jo went off to stay with a friend. Nick was off to study the cotton industry in the USA, I was at Durham University, Lucy was at Reading University and Jo was finishing off his grammar school education.

Beyond their family home, the decade loomed as another one of change. First of all, who did shoot JR? This famous episode aired in March 1980 left everyone wondering. MTV came out with the first music video, 'Video killed the radio star' by the Buggles; the first PCs were taking shape in 1982 with the first Mac Apple and the Commodore 64 PC competing and the mobile or rather 'the brick' was launched as the first mobile phone. Tragically millions of school children saw seven astronauts die as the January 1986 NASA mission combusted seventy-three seconds after it took off and Wall Street crashed, marking this decade of greed and excess and apparent promise for the future; between October 14 and 19, one trillion US dollars of wealth were lost with the crash that reverberated globally.

If it was a time of massive global change, it was also a time of real personal change for Mandi. With all of us journeying into our own adulthood and life choices, Mandi had to adapt again to a changing life. She still played second-fiddle to her husband's career, but had managed, like many women of this age, to carve out for herself a satisfying side career, with her family's needs still taking front and center.

Jo, describing his mother as one of the 'best communicators that he has ever met in his life', remembered this time when he was fifteen at the local grammar school.

'It must have been around 1980 and I was a teenager, more interested in myself, beer and my mates. Poor old Mum was subjected to the rather unruly last of her four children who was often badly behaved. At the time, Mum was about 44 years of age and had been doing Marriage Guidance quite a few years. My father was often away on business in West Africa, my two sisters were away at university and my elder brother had embarked on learning the cotton industry in the USA. I had a girlfriend, so Mum was not exactly at the top of my list. Fortunately, she had lots of friends and played plenty of tennis, but she liked to discuss her work. I was a constant in her life at that time and there day in and day out, so she would tend to tell me a lot of her stuff. It honestly drove me nuts listening to her marriage guidance stories, but I am also sure that a lot of it sunk in without my realising it and definitely helped me understand relationships. 'Jealousy is one of the things that destroys relationships' is one of the things she constantly rammed home and I never forgot it. It held me in good stead with the girlfriends I had in my teenage years and I never forgot it. It helped me learn to make my relationships work. Her true life examples of relationships also spilled over into my work too and I soon realised that if you got on with people, it was likely to be far more beneficial than walking out of school with mountains of A grades, but poor communication skills. At 55 years of age, this seems more relevant than ever and I know that the lessons Mum afforded me and my siblings helped us to achieve much of what we have done'.

So Mandi hung on for Peter, through his first flush of excitement for another woman, her own suppressed and deep hurt, his various trips abroad, job changes and uncertainties, and the growth of their children into young adults, until he began to come back to her. This was not an easy return and an inevitable distance grew between them until he was ready and able to give more of himself. It makes sense of that letter signed by himself and his secretary in which he did not ask one question about Mandi or his children, very unusual for Peter, but a mark of this strange time for both of them.

Mandi's diaries tell more of his tennis matches and dinner parties in those late-70s than family life when it came to Peter. Later, when she was able, Mandi would realise how many of those years he missed of his family, away on trips, just absent. She waited for him to come back, she loved him deeply and believed in that love, throwing herself into her children, working through those teenage years, until ironically Peter was made redundant and the children had left home. It was made even harder for her and for Jo that they did not have each other for the last two years of his home life. Peter had really wanted Jo to go to his former school Uppingham and he could afford it at this stage of his life. It wasn't a huge success though:

> 'When I was away at school for my A Levels I would count the days until I went home. I wasn't much fond of boarding school particularly my first two terms! I wasn't bullied or anything like that but I was always a home bird! Mum's great epistles were a constant source of support to me and still are to this day! Huge amounts of news and pictures, funny stories and advice streamed from her letters. Loved them then and still love to have them now! Mum you are a legend'.

William, Jo's son, took up exactly the same theme twenty-nine years later:

> 'Gran's letters to stay in touch were always so welcome, especially when life seemed hard. They would always give me a huge lift. Her unconditional love always made/makes me feel warm and whole, whilst there would have been something fun or hilarious thrown in to keep you smiling. Hearing about what she had been up to whilst we were apart was wicked, but it never quite compares to the treasured moments we have all had on her couches and bed reading through her diaries. Need I say more!?'

Nick had made a great success of his trip to the USA and the whole family had flown out to Dallas for the first family wedding of the next generation. It was so exciting to actually be in the place where JR and the Ewings resided and to discover a whole new and confident Nick, so in love with this beautiful, shining and all-American bride.

Nick and Paige were married and Mandi and Peter welcomed them back to the Wirral where they were to make their home. Paige was to become an important part of Mandi's life at this time and henceforth, initially as Nick's new wife and then in her own right. She wrote about the Mandi she met at the time as a stark contrast to her own much loved mother, whose attitude towards certain topics was more Victorian and who had sadly died when Paige was only seventeen, leaving her with no preconceived ideas of what mothering might look like at this stage of her life:

'You can only imagine the contrast to my mother-in-law trained as a marriage guidance counsellor. My second day of my very first visit to England saw her enter the kitchen with a happy smile and said that Peter had made love to her beautifully that morning. I nearly fell over, but I loved the open way she was comfortable asking people things and bringing people out of themselves. She has a rare gift and relates to people from all ages and I was totally in awe at her multi-tasking abilities. She was working in West Kirby Concourse for a local doctor (part time) and doing Marriage Guidance so she was constantly putting her skills to work, not to mention still looking after her own family from a distance as they all started to leave the nest.

During my first week in England, once Nick and I returned from our honeymoon, Mandy found out that one of her close friends had committed suicide which must have been such a terrible shock'.

Jo also wrote about that:

'One of Mum's great friends as I grew up was Penny and she was my godmother. I was only 16 and rather homesick in my first or second term at Meadhurst at Uppingham when I received a call from a very angry and upset Mum who told me how my godmother had chosen to take her own life! It was really an awful shock to me over the phone, but Mum was truly livid that her friend had done what she had done and left a husband and four children. Family was everything of course and we were all taught that when we were growing up! She had deserted hers in Mum's eyes and that was unforgivable; I will never forget my Mum and the way she reacted, even more than the tragic death of my presumably traumatised godmother of whom I was truly very fond!'

Paige continued:

'She still focused on the positives, helping to support the family with four children. Despite her sadness, she made time to help me settle into life in a new country.

She threw three welcome parties to introduce me to their friends and to meet some of Nick's as well as the rest of the family. She very kindly lent me her car so I could practise for my driving test and start to regain my independence. During the early days, she really had to pick up the pieces like the day I was told I had to leave work immediately even though I had a work visa because I was an 'alien'. She helped with our new home by making curtains and introduced me to the second-hand sale room. I am not sure I was quite as good as she was in spotting the good pieces. I bought a beautiful antique wardrobe that fell apart upon delivery for £5.00. We used the door for wallpapering and took the mirror out to hang in our bedroom.

She knew all the tricks.

She had already done a lot of work trying to make our house into a home ahead of my arrival. As we started a family and Matt was born, I had no experience with newborn babies, and she was especially good at giving me confidence in looking after him. I had always worked and really had never been taught much about cooking, etc. so I think even she was surprised when I told her I had managed to make an English fish pie with some nice English fish I found called tripe. She even happily ate my rendition of a Sunday roast dinner with sour cream chicken enchiladas. We shared a lot of giggles during this time as there were so many new things to discover and she seemed to enjoy discovering them with me.

We soon settled into a lovely friendship where she helped me and when she went away with Peter, I would look after their dog, Evie Jones, and check on the house or water the garden. She was very good at not judging, as I am sure an all-American girl used to tumble driers and accessing things quickly was something interesting to observe!

I loved the discipline she had in writing her diary every day and whipping up a dinner party with ease. A Gran at a very young age, we would spend hours playing silly games with the children when they were young. In some ways it was therapeutic for both of us as all her children had left the nest and after years of raising children, it was a big adjustment. A new season was starting.

Mandy and Peter were getting prepared to move to London which was not a move that they had previously anticipated. I missed them terribly when they went as we had spent some wonderful time together and they had become such a special part of our lives on a regular basis; Mandy's amazing support was very instrumental in my settling into a life in a new country.

We agreed to buy their house as they reduced the price and kindly permitted us to make whatever changes we wanted; this way they could move down south and we could acquire more space with an expanding family'.

All of this is written up in the diaries in various ways, but in a letter to Jo about Paige and Nick's return from honeymoon, the pleasure she took in welcoming her daughter-in-law to England was evident:

14 SEPTEMBER 1981

I'd stocked the fridge, cleaned and polished, laid the table, prepared a meal and put in flowers. I found a super mirror in the second hand shop and they gave me an old ironing board for nothing. I came home and recovered it. By the time I had finished there and put in the music and speakers Pop had given them, it really looked not half bad. We put down a minute piece of material in the front porch (red carpet treatment) to welcome them. I put in a bit of booze and we all sat and drank G and Ts and looked at photos.

It was 1982 and Paige was featured in the local newspaper and that question of who shot JR was still not answered. Paige drew attention to the position of women in society, saying that it was much easier and much more accepted for women to reach the top in the USA than in England. As Paige had her first baby, Princess Di had her second and I was making plans for my wedding with Richard. Mandi reflected in her diary:

> *Before January 1982 starts*
>
> *I suppose I am the sort of person who looks for the best in people and usually finds it. I am optimistic and good natured and because I expect to enjoy myself, it is like measles, those around me catch it and enjoy themselves too. Some of my life has had some very unhappy moments when trust has been undermined. I have been slapped in the face with awful pain, but through it all the will to make succeed what I wanted to succeed in has been in me like a seed. I am not prejudist* and I do not expect too much or too little. I am not a critical person, enjoying the differences of individuals and capable of thinking things through in my own mind. Definitely not easily led, I suppose I am an open book and therefore people feel that they can be so in my company with safety. Flea remains my best and most trusted friend and confidant.*
>
> *14 FEBRUARY 1982*
>
> *Get a lovely card from Flea. Give him one too. Romantic snoos we are.*

On February 20 1984, Nick and Paige's son, Matt, was christened and Lucy was giving up smoking. Both the Grans were at the christening and they were still watching Dallas. Mandi was struggling off and on with the very busy Peter who was here one minute and gone the next.

> *24 FEBRUARY 1984*
>
> *He's so unfeeling. He's so so precious. I feel so disjointed, but it was familiar behaviour now and she was so glad he rang*

Her diary entries reflected how confused she felt around this time. One minute, Jo had a brick put through his Mini window, but it was for him to sort that out and he was enjoying life, there was no doubt about that. The next we learn of Mandi's preparations for my and Richard's wedding, making the bridesmaid dresses, organising the marquee in the back garden, the guest accommodation, getting to know the in-laws, ordering the flowers, making the cake, sorting out the dress. She and Peter had been to visit us in our little house in Felsted too and were satisfied that this was a good move. It was to be one of the first weddings of its kind, from their house, not just a service and a reception, but an enormous party, complete with

dinner and disco. In fact it was a wonderful day, the garden in all its
glory, including the bedding plants! Peter was meticulous about it,
to the point that he was memorable in his speech and amused himself
greatly:

> 21 JULY 1984
>
> *Six months ago, my dear daughter said to me, 'Father this is an*
> *emotional experience, not a military operation'.*

Towards the end of 1984, Peter was made redundant and worked
hard to find another job. Peter had taken his redundancy from Ocean
hard and had never made it to the coveted position of Chairman which
had been given to a friend of his who was well connected and seemed
to get the top job for this reason. It had been terrible for him to watch
and for a £100 a year more, he had been side-lined to a relatively
easy position, but a painfully frustrating one, and his family had yet
again born the brunt of what was a very difficult period of anger and
rejection in his life. He was to be seen doing extraordinary things
such as hoovering the lawn and speaking and behaving with a brittle
pomposity only seen before in his teenage years. Under this new
leadership, Ocean was not to last long and was soon sold on, leaving
Peter redundant and facing an uncertain future.

> 7 JANUARY 1985
>
> *P's pipe and incessant coughing drives me round the bend. Gran*
> *rings all the time. There is always something, her bowels, her*
> *bladder and I don't know how long I can live alone.*

As happens for so many women, menopause was a hugely challenging time for Mandi. She bled too much, would feel low and moody
and would miss her tribe desperately. Her relationship with Peter had
been on a roller coaster and was not as yet back where she wanted it;
she had made huge progress and held her marriage together, fighting
to keep a lot under control and many balls in the air, but these had
been and were still going to be challenging years.

She was kept busy which was fortunate and provided a vital counselling and nursing service to her local doctors' practice. She took
bloods and did ECGs and provided other key nursing services, but the
doctors of her practice had realised by then that a lot of their cases
were being caused by stress or anxiety and people were returning
for physical ailments which were clearly triggered by non-physical
complaints. They had the foresight to ask Mandi to see these patients

and by the time she left this job in 1987, she had helped over 200 emotionally and this was undoubtedly a pioneering and inspired service. She also continued her vital work in the local convalescent home or residential home as it became known. She was both the diabetic nurse and the counsellor there. Now she insisted on seeing the children from the home in small groups of six or seven and was being paid for her visits three times a week. She continued to be a trusted and key visitor to those with whom she discussed relationships and did her best to provide much needed support. She worked through their feelings following exposing their teacher who was abusing the girls and much of what he did came out in her sessions.

One day she turned up beetroot red from a trip to the health centre's sauna which caused considerable comment and she felt she had to promise the students that she would take them one day when they were sixteen. She thought that she was safe from carrying this through because they tended to leave at fifteen. One, however, had to stay an extra year and held her to it; she is one of two that remain very much in her life today. Mandi told them in 1987 that she was leaving and heading to London; they were clearly devastated and the two who came from the south, Croydon and Swindon, made her promise to keep in touch. She could not refuse them in that era where the rules of today did not apply and she has remained firm friends with Donald and Owenka all these years and has enjoyed being part of their lives.

With some much-awaited good fortune, Peter became the Chairman of the Canadian Atlantic Freight Secretariat Ltd based in Crawley in 1987. It was time to leave the Wirral family home, Pinhey. Nick and Paige bought it and made it theirs, Richard and I had been posted to S'Hertogenbosch in Holland and Lucy was working away with Twinings, being escorted to lots of exciting social events by yet another lovely young man. Jo by then was doing his timber course and was planning to start with stockbroker Tilneys fairly soon and was then going out with Lynne. Mandi's tribe had left and yet she had her hands full.

Once again, Mandi was asked to leave her life and support and follow her man. She put her foot down with Peter over where they were to settle and refused to live in a distant Surrey suburb, insisting on Granville Road in Southfields, close to the very familiar Wimbledon and her old stomping grounds. Life was so different in the time that they lived in London. Their house was a Victorian terrace of sizeable proportions, but without distinction. Peter had wanted to buy more of a statement place in Surrey, but Mandi would always celebrate the fact that she exercised her will in favour of the London base.

They began to make it home, meeting people and making connections. Peter had always loved his tennis and was well connected to the All England Tennis Club. He began the long process to join this and the local Roehampton Club with his sponsors. Mandi went to find herself a job as a nurse again in the hospital just around the corner.

Very early on in London in early 1988, Mandi was to have an emergency hysterectomy. One of those ghastly cycles was just too much and she lost too much blood and had to have her womb removed at once. This led to hormone replacement therapy and a new stability for Mandi which was life changing and such a revelation to her husband and family as to what she had been suffering all those years hormonally.

As Peter sat in hospital eating the dinners Mandi could not manage after the operation, because of the pain, he was to really understand medically the lack of control Mandi had had over her monthly cycle and menopause. It was a long overdue medical explanation. With that hysterectomy, gone were the tension, the moods, the instability and her monthly battle with herself, although they had left their own scars. Unfortunately, a tendency to pass wind inadvertently seemed to result, which Mandi would pass off confidently as the result of her hysterectomy.

Explaining this just after the operation in front of the family, her future son-in-law, Stuart, scoffed:

'Hysterectomy? Rectal history more like!'

Stuart's is believed to have been the more likely explanation, but no one has yet to come up with a solution and Mandi's tendency to pass wind has been the cause of much hilarity to her and occasional embarrassment to others over the years.

By this time, Mandi had been left two properties. One was of no value and sold on quickly. The other was to build in value and required some attention. It was called Arva House in Wandsworth and consisted of three flats. On 26 January of that year, Mandi set off to clean them, ready for letting. The handle of the pan of boiling water she was using for cleaning broke off, pouring the scalding water down her left thigh, melting her flesh and leaving a gaping hole. She had the presence of mind to remove her track suit bottoms despite the pain and called an ambulance. She claimed no next of kin to the ambulancemen and dealt with the whole matter herself. The entire episode was indescribably painful and even worse when she returned to St Mary's 12 February 1988 for her two skin grafts.

She was helpless for a time and all the family came to look after her at various points. Peter was largely away, but luckily she had Jo's girlfriend, NickNack, on hand in London, who was invaluable. Jo and NickNack were nearby with both working in London. When NickNack met Mandi, she was not even fifty years old. Jo was living in the house that Mandi had been cleaning when she was burned, Arva House, and was working as a stockbroker in Tilneys. NickNack was a Norland nanny and loved the way Mandi always showed such an interest in her and any of the children that she nannied

As they got to know each whilst NickNack was going out with Mandi's youngest son, she was to discover that they had a great deal in common and were remarkably alike in their common sense, practical approach to life. Both loved the great outdoors and liked nothing more than the daily constitutional with a couple of lively dogs with which to let off steam, although that was rather on hold during her recovery. Both belonged to the caring professions and put family and looking after others high on the agenda, with homemaking, cooking and providing creature comforts a priority. When Mandi burnt her leg so badly, NickNack would spend hours with her and had the chance to find this out. They both had a very positive outlook on life and Mandi's determination to get better resonated very strongly with NickNack and she wanted to help her. She laughed with her and listened to her stories and jokes.

'What do you call a judge with no thumbs?'
'Justice fingers!'

NickNack got involved with the diaries, noticed how these jokes, often Jo's, punctuated them throughout. She played twenty questions with Mandi whilst they were at the hospital. It was the time of the terrible King's Cross Fire too and Mandi met Luke, an amazing musician who had had to put his hands over his face and run through a wall of fire to save his life. He was a regular commuter and knew that was his only hope. When he got to the other side, he had lost all his fingers and a fair amount of his face. She certainly did not tell her jokes to him, but they shared so much about their lives. His career as a musician over, both he and Mandi both noticed that they recovered remarkably quickly and put it down to their upbeat and positive attitude. An unfortunate lady in the unit who had burned her face severely because she opened the back door to put out her chip pan fire was far less positive and had showed no signs of recovery over the three months that Mandi had known her. Food for thought!

Lucy and Stu visited frequently before buying a house near Winchester towards the end of the year. Paige and Nick were just about to have their third child and Mandi had recovered sufficiently to help when Katie was born and again when Nick and Paige went to the USA in May. Richard and I were living in Holland and Mandi had already been out to assist with the births of our two first children and she and Peter loved their stays in S'Hertogenbosch. Mandi had biked round with me on the cobbles trying to initiate labour and once this task was achieved, then happily engaged with any tasks required whether in Dutch or not with her customary and generally successful generic French accent.

They had had such a good time celebrating Emma's birth in a local Dutch restaurant that when Mandi went to leave, she was utterly confused as to how her coat had grown and was puddled round her ankles causing her to have a fit of the giggles. The very gentlemanly owner of the coat had to come over and explain that whilst their coats were similar, their height was not! Fortunately 'Sorry!' in whatever accent is definitely understood in Dutch, so Mandi charmed the very tall Dutchman. This was a time with lots of friends visiting and many weddings. Christmas 1988 was held in the London home with Peter leading the decoration of the tree as always and two boisterous little ones to liven the celebrations, along with Richard and I and Peter's sisters and Mum Mum. It was a very happy, active time.

'The tongue can paint what they eyes can't see'.
— CHINESE PROVERB —

A TIME TO BE SILENT
AND A TIME TO SPEAK

In late February 1989, Mandi and Peter were to set off on a much-awaited holiday together on Madeira. They had worked hard to get organised for it and had found time to pop in to see Samuel James, Richard's and my third child, only just three weeks old, two days before leaving. Peter had gone into the study and held him to his chest; they had fallen asleep together for an hour, a sight recorded on camera and that everyone would treasure in the years ahead.

An early morning game of tennis and Peter returned to Granville Road feeling very cold. He had a hot bath and then a meal at Roehampton. Peter had asked Jo to drive them to Heathrow only the day before. He admitted to being slightly reluctant because the big Frank Bruno/Tim Witherspoon fight was showing on the Saturday night and he knew he would have had a few beers. He did it anyway and remembered joking with them on the way:

'Did you hear that Frank Bruno's opponent got stabbed last
night?
Witherspoon?
No, with a knife!'

He also remembered giving his Mum a kiss goodbye and went to shake his Dad's hand as he had done for the previous ten years and instead his Dad gave him a massive hug and Jo said: 'I love you, Dad'.

He will never know why they did that, but Jo is very glad they did.

On the flight, Peter gave Mandi a gold pen; when Mandi questioned this, he said she would need it. Another unexplained moment or perhaps not.

On arrival, they drove the twenty miles or so from the airport to the Savoy Hotel at Funchal and checked into the only double room in the hotel. The boy opened their hotel room door and Peter fumbled for some escudos to give him, before falling across the bed. Mandi thought he was fooling about, but quickly realised that he was unwell and went down to reception. They called the doctor, but the doctor would not look at Peter until he had received some escudos. Once paid, he took appropriate action.

On arrival, Peter was too big for the lift, so his tall, heavy frame had to be manoeuvred down three flights of stairs to the small, white van claiming to be an ambulance. English and communication were a real difficulty, but Mandi understood that she was not required. However, she was not going to pay any attention to that and forced her way into the ambulance, travelling the short distance to the hospital with Peter. At this point, the doors were shut in her face.

Hard as she tried, she got no news for four hours and only her desperate searching and making a nuisance of herself got her a porter that led her to the hospital mortuary. Here she found Peter, dead by then for some hours, half-covered with a mortuary sheet as again he was too unfamiliarly large for the standard size, so his head and feet were exposed.

Mandi lingered over this new and shocking reality, kissing him and whispering to him, totally alone in the mortuary, before eventually making her way back to reception and asking the way back to the hotel. At least they cared enough not to allow her to walk back alone, saying it was too dangerous, and a taxi appeared. She had no money and had to run upstairs to find the escudos to pay her driver.

She called Nick and he remembered that day so well with the sun shining in the bluest of skies:

'I received a call from Mum to say that Dad had been rushed by ambulance to hospital on arrival in Madeira and that she had been waiting in the lobby of the Savoy in Madeira and not been able to speak with anybody. She gave me the name of the hospital and I said I would arrange somebody who spoke Portuguese to find out what had gone on. I called Roberto in Brazil and asked him if he would mind calling the hospital and call me back with an update. A little time later Nigel MJ who was my Boss called me into his office and told me that Roberto had called him as he didn't want to pass on the message directly to say he had spoken with the Hospital and been informed that Dad had died.

I had to call Mum and just explained what had happened. 'Hang on in there', I told her and said that I would be on the next flight'.

Jo got on a flight too. It was all so confusing. Mandi tried to sleep whilst her boys made their way to her. As soon as possible, Paige took Mandi home and Nick and Jo stayed to sort out the return of their deceased father. Jo remembered their shock, their father dead at just fifty-seven years of age, their mother just fifty-four. This was not the expected order of things. Jo recalled getting hammered and throwing oranges out of the window, somehow in memory of his father.

Mandi, popping to the loo in the airport, gave all her 300 escudos to the loo attendant and received such a sustained hug that she has never forgotten it. She came out saying that she had just done her good deed for the day. Paige hasn't forgotten it either! Paige recalled the two men trying to buy them drinks on the airplane home, making a pass, and how they giggled over how unbelievably inappropriate it was.

Once home, the shock, the reality, the pain hit. Everyone rallied, but the journey had only just begun. Peter was returned, laid to rest and made up in the funeral parlour and remained there to be visited before his funeral. Mandi encouraged her children to go and say good bye to their father, partly so that it became real to them. This was their first encounter with death and they were not familiar with it in the way that Mandi was. It was to prove a life changing event for the whole family. Nick wrote later:

'I immediately flew out to Madeira with Paige within a couple of hours and arrived in Madeira that evening. Probably the most scary landing strip that I've ever been to as the plane has to bank into the side of the mountain before squaring up for the runway.

I remember just hugging Mum on arrival telling her we would all be OK and we got her and Paige immediately out on the next flight to London while I stayed in Madeira to sort out the formalities. Joe came out to help me for support. I was so focused on getting everything done properly and supressed my emotions, which never truly came out until Viv Clayton's funeral when she died giving birth to twins a couple of months later and my tears didn't stop flowing.

We both flew out two/three days later with Dad's body on the same plane we were on and were met at Heathrow by Lu'.

When someone you love very dearly dies, often it is a time of reflection and when Nick looks back on his father's role in his life:

'I remember Dad primarily for practical things such as pocket money, boats and trips. I loved and respected him greatly but he stayed in the background as far as I was concerned, except when it came to important milestones, and he did not really seem to involve himself emotionally with me— it was only in the last six months of his life when I was in my early thirties that we started to really bond. I remember a couple of lovely tennis games together and some great chats sharing lifts back from Liverpool at that time. I think he really bonded with Matt as his first grandchild, but when I was born his focus, maybe because of his upbringing, was on career and supporting his family practically as well as his many outside interests. I think his career allowed us all an international perspective rather than a local one. I do as his son remember one occasion where his determination shone through, when he was playing the number 1 player in Cheshire in the Men's Singles Final at Hoylake. I was probably about eleven at the time, but I distinctly remember his saying, 'I know how to beat him' and he absolutely did, winning in style'.

Peter, it turned out, had died of an aortic aneurism and there was no saving him from this cruel heart attack.

(In the beginning of the JANUARY 1990 diary, but undated)
My darling Snuffy died in his prime and dramatically and his thanksgiving service showed what a special person he was with over 400 attending. (I miss you Flea and still see you so clearly darling) You would have loved to have been at your special service. You were in spirit I know, but to have indulged in your short and long term friendships, the food and the drink and the puff of your pipe as we all reminisced. You would have loved the music played by Jonathan Newell; the children would have touched your heart with their moving and inspiring words. You would have loved the memories it conjured up. Remembering should not be morbid and you loved life and gave to it fantastically too. I was bleeding inside Flea, but you were holding me, comforting me and I know that you have never left me since we

had such gorgeous times together. We created so much, like a
pebble in a pond, there are so many ripples of happiness that I
now cling to.

Nick also recalls that Thanksgiving Service:

'I remember the love that surrounded us all at that time
and the worst sight I can ever remember is my young
3-year-old son Matt chasing after Grumpy's coffin at his
funeral service as the hearse drove him away'.

Ten years later in granddaughter Emma's English homework, he
lived on.

Emma 25 March 1999

"Mummy, how far is heaven?' asked Emma aged just 3.
'A very long way away, darling,' replied Emma's tearful
Mummy. 'Well, why don't we just get in the car and go
there and then you'll stop crying?' asked Emma logically.
This conversation took place just after the death of my
grandfather and the birth of my younger brother Sam. It
was strange as one life was born another died. You may
think that because I was only three my grandfather is of
little importance to me, but he lives on in the people around
me and through the fact that we still talk about it.

In our family, everybody works very hard and he was the
example of it, he never had time to read and he was always
on the go with a new project. He is also remembered for his
tennis as he taught his children to play and in their turn
they have taught us. He also loved to travel and Mum says
she got her interest in travel and languages from him. I too
would like to follow in his footsteps. He adored sailing and
had a huge love for the sea. His favourite place on Anglesey
is now the favourite holiday spot for all his children and
their families.

We still wave to him in the sea when we walk past the
place where his ashes were scattered.

Much of what I remember about him comes from a poem
that Mum wrote for us after his death. In the poem, she
remembers how he built sandcastles with us, stole the jelly
and chocolate fingers at our birthday parties, stuck up for us
if we got told off, smoked a pipe, loved peace and quiet and

always loved to hold a new born baby. She called the poem
'OUR GRUMPY' which was what we called our grandfather
and my Grumpy lives on in me'.

That place where his ashes were scattered was the first time we
had returned as a family to Lamare after Peter's death. We decided to
scatter his ashes off the cliff near where Hebe, his boat, went down
and into the sea where he had spent so many happy hours and which
he absolutely loved.

Mandi went up the road and onto the cliff path with her four
children, a sombre party on a typically gusty day. She stood and
solemnly let go of a small handful. Within a second or two, everyone was picking them from their teeth and spitting them out and
unable to keep serious. Laughing now, we decided to hold her over the
cliff to complete the task. Imagine the scene, both the boys holding
their mother's upper body over the cliff and the girls holding her legs
firmly to the ground as she scattered the ashes. It was not a reverend
scene, but it was somehow fitting. Lucy then went to fetch a gin and
tonic and peanuts and they went over the cliff too. She has repeated
this ritual annually in her father's memory. RIP!

Mandi was still very busy socially at the start of 1990, caught up
in her family, her friends and their activity. New year was spent
with the same old crowd of friends, but in that first year it was very
intimidating. Nick had just negotiated himself a strong position in
the cotton firm he started in and was established with Paige and their
three small children and still in the former family home, Pinhey.
Richard was established in London and I was a busy mum of three
by this time, based in Westcliff-on-Sea. Lucy had just got engaged
to Stuart on their wonderful skiing holiday and it was announced
formally in the Times on the 10th January 1990; she was still selling
yachts, doing her coastal skipper exams and was featured in Yachting
World at the Boat Show. Jo was planning a worldwide trip with his
girlfriend NickNack and was considering leaving his present position
and establishing himself in Liverpool as a stockbroker. He was also
very keen on sailing, but had missed his coastal skipper exams due to
his trip to Madeira.

A round of nursing, bridge, tennis and theatre kept Mandi busy
with work and socialising and she was forever taking calls and having
long chats to her many friends. Her diary is very full in this year as

well, and more reflective than usual, perhaps a really close friend to talk to. In the early days after Peter's death, she behaved as though without a care in the world, with no responsibility to herself and all of her family were terrified for her as she drove many miles at speed through the night from one venue to the other, worked long hours in the hospital, did not notice if she had eaten or not, drank a lot of wine and was rather out of control. After a skiing trip with a group of very established friends, they reported on her kamikaze style. Mandi's response was that she could not have cared less if she lived or died.

> 2 JANUARY 1990
>
> *Relationships in life are vital to me. I value them highly—A TRUE*
> *LIFE with anger, passion, fun, laughter, the spiritual and material*
> *integrated.*

She stated she was in the power of God and his will and wonders about the purpose of her life. The very next day she was relating her story of listening to the male nurse whose British Columbian wife was just too much for him after three months of marriage and he had walked out. Apparently, the wife and all her family moved into his flat and started ordering him around. He certainly found the ear he needed in Mandi.

She had clearly been talking to young impatient parents or indeed her own very demanding mother when she wrote:

> 4 JANUARY 1990
>
> *When will parents learn that children need to be listened to;*
> *they want their views respected; they need support and esteem.*
> *Otherwise we get rebellion and anti-authoritarian behaviour.*
> *We need listening, caring and compassion.*

The diary entries of this year record a range of events from drug scandals in Panama to the endless round of babysitting and visits from small grandchildren and their parents, the 'me, me, me' behaviour of her mother, deaths of acquaintances or parents of friends, much enjoyed concerts and plays; some, such as the much-loved Messiah, bringing back haunting memories. Her nursing work in the 'Royal Hospital for Incurables', now called the 'Royal Hospital for Neuro-Disability', provided important occupation at this time, but also key perspective and Mandi always cites this as a reason for emerging from her own sadness within.

14 January 1990
Seeing the trauma in Clifton ward puts my own grief into
perspective. Suffering is very personal, but next to these patients
we had had such a happy and fulfilling life.

Mandi wrote of them in the 1990 diary at various intervals. She tells of the young woman aged seventeen who was marching jauntily swinging her handbag for fun when the strap somehow got caught up by a passing lorry and she got swept along, only to end up in a permanent vegetative state for the rest of her days. Mandi watched her father come to visit her day after day and just sob with his never-ending grief and loss of his beloved only child. She watched the parents of the young man who lost his active brain and body in the road traffic accident come every day in grief to no reaction, every week to no reaction, every month to no reaction, every year to no reaction and then she did not see them again and he was left alone with the nurses. There was seventeen-year-old Lawson awaiting the pointless £1million compensation for the regrettable mistake where caregivers gave carbon dioxide instead of oxygen during a haemorrhoid operation. Walter who fell off the scaffolding leaving his inconsolable wife whom he had just married and could operate the computer enough to blink out at great length: 'Don't let me die until my wife gets the pension'. There were various road traffic accident victims whose lives were forever changed. There was Jeff who would only say, 'Piss off', and you never knew if he could or would say any more. He wasn't the only one who was angry; a fair number tried to exhibit their frustration as best they could. Mandi noted how young most of them were.

There was the time that Mandi was left in charge and thought her patient with a reference to MI had had an accident on the M1, but in fact was suffering a myocardial infarction or heart attack. She just had to laugh at herself over that one! Once she tried to question the £14,000 cost per week with the other nurses over coffee and had barely even opened her mouth when one said: 'If you are going to question their right to live, you should not be a nurse'.

Mandi did question it though, just as she questioned the value of her own life at that time, just as she questioned all that had been in her life. In among the frequent entries in her diary about grief and suffering are her questions about life, its value, her own value, the place of family, friends, acquaintances, activities in her life. This was a time of grief and so a time of reflection and change. Her diary was a listening ear as she worked things out, voiced her thoughts and became a more intimate account of her inner self than ever before.

18 JANUARY 1990

Oh Snuffy darling, I talk to you as if you were here. I act out things you would do as if I have internalised you and we have become one body. I can't quite take it that we will never be physical again, that I will never saviour those delicious kisses or have your arm around my shoulder, sharing the daily happenings, the fluffings, my comforter, my protector, my bestest friend. Where is your smile now? Your splendid laugh? I miss the saga of the socks, not having to tell you off for port drinking, forgetting to stop and remembering to tune into me for a bit, ironing your shirts. I can see your body as if it were laid out in front of me, tormenting you with a tumbler of cold water when you were in the bath, ruffling your gorgeous hair with my hands and listening to La Mer on the piano. My precious Snoopy. I am so alone, yet you left me an incredible legacy, your babies spoil me every day, you left me enough money to have an impy time. Oh my darling send me a spiritual hug. I am bleeding inside. I love you my darling Peter. I wear your rings with great pride. I love you so.

Mandi contemplated life very frequently, often disjointedly, just noting, not concluding.

20 FEBRUARY 1990

I suppose I could be described as having a sense of humour, which when combined with the fun of life, could often defuse tension at critical moments in life.

She wrote of the class system:

20 FEBRUARY 1990

I have always hated the class system. Most of my education has been since leaving school. I never enjoyed school except the companionship.

Mandi was always grateful throughout her widowhood that she stopped Peter investing all they had in Lloyds, which would have left her with no money as a widow. She had her own legacy in the three flats in London and Wandsworth, and she would not allow those to be part of the investment package.

On Peter's death, first Nick and later Jo, took over the running of her financial affairs and both did an excellent job for her, ensuring that she had a perfectly comfortable sum to live off and more if she ever needed it. Jo put a huge effort into converting the London flats she had been left into a lasting legacy and this was to provide her with funds for years to come. Mandi was never an extravagant person and never overspent the budget she agreed with Jo. A wartime upbringing and carefully controlled housekeeping with four children had taught her to be thrifty and she knew no other way. The running of Lamare in Trearddur Bay was in theirs and Lucy's hands too until the latter moved to Australia.

> *27 FEBRUARY 1990*
> *A year ago today, my darling Flea went to heaven. God bless your*
> *soul darling. I think of you so much and with so much love.*

All the children call and this anniversary was to become an important day in family life henceforth with flowers and tributes coming every year until the present day. Further tributes arrived on Mother's Day, barely a month later.

Life was going on around her in a constant confusion of close knit, local, national and world activity and it is all recorded in the diary in a frenzy; Nick's business trips and the growth of his little family, Mandela on the verge of being freed, floods in North Wales, the Lithuanian and Russian governments fighting it out, Lucy organising her wedding, her hen party, the Tory crisis, Maggie Thatcher, John Major, the boat race, the Poll Tax riot, granddaughter Sarah swimming her first length, Jo and NickNack staying with their many friends popping in and out for suppers and drinks, visits to and from her ailing or exigent mum, Nick running a marathon, Richard and I moving house, I got epilepsy, small children's stories shared on the phone most evenings, more birthday parties, the ambulance strike, April Fool's tricks, dinner parties either at home or away and charity events locally. There were theatres, concerts, more birthday parties, regular keep fit and tennis classes, nursing most days and deliberations on patient plights, Wimbledon and Ascot, surprise winners and losers, her new Honda Civic, named 'Hornsby', a visit to dear brother Ant's place on the Mull of Kintyre, out with other brother Dave and wife Pam, her children with grandchildren all holidaying in Trearddur Bay in the summer and a new era underway. The children's friends were getting engaged, married and having babies, the IRA was bombing, anti-pollution campaigning had begun in earnest and Saddam Hussein and the gulf crisis were looming large. Jo and NickNack's plans were progressing and Lucy was going to be married to Stuart on September 1st.

6 MARCH 1990

I sometimes scream to crawl away somewhere, like an animal, and think things out with no interruptions, but always the phone rings, Mersey needs exercising, something needs to be thought through. Oh my darling, I hope you are happy, free, and unencumbered.

29 APRIL 1990

I believe in hope.

10 MAY 1990

My mind is still so often in Peter's camp and despite my own great personal tragedy, I know deep down that I am a very lucky person with good health, a loving family and good, loyal friendships of every colour, class, creed, every walk of life. It is in opening yourself up to them that you see the joy of living and life. Nursing taught me to be adaptable, through having to move to another ward every three months and seeing my carefully tended patients go off into the unknown after their time at Guy's. The love of human relationships is so sustaining, the joy of my own four children and the challenge of motherhood goes on.

This kind of profound thought is juxtaposed with an entry about Wendy's very frisky cat and how she will talk about her 'grey pussy' and a joke about how you should not wear nuclear underpants as 'Chernobyl fall out'.

18 MAY 1990

As I lie in bed meditating, I think of the many friends and acquaintances who have influenced me and have enriched my life. I give thanks for the gift of communication, an essential ingredient of life. There are so many wonderful people in the world, but too many are locked in and unable to show their feelings. This is a crucial time in my life. My family and friends have been real friends and I am so thankful for them. I am thankful for living in London and its accessible hurly burly existence.

Our marriage Flea was a success don't you think? So many

*relatives and friends have been incredibly kind and thoughtful.
I've been physically faithful Snuff as you know, but am I to be
celibate all my life? Why am I abstaining? Not virtue, well no, in
memory of Flea, well possibly.*

10 JUNE 1990

*Coming to terms with what the future holds and where I go
from here. I must feel free to pursue a new life and make stable
relationships again. We had known each other 40 years, we were
married for 32. I know he would want me to be happy. My life
is a mess, but I must rebuild again. At some time or another we
all have to cope with intolerable pain emotionally. We all feel
helpless and burdened at times, but floundering can often
strengthen those that flounder too. My experience is not unusual.
Pain at parting is the price we pay for love. It is like a tide of pain
that engulfs and comes and goes. Sometimes these days I feel
more of an outsider looking in on the outside.*

27 JUNE 1990

*When I think of my childhood, Mum obstructing any free thinking
I might have been able to do, it is such a joy to know that I have
not been that sort of Mum. I am able to confront and examine
myself more objectively now.*

8 AUGUST 1990

I feel very depressed. Painting reminds me so much of Flea.

This was after a summer of sailing with Nick in Argo, the 14-foot
sailing dinghy, races, the running sports and Richard, her son-in-law
painting the outside of Lamare. It was all too much!

27 AUGUST 1990

My horoscope says I must change my life now!

Attending Lucy's wedding without Peter was an important mile-
stone for Mandi. Nick gave his sister away and Mandi was on his arm.
Both Lucy and I wrote to Mandi afterwards as follows:

6 September 2020

'What a day! I could never have dreamt it would be so
magic! Good organisation helps, but on the day, it is the
people that make it. Thank you for everything, Mum. Dad
was smiling, I know, though perhaps crying with all of us
during Jerusalem. He will have been proud of you. Love to
the 6th bridesmaid Mersey Moo.

Lots of love, Lucy and Stu'.

6 September 1990

'Memorable and very special time at Lulu's and StuStu's wedding. The military was to give way totally to the emotional in the end. I have just sat down and rendered Jerusalem tonelessly with Dad's top hat on my head and followed it with a good howl. There is no escaping the fact that Dad would have added an inimitable presence to the occasion had he been there physically. Lu and Clive toasting him was so special. You looked absolutely stunning in your red and you got through despite your fears. I think it proved an enormous step forward for you.

Much love, Jen'

Mandi attended philosophy lectures over a couple of years at this time and wondered a great deal in her diaries. There she asked questions such as,

11 OCTOBER 1990

What is wisdom? Can you be wise and not know yourself? Can you be free from desire? Is perfection in the moment? Are you born perfect? Is perfection the moment between one activity ending and another starting? Does making judgements forbid perfection?

She did not answer these questions and at various intervals asked more and wondered about all manner of things.

13 OCTOBER 1990

I suppose I could be described as having a special gift for hospitality.

21 OCTOBER 20

Throughout the life cycle loss is encountered, the baby leaves the security of Mum's womb, the growing child tests out his ability to separate from his parents, the adolescent wrenches away from his home to form a separate identity. At each phase of change is loss. Loss and renewal from birth to death and the finality of death can lead to renewal for those who mourn, those with the ability to mourn and change, carry hope. Fresh challenges and psychic growth. Guilt and pain are inseparable from loss. The multiple challenges and changes of family life. The greatest need is to maintain significant personal relationships for life and growth. The survivor often comes to incorporate some of the qualities of

the dead person and finds new value for herself. Learning to die
is the continuation of learning to live and to love. He who has no
fear of life and can relate in love is much more likely to let go of
life with acceptance and confidence.

Perhaps by writing a diary, the end of a year brought closure and the start of the year, freshness; Mandi certainly attacked 1991 with vigour. She described the crazily busy lives of her children and kept in touch with them all as ever, but wonders about the return of her own feelings. The marriage had taken place, Jo and NickNack were travelling. I was crazily busy in Westcliff with my tribe. Nick and Paige had bought a flat and set up their own business with Mandi supporting it financially and becoming a partner. A trip to Liverpool to admire the offices, to become involved, to see the children and to whizz back to her London life.

Nick wrote many years later:

'She was incredibly supportive of us when I married Paige and we had young children.

I guess Dad's death and all that followed crystallised in me that I didn't want to reach the age of 50 and be made redundant as had happened to him and 1990 was a pivotal year for my family as it was the year I started Plexus and went out on my own.

I am not sure that Dad would have approved but Mum backed me completely, lending me £75 thousand, all of which was paid back and to which she received a 10 to 15 percent preferential dividend every year'.

Diary entries continued to be very chaotic for a while. Mandi recounted accounts of the terrible storms in Trearddur Bay, the cost of living, Salman Rushdie, Australia/England cricket test results, the Saddam Hussein horrors of war and Liverpool results. These are mixed in with letters and visits from friends along with news of her children's jobs and her grandchildren's small triumphs in life; a juxtaposition of world events alongside the domestic.

However, Mandi's life seemed to slowly settle into a greater order, the wider world, her own and others' experiences and her personal experience of ongoing grief finding their place more logically in her mind. Mandi had loved Peter completely and totally, but now she focused on her new-found freedom of her career and her family.

The freedom created in her a profound respect for the personality and values that she had always had, but which had been somewhat hidden beneath the many duties of wife and mother over the decades of marriage.

At the start of 1991, she wrote a lot about what was going on in the wider world. The Gulf War, pitbull terriers registered, child abuse exposed, recession and depression, snow impeding the smooth running of British Rail, Elizabeth Taylor's eighth wedding, Filipino First Lady Imelda Marcos and her shoes, John McCarthy and Terry Waite released, the Kurdish people fleeing into the freezing mountains, Senator Edward Kennedy up for rape in court, Robert Maxwell plunging from his yacht having plundered the Daily Mirror pension fund, Princess Di's friend Adrian Ward Jackson dying of Aids, Mikhail Gorbachev surviving a coup which precipitated the end of the Soviet Union, Gerald Ratner describing his jewellery as crap, the first woman in space, the Birmingham 6 and Guildford 4 walking free, Palestine and Israel sitting down to peace talks, Sir Allan Green, the Director of Public Prosecutions, caught kerb crawling, the NHS continuing as a major political battlefield, India's Gandhi assassination and the Lockerbie bombers named through Gaddafi and Libya.

Girl power had taken off, coinciding with the very point that Mandi herself was really beginning to find her freedom. Though Mandi didn't necessarily reflect on how the cultural moment coincided with the emotional, social, and familial moment of her life, it had an enormous impact. Mandi was living her life to the full, refusing to be shackled to the ideas and traditions of her own coming-of-age. She was and is a beacon of change, of personal growth.

But even if the full impact was not completely relevant to Mandi, she slowly sensed a change in herself in this year as she reflects about herself whilst preparing for her own mother's eighty-sixth birthday party:

17 JANUARY 1992

What do I really feel about now? I am free. Who am I now I live alone with Mersey? I can be incredibly generous, passionately demonstrative, fanatically loyal. I can be exhausting, but seldom exhausted. All my childhood I felt under a microscope, unable to be me, forced to take on the rules and ideals of my mother and grandmother. As a character I felt ugly. I love roaming about London in my silver civic Honda. I have a strong sense of right and wrong. I love and respect other people's differences. Peter was a woman's man though due to his upbringing too. I was attracted to his love and caring for me. I've been alone with my thoughts for nearly three years now and I am finding me. Family is so so important. We are all workers and frown on shirkers. Life is exciting like a long cool drink in the summer with bits in it. Yum!

A TIME TO MOURN
AND A TIME TO DANCE

Some three years after Peter's death, the four of us and our partners in our various ways, sat Mandi down to talk to her about her own life.

'You are still so young'.

'You still have so much ahead of you'.

'There is still time to build something new for you'.

'You have so much to give'.

These were among the many messages that Mandi heard and had already begun to realise in her own way. She knew that somehow she had to put her love and feelings for Peter firmly in place in her heart and let them reside there whilst she found a way to move on.

She had never lacked courage, but it was not so easy. She was still relatively new to London life, and her local friendships were largely from the Senior Wives group and Roehampton Club, so meeting other men was extremely difficult. She had also noticed that she could be something of a threat to her friends unless she was very careful. Waning marriages and an attractive lively widow were a dangerous combination or so some of the more threatened felt and Mandi had already had to let go of some old friendships on this basis.

So began her dating life. No one really knew what actually happened on these dates and her dating behaviour became legendary and rather worrying at the time. The diaries are missing from this period and do not reappear until 1993 when she began to build a real and lasting relationship. However, the stories she told caused both anxiety and gales of laughter. Interestingly and probably surprisingly, her daughters were all in favour of her dare-devil approach and her sons much more protective.

She began by joining a dating agency and making a video of herself saying that she had recently been widowed, was not ready for a relationship yet, but that she had always really enjoyed sex, so this would be a good place to start. Any offers? Luckily it was through an agency, so some filtering was in place. The dates came, sometimes through the agency and sometimes by chance.

There was the plumber who wanted to chance it because Mandi was in her nurse's uniform and eating a banana and the plumber was, it would seem, unable to concentrate on unblocking the dishwasher with her enticing him like that. Anyway, she did get her dishwasher mended that day and has always said it was one of the best services she has ever received.

The one who turned up in his Jesus sandals asking for a sweet sherry got shown the door and made a very reluctant and somewhat outraged departure. It was difficult to turf him out and a bit scary. The only explanation Mandi has ever proffered for this harsh treatment has been that he was not worthy of her very tasty homemade fish pie. That is when she realised that it was best to meet these strangers in a central place and not entice them with any overtly sexual behaviours or promises of fish pie, at least until she knew them a little!

Then there was the chronic, miserly smoker who met her at Hampton Court to watch the rowing on the river, told her a pack of lies about himself, expected her to pay for tea in the café and pronounced over the cuppa that she would do. Mandi by then had taken in his yellowed teeth and browned fingers and the fact that she was going to have to foot the bill for tea and had made her decision early on. He, however, was most surprised by Mandi's response that he would not do and that she still loved her husband and so ended another.

The chap who asked her out on a barge for a day only lasted that one day too. Mandi claimed and still does that after one day on a barge with someone, especially if they have terrible body odour and wear a nylon shirt, you know whether or not you ever need to see them again.

The officer in the Fleet Air Arm with the very pleasant voice promised to be a better proposition and came to pick her up in his car. He looked her up and down as he picked her up before escorting her to his car and seemed pleased with his assessment. She went to open the car door and was rudely stopped in her tracks. It was for him to open the door apparently. He then whirled the car around and in a powerful, show–off way, shot off down the road, speeding too fast over the speed bumps, making Mandi bump up to the roof of the car. He arrived too early so they had time to look at the Harrods windows, which she enjoyed, but they seemed to be headed for an apartment, which made her feel uneasy. He had a card for a building that turned out to be the Fleet Air Arms Club and ordered Mandi a schooner of sherry. After that, they went into the restaurant and he ordered their meal. Mandi had no decision in this as he knew what was good. Soup, lamb chops and ice cream later, a tasty enough meal, they returned to the Jeep and she knew for him to open the door this time. He was clear about the deal in that he had given her dinner and now it was her turn.

Mandi had learned by this time that it was not just sex that she wanted or with just anyone; she sought something much more meaningful and profound, but how to get rid of this one? She fiddled about with the key, pretending incompetence and asked him to shut the outer door; as he turned to do it, she turned the key in the lock and ran in and slammed the door. Through the slammed door, she thanked him for the lovely evening and explained that the deal he had set up did not work for her. He ranted and raved for a while before eventually departing, never to be seen again.

Those early years after Peter's death were indeed a time of meeting new people for Mandi and finding her feet as a young widow. She described her hot air ballooning adventure with the Wandsworth over 50s. 'Set off at 4.00 am'. Mandi gave a detailed description of every character involved and how the day was organised and the ballooning worked. She met lots of new people that day and had a fabulous new experience.

26 MAY 1992

Flew at 2000 feet. Fantastic sensation.

Mandi was to get one of those calls to go and help Nick and Paige at the very moment when she had just employed Freddy, her Rastafarian decorator.

6 JUNE 1992

Freddy has been decorating the sitting room. He is 25 years old, black, the youngest of 7. His mum died when he was 12 years old and his dad when he was a teenager. He's got a problem in that he vomits every day when he wakes up, perhaps antacid. He asked me about it.

With this knowledge firmly on board, she made the decision that he was absolutely trustworthy and, leaving him a set of keys, set off to the Wirral for a week of keeping house and home with three small children. There was not a moment to draw breath and goodness knows what she might or might not have found on return. At that stage in her life, in truth she did not really care, but equally her gut instinct was right and trust was rewarded with trust and she and Freddy have been firm friends ever since.

Mandi has many stories to tell of such chance friendships based on trust. Only recently he was doing lots of odd jobs for her, updating her with his life story and improving her music selection, having seen that she was still listening to the same selection of songs that he had set her up with on his previous visit.

When Sam, one of her youngest grandchildren, who had been staying with her to study for his law exams in London years later, was hugely disconcerted by what he felt was stage whispering between Freddy and Gran downstairs, he popped out to ring his mum, me as it happens. 'Mum, Gran is behaving very strangely. There is this Rastafari guy with handcuff marks on his wrists, saying that he has been locked up unfairly and that the police are after him. Do you think Gran is OK? Is she having some weird kind of affair with him? Why is she whispering like that?'

I was not able to answer any of his questions, but I was able to reassure him that Gran would be fine and of course she was.

On 17 June 1992, Mandi resigned from her work as a nurse at the Royal Hospital Putney as they refused her request for a six-month sabbatical. The opportunities to go and travel were arising and she wanted to take them up. Suddenly what had made her feel safe and secure and had helped her through her grief was now a tie. She put herself on the bank of nurses, but this was a big and final step career wise as Mandi knew that by not working regularly, she risked losing touch with nursing and modern practice.

Ultimately Mandi was to meet Lorenzo, her 'Italian stallion', as she came to call him.

Perhaps initially the relationship was built on that pure chemistry that made them work so well, pure physical need that came through their mutual grief, both of them having lost lifetime partners. They worked superbly together as two bodies long before they became two minds and spirits, but that was absolutely what was needed at the time. Mandi was comforted, lifted to the heights of sexual ecstasy time and time again and moved by that so much that she could see a way forward, a way to cry and let out the lingering pain that still hurt so much. Lorenzo understood this so well just as she understood his pain, something that their children could not be part of, however much they thought they could.

Their relationship provided the real healing, the road to truly moving on. Mandi started to really feel again, physically and slowly, but surely, emotionally and as she stopped a little to really appreciate, spiritually too. With Lorenzo, they teased, tickled and played with each other and Mandi began to really notice how she felt, how blue the skies were, how the birds sang, how the flowers burst into colour; how they enjoyed the wondrous tones of Andrea Bocelli, Pavarotti and other splendid Italian singers; how she enjoyed the sound of his voice in Italian, his passion for her in Italian, his temper, his expletives. She wanted to learn his language. He was impatient with her, but she persisted, found herself a course. No longer the attitude of 'I can't' when he laughed at her efforts. This was her time now, her choice, her voice and she wanted to learn Italian, so she did.

They went to visit his family in Udine, eighty miles north of Venice in Italy and she got to know his mother, his children, his birthplace. They fought passionately, especially if he was in the driving seat, but loved each other even more passionately. Holidays together were intense and memorable. Back home, it was a relationship for Wednesdays and Saturdays. Lorenzo was a romantic, gave Mandi attention, brought round ten red roses every week; he never faltered. He had always worked in restaurants and had so many contacts in different establishments that he would take Mandi out all over the place. Harry's Bar was a familiar haunt and here and many others afforded so many fabulous nights out. Mandi always kept those days for him. Sometimes he would stay longer, but she would retain her new found independent life, which he was not part of unless she occasionally decided to include him.

If one of the children phoned, he would sometimes answer in his emphatic Italian accent explaining her whereabouts: 'Your mother is gallivanting. I don't know when she will be home'.

It was irrelevant that Lorenzo did not wear the expected clothes to formal events that he was invited to, or that he played games with the young grandchildren to win, and lost his temper when he did not, or that he did not fit in easily with Mandi's established friends. When they went to stay with one, he was put in a separate room and he failed to understand what was required in the croquet match or over the rather smart dinner that was laid on. Concern was expressed, but Mandi was oblivious. She had chosen Lorenzo and she was quite clear about that. She knew her mind on this and she did not change it ever.

He asked her to marry him many times, but she did not want that and consistently wore her wedding band from Peter. However, to pacify Lorenzo and as a gesture of commitment, she did wear a ring as a symbol of their relationship and promised herself to him so that he could feel safe and secure. Somehow she no longer needed a formal commitment or certainly not a religious or social definition of that. She stayed with him loyally and lovingly until his death on 2 June 2010.

'Whatever the mind can conceive, man can achieve'.
— UNKNOWN —

A TIME TO TEAR DOWN
AND A TIME TO MEND

This understanding that she had freedom and choices became a very important part of the following years of Mandi's life. It was understandably still rather confusing in that family remained central to her values, to her recovery from grief and to fulfilling her life, but it was time to find a different way to know and live it.

Mandi was already a grandparent when Peter died, but this role and all that it entailed was to become an increasingly fulfilling part of her life, lending deep meaning and purpose to the new great matriarch in the making.

Her mother-in-law, Elsie, died on July 23rd 1993 with just three weeks' notice when cancer took her. Her mother became the matriarch of the moment. She entertained splendidly in her flat in Pembridge Villas in Notting Hill and her considerable family spent wonderful times in her apparent B&B, either stopping over for dinner or breakfast and always drinking too much. On hearing on one of these occasions from Jo and PaddyWhack, as NickNack was now known, that PaddyWhack was expecting, GG immediately announced that if the baby should be a boy, she would like him to be named William. She proclaimed, 'I have waited fifty-eight years for a William. Mandi was not expected to be a girl'. All those years later, she had not let the subject drop!

With her own beloved father long gone, her mother had come to rely on Mandi just to be around for all manner of support, and Mandi, now conveniently nearby in London, was. Enid had a party at White's Hotel, Bayswater, for her eightieth birthday and her son David proposed the toast:

'The vintage GRAN of nineteen-six comes highly recommended.
Provided (due to age) it is assiduously tended.
This priceless vintage has a charm whose reputation grows...
How generous the character! How delicate the nose!
What classic style! What eloquence (so very seldom corked) !

With just a hint of sharpness (of which I've sometimes talked).
So fresh and fruity the attack! So elegant the taste!
The merest sample leaves one feeling consummately braced!
As time goes by, some connoisseurs increasingly detect
A slightly nutty quality....(I mean no disrespect).
(Keep well below room temperature, and NEVER serve with pies;
Instead, a Dover Sole, a Rack of Lamb, I would advise).
Though mellowing a little, still remarkably robust.
With an earthy sort of honesty that one has come to trust.
Maturing imperceptibly – but clearly drinking well ––
And guaranteed to sparkle, when uncorked, at White's Hotel'.

Enid, Mip, Mum, Gran, Great Gran, GG ultimately had to give up her wonderful flat in Notting Hill and move to her 'rented room' in Lancaster Lodge, Wimbledon, just up the road from Mandi, where she was to spend the last thirteen years of her life.

Mandi would visit or take her out every day and she recognised the steadfast will and views of her mother that she had known all her life, but a declining strength and capacity to make things happen around her which left her more needy and vulnerable. Without questioning, Mandi stepped in and tended willingly to all those needs, in the full knowledge that her mother was unlikely to be appreciative of it. She was not, particularly, but Mandi had never needed to be thanked and had come to understand the way the relationship had shifted at this stage of their lives.

Her mother's dominance and tyranny, which had always under-mined Mandi in those early years and still shook her confidence later on, had also manifested themselves as fierce and passionate love and loyalty for her family and the way things should be done. Mandi too understood duty, loyalty and love of her parent, though she comments to this day that her mother never hugged her and that their two approaches to love were from opposite ends of the spectrum. In the end, it was not to matter; there existed a decent respect between the two women and Enid had come to learn that Mandi would not argue with her or take her on, but would simply leave and return again the next day, fresh for what that day would bring and unable to recall what might have been on her mother's mind the day before. It was an effective tactic and allowed them to enjoy their relationship for many years and undoubtedly Mandi helped her mother to achieve the fine old age of 102.

It was quite an achievement when you think back to what her great friend Jen Jones had written about Enid all those year ago:

'I'd known the Hornsbys for 65 years. School with Mandi and Bridesmaid at her wedding in St Martin-in-the-Fields. Mandi's Mum and Grandmother were powerful characters and wanted their own way...not easy at times. Enid, I recall, disapproved of David's girlfriend. 'Dirty feet', so unsuitable. I remember an incident with brother Ant at Mandavant, his Mum was in hot pursuit yelling and wielding a golf club and Mandi yelled, 'Hide!''

Enid had not forgotten her voice, however, and the staff at Lancaster Lodge certainly knew it. She was still quite a character and when one of Jo's friends popped to see her, having completely forgotten her room number, he simply reminded the home staff that she loved a gin and tonic, and was shown straight to her room. Did this penchant for a tipple or few also contribute to her longevity? An irrelevant aside, but one worth wondering about!

At her one hundredth birthday on 28 February 2006, she was delighted to be celebrating with fifty members of her splendid family, receiving that vital card from the Queen and confirming the tradition of alcoholic celebration.

In Enid's family book, *A Fantastic Innings*, dedicated to her from her own children as a celebration of this great matriarch's life, there is an overwhelming love for this splendid lady who lived two years past her one hundredth birthday and celebrated it in style with her three children, their partners and her twenty-eight grandchildren. All of them wrote warm and loving tributes to their mother, grandmother and friend, feting her, her love, the influence of her voice, her views, her outspokenness and her energy. It is a truly magnificent tribute and a mark of the woman she was, but those who had been around the longest, perhaps reflect the power that she had had over Mandi, particularly in those formative days and answer the question that a fair number of Mandi's grandchildren ask today. 'Why does Gran never praise herself or openly recognise what she does well?'

As Enid aged, so hearts softened and when her mother died at 102, a genuine love had been shared between the two women, a love based on very different giving and sharing, but certainly giving and sharing, with a common love of family at the centre of each other's purpose and perhaps a better mutual understanding of being a woman of their time with the individual right to do things in their own way.

> 'I think the biggest teachings that come from Gran is her outlook and approach to family. She ties together the best family in the world and has infinite love and squeezles for everyone. Her eyes twinkle as she talks about everyone in the family and they always seem to be at the forefront of her mind. It's an outlook that has set a major foundation for me and something to consistently strive for'.

Her grandson Charlie wrote this in his second year of training as a doctor and it reflects the importance that family has for Mandi and how she held the network of her family together over the years in lots of different ways. It was that ability to work out how to be adaptable, to learn what to hold on to and what to let go of that was the secret of her success with her family.

So photos of Mandi's eldest grandchild Matthew with his grand-father on the beach at Trearddur are treasured. He managed to see his first six grandchildren come into the world before his unexpected death, but sadly had no time to really build the relationships as Mandi did.

Mandi recognised that stage of life that her children were going through or about to go through. She remembered it as incredibly demanding and there were often two careers to work out for her own children in a world where women had achieved greater opportunity and equality in the workplace, but few solutions to the reality of biological, domestic, work and financial load. Mandi knew about that life in your early to mid-thirties with one, two, three or even four children, the usual range in age from newborns to seven-or eight-year-olds.

30 APRIL 1999

Lopsy on the phone. In laws have gone and no help. Lu has lost it. The last 2 weeks she has gone silent and absolutely has had enough. Stu sounded as if he was in for a pounding as he has been in Sydney most of the time they have been there. A very sad and tearful Lopsy went off the telephone, leaving me feeling very helpless. 3.00pm go and collect Jamie from Avalon and William 3.30pm from St Bridget's. Jo has got awful sinus, so give him

olbus oil inhalations to clear them a bit. Paddy is excited about
her time away. Cook chicken, veg, milk jelly. Bath time and stories
and 8.30pm all asleep.

Jo and Paddy ring 9.30pm. Safely there. Play with the dogs.
Do washing. A good day.

She knew about the need for resilience and boundless energy
to overcome the exhaustion, mental, physical, and emotional, the
relentlessness of every day, every hour, every minute, every second
and it is reflected in the phone calls she had with her children and
then recorded in her diaries. She has kept this Christmas letter from
me from 1991:

'It's hard to believe that I am sitting here thinking about
Christmas again. Whilst Christmas is a happy time for us,
with lots of noise, excitement and laughter, it also brings
home how rarely we see many of our friends. Mum reas-
sures me that she used to be in exactly the same boat when
she and Dad were bringing up the four of us and used to
send an annual Christmas card'.

I went on to describe Richard doing a new job and a distance MBA,
and his main responsibilities as getting the children to Sunday school
and tennis and making sure that they watched enough television.
Emma is depicted as boisterous, bossy and organised and absolutely
committed to life aged five with Badger aged four really coming out
of his shell now and getting very chatty and becoming his own man.
Sammy, it appeared, had moved on from being a fire engine to being a
police car and ran round the house aged two going 'WOO, WOO, WOO',
and driving his cars through his breakfast if he could get away with
it and feeding his greens to the dog. I explained that I was unable to
drive due to epilepsy and was to be seen, one child on the front of her
bike, one on the back, various bags and a dog attached, another child
on a bike behind. I continued writing about my private teaching to
help make ends meet and life was clearly both very full and fulfilling.
I finished the letter thus:

(Christmas 1991)

'It seems incredible to think that my dear Papa has been
dead for nearly two years now. He is often in my thoughts
and it is still very painful to watch Mum come to terms
with a life she would never have chosen. She continues to

be very brave, but it seems a cruel fate for one who sets so much store by relationships and family. She will be with us for Christmas which we are looking forward to very much'

Mum and I spoke on the phone every night for three years after Peter died, but did not visit each other that often and that was as it should be. During the time that Mandi's children were having and bringing up their own little ones, Mandi was as helpful as she felt that she could be, but it was for them to sort out their lives at this stage and she could only give so much; giving to them physically was not always her first choice or indeed the right choice. Jo and I had other in-laws to support us as well, Lucy had moved to Australia and etched on Mandi's mind will always be the birth of Tom, Lucy and Stuart's youngest of four:

14 JULY 1999

Thomas Allinson born 6.10am. Waters broke. Stu in the air. Children to neighbours. 2 hours labour...one hour gentle, half hour strong, half hour hell. Breach birth. 8.45 am having general anaesthetic for ballooning operation. On respiration.

Two days later, Mandi had got herself organised and was in Melbourne to help with the three children and the reality that Tom was a very sick little baby with the severe risk of not surviving an operation to switch his aorta and pulmonary veins. She got to know Lucy's friends and her grandchildren well during that time. However, the reality of not being able to solve a problem for your child really hit home and she had to leave them to the tough challenges that she knew awaited whilst she flew back to the other side of the world, no easy thing for any mother to do. Tom survived and is a fine, funny and much treasured young man.

Mandi could not visit often, but did when she could and some brilliant and memorable trips to Oz were to follow and equally she has welcomed all of Lucy and Stuart's children on pre-teen unaccompanied trips to her London home. Fortunately, Lucy was a chip off the old block and hugely independent and the Allinsons have thrived.

Mandi always felt that Nick had more of a need with Paige's family so far away in the States and no one to support them in the same way, so she looked after their three quite a bit, but they still had enormous challenges with Nick's work taking him away frequently and Paige often needing to accompany him.

However, they all had to stand on their own two feet just as she had and she now needed this time away from the kitchen sink, the constant demands of family life to rebuild, to reshape, to create her life of choice back in London. This was not to say that she did not support them and it was not to say that her children and grandchildren were not immense in her life. Much as they valued her pleasure, her joy and her support of them and their families, everyone in the family had to go through this process of understanding Mandi's changed life, her independence, her right to choose.

13 August 1999
Jen Jen Pen rang. Both boys crazy on ping pong and tennis. Emma initially a bit homesick on the Spanish exchange. Lorenzo and I had a lovely sesh together and did Italian pronunciation afterwards. GG is growing amaryllis in plants pots. Lopsy rang. Stu in Sydney for next 3 months, returning at weekends. New baby got a few problems, hole in the heart, so will have to go into a major hospital for big heart op. The paediatrician is confident that they will cope. Told 'I am not to worry', but with four tinies and Ben's kidneys, not easy. Long chat to Jill Pye. Go to The decorative Antiques and Textiles Fair. Paige rang and planning to come and play with me in London for a day. Hooray. Sarah leaving for Belgium to cook at Battlefields, She came 1st in French and 4th in History. Paige delighted. Computer is being a disaster. Noodle coping with all the pressures. New house pretty uncomfortable but will be spectacular when done. Went to Isabella Plantation with Sarah Rathbone who came to lunch and 2 dogs. Azalias, heathers, rhododenrons and camellias all out—gorgeous sight, black swans with red beaks and I talked to Jenny Wilmott about pony trekking and planned that. Long chat to Ant and hope to meet up next week.

Mandi knew about the juggling of naps, feeding, dance class, cub and brownie schedules. A million balls she knew about for she had juggled them all before and she knew that feeling of being unsure if one could keep them all in the air. She knew about those days when you dropped a few and just could not keep them all up there. She understood when Lu or I would phone to chat about how we were not enough, how we felt guilty. Guilty about trying to be too much, about not being enough, guilt over having a career, and not spending enough time with the children, guilt over being too harsh with the children. I wanted to know why the only time I used the wooden spoon as a punishment was the only time they remembered and it only happened the once after they had painted the garden gate, the car and the garage door with the kitchen paint I had stupidly left on the sideboard. Then to cap it all, the children had hit my tennis coaching balls to kingdom come. Those naughty, outraged ringleaders, Emma and Mark, wanted to know why they got the wooden spoon harder than their innocent, little younger brother Sam. Mandi just laughed, not because she did not understand not being enough or that guilt, but rather because she knew that over time, it would not have that importance. Indeed, it has become a funny story!

She was there to witness it all, able to be there at key moments to share and give each family a lift and at the same time remind herself of some of her own purpose. Her daughter-in-law, Paddy Whack, wrote:

> 'Gran has always been such an important figure in the upbringing of our three children. They would literally walk over hot coals for her. She is their greatest confidant, friend, listening ear and comforter; she fills a very unique role. I consider myself a very, very fortunate daughter-in-law to have had her by my side when Freddie was born in March 1997. Towards the end of my labour, my midwife realised she had left the umbilical cord clamp in her car and went off to fetch it. She didn't seem to be in any hurry, and whilst she was absent, Freddie chose to pop his bonce into the world, and Gran was there to witness the action unfold. Incidentally, Jo had chosen the top end third time round! Gran was as cool as a cucumber, and uttered, 'Iit must be a boy, darling, it looks just like William', she promptly washed her hair to look respectable for the visitors and ensuing photographs and then she made a 'Gran mince', to make the house smell homely. Classic Gran!'

Mandi shared the highs and the lows with her children and their partners, recorded their friends still getting married and having babies, but some struggling in their marriage, and even getting divorced and she was actively involved in supporting at least two, via her daughters, because Lu and I had phoned and bent her ear for hours. Indeed, she was genuinely upset about my dear friend Lori, having spent a lot of time with her in Holland; to hear that she had lost custody of her four children was very tough for everyone. Lori and Mandi were to become firm friends over the years and she is a regular visitor to Mandi's and my home now.

Mandi as ever was there to listen, to ask key questions and to consider options. She really did understand about the pressure of those early years, but was objective and wise enough to help get them through. It's a phase where you have to put in the time, the effort, the work and the energy to make sure your individual marriage stays as healthy as possible, but where does that time come from? Mandi recognised that the divorce rate had shot up noticeably from her time in this stage, perhaps because societal values and norms, the role of women, and the church at that time encouraged a couple to fight for their marriage more strongly.

Mandi didn't need the church, government, or society to tell her what she believed was right. She was there to encourage her children to keep going, sometimes discussing the trials and tribulations, sometimes writing meaningful and understanding letters. Between them all, they had a friend who had experienced infertility, miscarriages or loss of a child just as she had all those years ago. Between them all they had friends buying, selling, redesigning, redecorating, packing up and moving houses. They seemed to be sharing a fair number of hormones all out of tune because one or other of them had been pregnant, postpartum, or breastfeeding over the years and Mandi was certainly good for advice. That was a hormonal phase that Mandi was so pleased to be out of post–hysterectomy with her recent hormone replacement therapy and she had enormous empathy for any woman battling with the female anatomical curse!

It interested her that it was no longer taboo to talk about those things now and to ask for help and medical and emotional support. She openly discussed her own difficulties at the same stage and wondered at how they dealt with it all so much more easily with the pill. She empathised with that phase where you are struggling with identity. Are you just 'mummy' or 'daddy'? Is there any part of you which is not about parenting? Is there something more glamorous still lingering? It's a stage where you are on a constant quest for balance, and can never find it. Mandi recognised that time; it was the time when she took up Marriage Guidance and pushed herself over the edge sometimes, but equally dealt with some of that identity question.

These were hard and challenging times for her four children and their partners and they had to ask for help and accept it when it was offered. For all the tradition of that 1950s conventional marriage, which most of us rejected, there was something in putting the children to bed early and enjoying that glass of wine in the early evening with your partner and discussing the day or having a conversation. Time out with friends was key, support from friends was vital and it was pretty handy having your parents, either in-laws or Mandi, around to love, support and reassure on the phone, in an emergency, when on business trips and at breaking points. That parent who would agree that it is OK to say 'no', OK and indeed important to leave the children with Gran for at least a week per year and go away for a break, who would remind you that an immaculate house is far less important than having fun, who gave you little presents to keep you going and who reminded you from her own regrouping joy of life that you have done something wonderful in bringing her grandchildren. That person was a very important parent and grandparent indeed. Mandi was just that person and her diaries are loaded with entries referring to phone calls about just such things.

Paddy Whack sent her the following notes for her diary:

22 April 1996

> 'Sat: Poppy Amelia Crowe born to Emma and Alex at Liverpool Women's hospital. 7lbs 6 ozs. Sister to Oliver. Her dad took her to hospital as Alex on call and still with her when her waters broke! Drove Willy, Jamie, Rod and Eunice to Margot's in Leicestershire for weekend. Jo on stag do in Paris. Played with their grandchildren and Jamie Lou delighted everyone with her happy, smiling ways. Sun: Missed Elizabeth Leonora Williams' christening and party afterwards at Granny Williams. All back home with Daddy by 6.00 pm. Nick Faldo great win on TV till midnight. Mon: Jo's stolen Golf found in West Derby, Liverpool after being used in armed robbery. All smashed up. All contents missing—10 CDs, golf clubs, sunglasses, various cloth-ing, prescription glasses, loose change, fleece jacket—ALL

GONE! Tues: Willy took the play scissors and cut Jason's hair. Praise be! Lunch out with Lori and all coming here next week. Jo's insurance claim = £1554.00 Skiddy coming on heat. HELP! Jasper the sheepdog is coming to stay at the weekend. Weds: Jo and Willy mowed the lawn. Grandpa took Willy swimming in the afternoon to the fabulous new Europa pool. Jo made £350 on the stock market today and paid for his weekend in Paris. Cooking, washing, cleaning, dogwalking, wifing—you know the scene. Thurs: Unpacked a huge amount of clothes and turned my sitting room into a boutique. 15 mums and their children for coffee, chat, play and buy. Very successful! Fri: Went to Sally's for lunch. Jamie Lou divine. Willy found a packet of sweets. Found him behind the bedroom door unable to speak as mouth so full and pockets full of papers. Went out for dinner with Jo and much needed time together. Looking forward to wedding tomorrow. Hope you're OK and looking forward to catch up and fun over Bank Holiday.'

Mandi could look at all that her own children were building and know how utterly she had walked this path and worn these shoes; her empathy was vital to her children and incredibly real and meaningful to her. This next generation truly exemplified the circle of life. They understood her perspective, that she could not do their work for them, but that she would do enough to support their role, especially at key moments.

She was that grandparent who noted and showed in her diaries that this stage of life was beautiful, particularly beautiful. She did this with her photos, her memories from her visits, her notes of first words, first steps and first teeth from her everyday phone calls with her children or their spouses. Through her diaries, Mandi demonstrated that this time for each of her children, their partners and indeed herself was so precious, a time to savour, a time to linger over, even when there was no time to linger. She noted that same open love of this age group that she had so enjoyed. She recorded her children and their partners coming closer in a tough and challenging way, watching the growth of their relationships, their learning together, being stretched together, building a oneness together and shedding that selfishness of their single lives together. When Lucy and Stuart were going through a stage of three troublesome and troubled children, her sage and simple advice to give them love above all proved to be the best advice. She joined in so many Christmas and birthday celebrations across the four families and saw them through her grandchildren's eyes, in that so much more exciting and magical way, than it would be just be through her very experienced grandmother eyes.

CHRISTMAS 1995

'A holiday in a million! View spectacular! My darling Nick/Paige spoiling me—ski pass, fantastic sheepskin boots, dog sledding, Breckenridge Hilton, skiing, ice-skating, hot cider and cinnamon sticks, gorgeous breakfast bar!...Lucy organised Christmas beautifully. She had just completed her bathroom. Present opening was a joy. Two stockings I had. Very spoilt lady! Ben a reindeer in Christmas play. Jen's trio do Scrooge for us and play in the snow with them and all Jo's lot'.

She wrote about the class outings, birthday parties, dressing up, swimming lessons, accidents, disasters, bath times, tooth fairy visits and cut knees as reported to her, but often it was for her to listen, console or write a warming postcard from afar. For Mandi, it was so poignant, so much fun and this time around, not too much, a time to savour indeed! She watched her own children and their partners be young enough to enjoy it all and old enough to have obtained at least some wisdom to get on with it all as they had to. In the meantime, she appreciated the wisdom of her own decision to step back and support from a distance. She got so much pleasure from it all, but had empowered herself to say no when she wanted and pick and choose enough to enjoy being Gran, Grin, Grin Gran and all that she came to mean to her thirteen grandchildren.

What she came to mean exactly and sometimes less exactly, they all talk about individually and their views all tie in with entries in her diaries throughout the years and reflect the time and effort she put in as both parent and grandparent. Matthew, that eldest grandchild, now a commodities broker and fellow Londoner, is settled in a happy relationship, and has a deep respect for his grandmother, valuing her thoughts and guidance enormously. His thoughts conclude this biography as a summary of key influences of his Gran on himself and others. Sarah, a married mum of two and marketing guru, likes nothing better than to come and visit and play the grand piano, so reminiscent of her childhood, all she has heard about her father's childhood and which she is now creating in her children's childhood. She has some very important things to say:

'I have a million things to say about my Supergran and all of the special memories we share; I struggle to know where to focus. Perhaps we'll pass over the moment you had sole care of all three of us at Burlingham Avenue when I was a child and I decided to run away, or when you came to pick me up from the Woodchurch estate where I was wearing my favourite tracksuit and high heels meeting some local boys. Or the moment Flora (who always wee'd in the lift) got in the same lift as us at GG'S nursing home and Katie and I burst out laughing. These moments were always met with a calm temperament and the look which told me Gran did not approve.

Believe it or not, Gran has always been my moral conscience—if Gran disapproves of my behaviour, I know I need to take a look at myself. She has helped in quite a lot of other ways too:

You have helped each grandchild at a pivotal point in their life. Your wise words, calm temperament, openness and generosity have made each of us able to open up to you and seek solace at 115. None more so than me when I came to London in 2007.

When we moved, I knew I wanted to be close to you and so we landed on Putney. It was my favourite thing to head to Gran's on a Sunday for a welcoming lunch and chats by the fire. Everything about your house was warm and inviting and we would chat for hours. I loved spending time going through your diaries, listening to what you'd been up to, playing your piano and hearing the familiar overshare of yours and Lorenzo's love life. When London got too much, I knew I could use my key, let myself in and I would always be given the warmest of welcomes.

I loved exploring London together. You taught me so much about this incredible city. The fun we had and the games you taught me: 'Where would you go if you were an angry monarch?'

I remember asking you to meet me at the Savoy with two fashion designers after a work event one day. You turned up chic as ever in navy with your elegant scarf knotted around your neck—you were an instant hit. You told us the stories of coming into the Savoy to go for a wee on your way to school and taught me about our incredible family history. We drank too many cocktails and they named you Supergran and asked if you would be their gran too (a regular occurrence amongst friends).

I have only touched the surface of the incredible memories we have shared. I am so grateful for your wise words when Josh was born, support with Seb, visits to Tunbridge Wells and the days you come and played in Epsom with the boys. Thank you for supporting me at every stage of my life, your impact has been extraordinary. I feel incredibly lucky that I got Supergran'.

Katie and her husband Russell in PR and journalism, and about to embark on the parenting journey themselves, lived with Gran for a while and dealt with basic needs first and foremost. A six-month supply of wine gums would arrive to fill Gran's much loved old sweetie tin left to the family by Aunt Eva. Gran's love of chocolate and sweets is of course a winner with all the children and there is not one that will not cite her milk jelly as an absolute childhood favourite. Mandi will often eat a whole bar of Cadbury's chocolate at a sitting, part of Peter's legacy perhaps, but she remains svelte with her smooth complexion. As Katie recounts:

'Living with you were some of the funnest days I could imagine and you taught me the ropes of the Big Smoke, encouraged adventure, instilled routine and discipline and mostly taught me to laugh at myself when things weren't quite going my way. You very kindly said I could come live with you for a little while whilst I looked for jobs and I took up residence in the Elephant room. But having graduated at the height of an economic crisis in 2008, my short stay soon became a year as your kitchen table was transformed into a recruitment office.

Every time I came back deflated from a failed interview or a disappointing chat with a prospective employer, you were there with your metaphorically broad shoulders to cry on and offering such kindness and eternal words of wisdom that I continue to recite to myself today. You have an ability to see every day as a fresh canvas, that will be better if fuelled by half a grapefruit and some porridge. But when things got just a little bit too desperate, you pulled out the big guns and surprised me with two tickets to an Abba Sing-Along at Wimbledon Theatre. At the height of my job slump, moody and depressed I found myself begrudgingly sat with a sparkly wig amongst the crowds. Your kind gesture had taken me so far away from the dark room I wanted to be sitting in. But you knew best. The highlight was when I nipped to go to the toilet, I laughed to myself as I made my way back to the seat having seen one woman at the front of the stage going hell for leather on ''Thank you For the Music''. Her blue shiny wig rocking back and forth as she stood solo soaking up the excitement with her hands punching the air. When I got back to my seat to point her out to you,; I soon discovered you missing and that you were the woman at the front of the stage. I've never laughed so hard and the journey to finding my way didn't quite seem as hard after that. I hold on to the memory and remind myself to live more in the moment, just like you did that night and you do! I call that memory 'Filled with the joys of spring!'

My final memory is about a good old romp and I'm not talking about a 5km walk....After getting settled in London and taking up a job at *The Sun* doing night shifts, my favourite daytime activity was to come hang out in your garden. I'd take my work clothes and sunbathe all day or sort out your computer woes or go for lovely walks before heading off to Tower Bridge. On one of the days, our conversations about computer woes and our struggling love lives merged and we took a look at your prospective suitors/matches on your online dating profile. Confused as to whether it was a technical glitch, we discovered you'd been 'winking' at every potential suitor. Having learnt a few tricks from you on how to get the most out of someone in a conversation—we sat down and had 'the chat' about responsible online dating. I lured you into the conversation by asking: 'Is there another reason, perhaps a deeper reason —you have been trying to get responses from all of these men?' You didn't waste two minutes, you ran upstairs and came back with your vibrator—given to you in 1989— slammed it on the table and declared: 'This!! This has stopped working! And this is probably why I'm prodding all these men online'. There, we had it. You had laid bare your frustrations.

'Have you changed the batteries?' I asked.

'Of course I have', you retorted, before adding: 'I don't know what to do. Shall I call an electrician?'

'Probably best we reserve him for wiring issues and we just go get you a new one. There's an Ann Summers in Wimbledon that sells vibrators, shall we just go there?' I asked.

You were very quick to turn down the offer and determined you didn't want to set foot in that 'sort of shop'.

But as one of the most determined women I know, it was unusual to see that determination waiver so quickly and just a few minutes later, you coyly suggested we go to Wimbledon for, perhaps, a look around the shops or to buy me a new dress?

On a mission to get you a new friend and you to get me 'a new dress'...we jumped on the bus at the end of the road and headed off to Wimbledon.

On arrival into the shopping centre, I forced you into Ann Summers and we began the delicate selection process. I'll never forget you asking me why so many were 'big and black or all wiggly and purple'.

But before I could answer, we were approached by the shop assistant who turned to me and asked, 'How can I help you?' I took great pride in telling her, 'Oh not me, my Granny,' as she offered her assistance.

As she talked you through the various functions and

designs, I stood back in pride; this was your Abba sing-along moment and I'd managed to take you out of your comfort zone and find something that was good for you! You really had taught me well!

After selecting your new pal, the shopping experience was not over and when they tried to wrap it for you, you quickly turned down the offer in case your neighbours saw it in your bins and in fact, asked if they could they take the box too, as you didn't want anyone to know where you'd been shopping.

After paying for the 'new friend', your torturous shopping trip was very nearly over. Quick stop by M&S to pick up a lemon drizzle for bridge that afternoon or, as I'm convinced, to disguise the nude vibrator in case beady-eyed passengers spotted it through your Harrods Bag for Life on the bus, and then it was home time.

After arriving back at 115, the excitement of your new friend all became real and after going through several Italian names, Pepe was born.

Off I went to work, safe in the knowledge that you were happy. I'd played you at your own game Gran and found a solution to a problem that for the first time ever, you had some difficulty in communicating. One of my proudest moments and the very skills you taught me, in action!'

My lot recall Gran coming to see us in Westcliff when they were tiny. She would support me as chair of the local playgroup just after Peter died and turned up to the annual fetes where Richard and I would perform the clown show, the children would dress up as three little pigs or other fairy tale characters and all their friends would put on the side shows. Mandi would joke with their friends about missing Peter and having to rely on the vibrator that Richard had bought her from a visit to Amsterdam in 1989 to keep her happy whilst she was waiting to meet the right man after Peter's death. She would recount how he presented it to her in front of all the family in a beautiful gift box.

The human fruit machine reflected how well those friends had come to know her on her visits to Westcliff. Three of the four dads sat with a bag of fruit and the fourth dad provided the arm that has to be pulled and the music. Mandi pulled down the arm and had to giggle when all three men pulled out a banana, holding them all bolt upright with an enormous smile on their faces.

'You are so naughty!' she admonished them with a naughty twinkle in her eye, clearly loving every second.

Much the same thing happened when Sam was christened at the local Methodist Church during a Harvest Festival service. Firstly, the passing of the marrow caused much mirth when the vicar invited everyone to feel and appreciate God's good work and Mandi was certainly passed the marrow more frequently than was necessary, by Jo of course! Then the church's own electric band was warming up with so much regrettable feedback that Tom, one of those Westcliff friends, was heard to say in a very loud whisper: 'Turn it off, Mandi. Not in church!'

Somehow where there is laughter and a joke, Mandi is in the thick of it.

My lot remember Mandi having them in her London home quite frequently in the very early days, with wonderful adventures on the tube and around London, all tied to a rope to ensure that they did not get lost. Shooting down the stairs on a duvet was equally good sport, although an unfortunate abseiling episode over the bannister using Gran's much loved abs device, Mr Adpinalp, did result in a broken arm. Visits to GG were always part of a visit to Gran and these would involve going up to her room in the lift that smelled of old people's urine, carefully constructed conversations based around pre-planned questions, promises of rewards for good behaviour and fake joy at GG bringing out a tray of smoked salmon sandwiches from the top drawer of her chest and then trying to hide some of them in pockets so that they appeared to have been devoured before departing. Outings to Richmond Park with Gran and GG and letting go of GG's wheelchair, whilst she apparently flew obliviously down the hill, was all part of the entertainment. As they got older, they became very interested in the suspect reading matter in Gran's spare bedroom and frequently discussed the sexual positions illustrated. The excellent cakes and the contents of that sweetie tin were very important sensory memories too.

Later, Mandi recorded endless support of their plays, concerts, matches and events at Felsted. Emma, Mark, Sam and Peg Pog, the dog, will never forget the day when Gran was looking after them at Stocks, the first boarding house that I ran. Whilst she was leading the first day of term, Gran took charge with a bright idea. It was a perfect day for picking plums from the laden tree in the back garden. All the children had hockey sticks and cricket bats with which to bash the branches whilst they had climbed into the tree and Gran climbed on to the small white drinks table. Unfortunately, it was a plastic, rather tired table and she promptly went through the middle of it. She stood there in a plastic white tutu, she and all her grandchildren in the plum tree, crying with laughter.

Boarding school life afforded so many fabulous opportunities for the staff and their children and Mandi was a regular in her theatre seat, pitch side, at a ball or Speech Day. She loved nothing better than the opportunity to go to chapel and sing 'Jerusalem' and 'I vow to thee my country', hymns that had travelled with her all her life and which she associates with her father.

Mandi certainly got a very different experience of school second time around. She came to know a great many of the staff and became an extremely popular member of the school family, known by many and often joining in. Much loved for her sense of fun, she even came on school trips as a staff member.

Her most memorable was accompanying me in order to stand in for me on a night off whilst I went off to celebrate my twenty-fifth wedding anniversary with Richard. I had been up all the previous night preparing and as soon as we reached our destination hotel in Salzburg and got our German students fed and into bed, I collapsed on the double bed I was sharing with Mandi and fell asleep. In the night, there was a knock at the door and Lily was there, aged ten, in her nightie, terrified and homesick. Mandi, being the kind and compassionate lady she was, invited her in to snuggle up with her and fall asleep rather than wake all the others with her anxiety. Lily at the end of the trip particularly remembers Mandi for this kindness, though I spent the next three weeks clearing my name from a safeguarding point of view, having woken up to find a small child in our bed. The staff thought it was hilarious and Mandi went on to entertain all the Salzburg tourists on that trip. Lily also remembered her for transforming into Mother Teresa behind a tree; being the oldest, but the first up the mountain; farting whilst bending down to serve the children with their picnic lunch; having a few glasses of wine too many one evening and having to be directed back to the hotel and removed from her duties. Everyone was thoroughly amused by her and all the staff ended up sharing their life stories and wanting her on every forthcoming trip. I, as the headmistress, never dared to take her again!

When Richard left me, pretty much at the same stage and age that Mandi had lost her Peter, Mandi understood what that looked like and stepped up to support my family, calling and writing every day, just as I had done for her all those years ago. She came on the camping trip to North Wales and nearly had to have first aid after the white water rafting expedition. Then she surprised everyone on the horseriding trek. When the leader asked if anyone would like to gallop on the beach, Mandi was the only one to go for it. I, who was trying to stop my horse from eating every hedgerow, looked up in amazement to see my mother, John Wayne-like, riding at speed with just one hand on the reins, flying along the beach at full tilt.

'Oh yes, darling, used to ride a lot as a child. Never had the time nor the money when you were young and it wasn't your father's thing!'

She did the same the following summer in Trearddur Bay on the golf course. Emma lost both the golf club and the ball in one shot into a neighbouring gorse bush whilst Gran placed her ball neatly on the green using her five iron.

'Oh yes, darling, used to play a bit as a child. Never had the time nor the money when you were young and it wasn't your father's thing'.

On the next hole, Emma hit a sheep and Gran hit the green again! There was no doubting her talent, although there was some doubt about Emma's. They laughed together till they cried.

She was invited to Seville on Emma's hen do and biked around the city with the best of them, following the bride to be dressed in her flamenco outfit. She went to the out of town strip show on the Saturday night, laughed when she was offered a phallic bread roll, drank her cocktails merrily and was so shattered by the time that it came to the various servicemen stripping that her ringside seat proved pointless. She sat, her head thrown back, catching flies, as the soldier, the airman, the sailor and the fireman all flung off their clothes and revealed their glory right beside her. They noticed her and tried to attract her attention, but she was only there in body that night and claimed later that she had seen it all before anyway!

For Emma, it says it all that her Gran was key to her hen do and wedding celebrations. Charlie, Emma's husband, always seeks out Gran if there is a family party: 'I love Gran and her passion for life and for people and how she always wants great things for them'.

This is all he will say as he comes back pumped up from a chat. Emma is now an established teacher and Charlie in social work, enjoying their two little ones, Bella and Matilda. They often come to visit and GG has been sharing their art lessons with Aunty/ Granddaughter Loubird over zoom during the Covid lockdown.

When we went on a family trip to Turkey before Emma's wedding, she was there too, enjoying the Dalyan mud bath and pummelling that went with it and doing the daily water aerobics to ensure that bodies were in shape for the much awaited Big Day. Mandi was hugely part of all that and so many family weddings, even asked to read the prayers at the wedding for Mark, known as 'Badger', and me in 2019, during which she recited the very prayer that had been read to her as a child and which she had repeated to her children and her grandchildren off by heart over the years.

'Jesus, tender Shepherd, hear me;
Bless Thy little lamb tonight;
Through the darkness be Thou near me
Watch my sleep till morning light.
All this day Thy hand has led me,
And I thank thee for Thy care;
Thou has clothed me, warmed and fed me,
Listen to my evening prayer. (Hymn Mary Duncan 1839)
Let my sins be all forgiven,
Bless the friends I love so well;
Take me, when I die, to heaven,
Happy there with Thee to dwell'.

Badger reminds Mandi so much of the Hornsby side of the family with his penchant for madness, singing, laughter and joking; the fact that he had quite a tough early school life resonated with her and they share a huge affinity as a result. On her eightieth birthday, he made a video of all the family's contributions to express their love for her and it represents how important she is to him and just how he described her at his own wedding, 'The glue that holds the whole family together, the one that is always there'. For him, she always has 'wonderful words of wisdom, a ridiculous energy that enthuses and inspires, her naughtiness permits more naughtiness throughout the family and everyone loves the boyfriend sagas, the outrageous stories, as much as they love the homemade cake, welcoming meals, squigs of wine and willingness to house a bike for months on end!'

Mandi is so delighted that darling Badger has found such a lovely wife and even more delighted that their particular hobby is wine tasting! Incidentally there is no greater lasting statement of what she means to all her family than that video made for her when each and every one of them created a heartfelt song, message, sketch for her in one long, moving and very funny tribute.

It is interesting how much Mandi learned about this third generation approach to learning difficulties through Badger. I was so interested in this area through running a school that Mandi often discussed with me how I was dealing with dyslexia, using her own aunt's by then famous book, 'Alpha to Omega' to help dyslexics. Beve Hornsby had set up the Hornsby Institute and was important in turning round the embedded attitudes of such as Enid Hornsby and leading educationalists like me and my team to helping many a struggler to success. Mandi also saw the incredible progress Badger made over thirty years from a child, initially diagnosed with ADHD, and ultimately becoming a highly organised and successful young man in recruitment after some time in the gym business, able to focus and achieve with the best of them.

Mandi in turn was able to reflect on how she had come through her own dyslexia, which indeed her difficulty with spelling was, and prove herself not only a highly effective kinesthetic learner, but also a worthy wordsmith, key to her finding her voice. Even in writing this book, it is challenging to persuade her of that, but that is more from modesty than self-belief these days. She also came to fully understand that her mother's attitude to left-handedness was inherited and that she had the right and ultimately the knowledge to reject aspects of her parents' upbringing and create her own beliefs, values and standards.

Like many of her grandchildren, Sam came to live with her in London whilst doing his pupilage. He had to study hard and Gran knew to leave him alone to get on with becoming a barrister. On the odd occasion he would get some space though, he, Gran and India, his girlfriend, would go out for a walk or a cycle. Gran remembers struggling up a hill on her bike and Sam coming behind her and just pushing her up the tough hill with one hand. She loved that as she got older and the hills became somehow steeper, a grandchild would always be on hand to get her up that hill. That time was meaningful to Sam too and in the 2016 diary, you find his thank you letter to his grandmother after his six month stay.

'To the legendary lodger lookerer afterer living on Granville.

A card is wholly insufficient for what you have done for me over the last six months. I will be organising a surprise adventure, but in the meantime, I can only offer this card and a squig of wine.

Thank you for amongst a million other things:

1. Saving me six months of crippling rent or a stint on the streets
2. Letting me have the master suite at the expense of your many other visitors
3. The endless gunge and vino
4. The fridge, that despite my best efforts, cannot be emptied
5. Noticing my partiality to cracked black pepper Ryvita thins and subscribing to a life supply
6. Washing and ironing all my clothes (particularly the collar shirt trick)
7. Cleaning my room
8. Teaching me how to use the printer!
9. Whizzing me to Clapham Junction in under 3 minutes at an average speed of 123 mph, which was impressive if slightly terrifying, and saved face with my supervisor
10. The art exhibitions of your excellent works
11. The whiteboard messages letting me know what was going on ('Gran 04.50 10 mile hike. Back later'. Probably my favourite)
12. Your silent whatsapp messages without words
13. Cosy fires
14. Accommodating India, the extra late night lodger

15. Putting up with my anti-social behaviour
16. Giving me so much freedom to be grumpy and stressed without rebuke
17. My various lessons on slightly befuddling bridge conventions
18. The advice, albeit unheeded, on how to soften my leather shoes. I will definitely have a bath with them on next time
19. Restraining to a large extent from talking about your sex life with Charles (some improvement still required on this front)
20. The farting (oh how I will miss the farting!)
21. For being so excited when I got my barrister's wig
22. The table time chats
23. All the advice on dealing with the funny people that I am dealing with and perhaps most importantly:
24. All the love, hugs and squeezles'

He finishes, unable to express his gratitude enough, and looking forward to their next encounter. India, his soon-to-be wife, also developed a really special relationship with Gran over this time, sharing their love of classical music and the Proms, the great out-doors, a warm love of Sam, homemaking and cooking and that zest for life. Gran could not be more excited that they are now expecting twins together.

Frequent shared holidays with Gran allowed for those wonderful relationships to develop; Gran would ski and join in with the après ski with everyone until it became just après ski. In her mid-seventies, Gran hung up her ski boots. Having done two gentle slopes, she ended up upside down off the drag lift on the first day. From here, she was ultimately launched into the soft snow drifts at the side of the lift from where she was rescued and this decided it for her; she was there for the party and ensconced herself in a bar where she never lacked a companion for the entire trip. Every day, she would put on her gear, including her boots, pick up her heavy skis, head up the mountain and find a bar. After a great week, she is still known to accept a skiing holiday invitation, but she is definitely there for the party!

Despite Lucy and her family being in Australia, Mandi maintained a strong bond with all of them. Endless telephone calls were recorded in her diaries and she painstakingly copied out letters from them.

CHRISTMAS LETTER 2006 from the Allinsons stuck in the diary:

'January: Ben and Stu do Lorne Pier to Pub 1.2 km offshore swim 'together' (Ben whips dad by 2 minutes'. Ben 'Duxes' his promotion camp and earns a flight with the Roullettes (Aussie equivalent of Red Arrows) Lu and Stu go off camping and walking—52 km in 36 hours, through Wilson's Promo National Park

February: Having passed up chance to be ball kid at Aussie Tennis Open for Cadet camp, Ben does stint as ball boy at the Aussie Wheelchair Tennis Open. Ben also does his first Olympic length triathlon (800m/24k/80k

March: Tom has check up—explains to Professor Menahmem that torso scratches are a result of 'farting on Jenny's bed'—Stu too late to stop detailed explanation.

April: Charlie, Ben. Lu and Stu see last Rolling Stones Melbourne gig before 'Keef' Richards falls out of tree in Fiji. The stress of queueing online for those tickets, but it was worth it! Ben and Charlie qualify as soccer (sorry football) referees. Jenny does Weetabix triathlon.

May: Charlie and Ben take up water polo—intrigued by the 'it's legal if the ref didn't see it' rules and stories of 'blood in the water' match between Hungary and Russia at the 1956 Melbourne Olympics.

June: whole family starts building a house, literally up a hill in Kangaroo Island. Back in Melbourne, manage to lose Kazu Toshi (visiting Japanese student)—found eventually!

July: Ben goes to Washington to attend international student conference. Lu and Stu return to South Australia to continue construction of house.

August: Ben and Charlie both (relief) qualify as ball boys for 2007 Aussie Open. Charlie gets academic and drama colours at school.

September: Stu returns to SA to repair wind–damaged verandah on house (AAgh!)

October: First carrots from Tommy's vegetable garden. Jenny hits netball courts coached by former Australian national squad member. (Tommy's girlfriend's mum from school)

November: Lucy co-founds Bayside Climate Change Action Group —(Go you activist) and inspires community with 'change begins with me!'

December: Charlie plays Stairway to Heaven in impromptu street concert with semi-professional 'musos' to wild adulation from some of the more outrageous mums. Jenny starts career as stand up comic in school talent contest. (She's got the timing—unfortunately Dad is providing the content!)

So we end older, wiser and a little more philosophical. It's been very enjoyable nonetheless. We are looking forward to seeing the Burretts this Christmas as well as hopefully two of Stuey's mates—out for the hopefully still undecided Ashes series'.

This one was sent to her from Ben, the eldest Allinson, when he was sixteen.

'Dear Gran,

Thanks for the Adidas shorts. As usual, you seem to have found a way into my mind and found out exactly what I needed. Christmas Day went down as usual with Tommy ripping my hair out and telling me to get up at 6-ish in the morning. I fended him off for an hour or so and then Jenny joined in the battle, so sleep went out of the window. Excitement lasted about 5-10 minutes for Charlie and I before we went back to sleep again, out cold till about 1 in the afternoon. I was sprawled out on the couch completely unwakeable, yet when I woke up, no one had drawn a single thing on my face. It's weird because most Christmases with you and other families are non-stop with just a few toilet breaks, but when it is just us six, everything reverts to slow motion, there's a lot more lazing around and contemplation. It's not necessarily bad, just extremely different from what we have done for the last few years. Apart from Christmas we have not done anything particularly spectacular through- out the year. We've had some pretty cool accidents though, like Dad splitting his head open whilst trying to put braces on himself and more recently, me nearly breaking my neck whilst body surfing. I got the entire spinal board, ambulance, hospital experience and the usual minor cuts and bruises and broken somethings. Aside from the interesting stuff such as injuries and Tommy, school's been going pretty well, though the end of year marks have ignited a fire in me to do better next year...no long term bird on the scene, but it's holidays, so not a good time for one anyway'.

Ben then gave a lot of detail about his plans for the coming few months, including hoping to see his Gran. Later in 2011, Ben came over for his cousin's wedding, stayed to do a trip, and at the end of it treated his Gran and his girlfriend to the Fat Duck, Heston Blumenthal's Restaurant and Pub in Bray. He worked hard for every penny of that trip and saved for the £700 meal bill.

13 DECEMBER 2011

I've never had 12 courses served to me by such friendly waiters and waitresses, attending to everything so beautifully. The fish course in 6" seashells with earphones giving us the sound of the sea. Unique! Perfection! A joy to be with them.

Ben, her eldest grandson of the Australian clan, was working in England in 2019 and came to visit when he could. He remembered that nothing surprised him and he is still delighted about another collection of memories from times with Gran.

'I have many fond memories of my Gran but I have decided to share a more recent one, fresher and less bloated by nostalgia. Whilst working in East Sussex I would sojourn at Gran's, with its multitude of beds and couches, whenever I could find time. Without fail, Gran would invite me to sleep in her bed and I would curl up next to her and spend eight hours in deep blissful slumber, like a baby in a crib. I think that it is a beautiful thing to be able to do after so many decades on the other side of the world.

I watch friends interact with octogenarians and their own grandparents and can't imagine any great percentage of them enjoying such a relationship. Where other elders might carry the callouses of previous relationships or the

slumped shoulders of those disappointed by their nearest
and dearest, Gran does not. She has erected no walls
to the world. She remains optimistic in the transient
wayfarers who enter her life for days at a time and hopeful
for humanity at large. She projects warmth and welcome
with a selflessness that is as rare as it is delightful to find in
someone who has lived so many lives in so many different
environments.

As I myself age and begin to wear my experiences in the
lines around my eyes and the arch of my back, I look to her
belief in people for rejuvenation. She has shown me that
there is nothing more endearing in a person than knowing
they care deeply and endlessly for the people they surround
themselves with. I'm very glad to have you as a part of my
life, Gran'.

Mandi's home is a place which many warm to. Paddy Whack and
Loubird, Jo's wife and daughter, see themselves as similar to Mandi
and pride themselves on sharing and enjoying her skills. Mandi and
Paddy Whack have done up Lamare together a couple of times and
their reflection of the seaside environment in the seagull curtains,
polished wooden floors and sand-coloured suite of sofas and arm-
chairs was both practical and memorable. Jo, extremely good at all
things DIY, does all the odd jobs around the house just as Peter always
used to. Both homes are enhanced with photos everywhere and
artwork; Loubird really identifies with that, saying that she and Gran
both share that creative passion, although interestingly, she cannot
help but notice how hard Gran is on herself and never accepts that her
creations are worth looking at, a throwback to that childhood again
perhaps. Loubird, on the other hand, is usually rather pleased with
hers! However much one decides or tries to shake off a childhood
legacy, perhaps it just leaves its scar; Loubird is of a generation when
effort as well as achievement are so praised. Gran was definitely not!
Loubird loves Gran's birthday cards, which are always creative and
cards are left up and pinned up at Gran's as a reminder of her family.
Gran buys the card and then cuts out the relevant face and if possible
makes the joke work. There would often be carbon paper with money
inside and a suggestion for what we might buy.

Loubird also learned that 'a tidy cook is a good cook' from her Gran and making cakes and flapjacks with Gran is a very fond childhood memory.

'Whenever I stay, it's what we do, grating the lemon peel and orange peel into the cake and licking the spoon and the bowl. I never knew spatulas existed until I started making cakes with my Mum as Gran always made sure there was always enough in the bowl to eat!'

Whilst Gran never actually taught her to sew, Loubird has gone on to become a fine tailor and Gran is still happily sewing all sorts of things, not least the recent upholstering of all my dining room chairs.

William, currently travelling the world as the bosun of a luxury yacht, lingered fondly on all those homely memories too:

'Some of my first memories of Gran are probably her flapjacks in Lamare with all the family leaping around the tray to devour them whilst they are hot. So yum! Following on a similar theme, when we'd go stay at Gran's in Granville road, I would always look forward to being woken up for a 'midnight feast' in the twin bedroom. Such vivid memories of Fred, Loubs, myself and Grin gathered around a plate full of salami, crackers and cheese. Wow! So much excitement, it puts such a smile on my face thinking about it.

Another memory that has stuck with me all this time that clearly touched me is that Gran kept a small white polar bear teddy (endorsed by CocaCola [probably from McDonalds]) above her bed for probably 18 years that I gave to her when I was about seven years old as a gift. It really ended up being the gift that kept on giving, but back to me, as when every time I came to Granville road, she would show me she still had it in her super sweet Grinny way.

There is almost nothing I love more today than coming to visit Gran and you to sit around and catch up drinking tea. If Gran's gunge is kicking around, then phwoar even better. Again, always giving me that grounding homely feel that is often so far away for me. That bloody sweet tin as well. We have such special memories based around all these wonderful things. Anyway, most of all when I think of Gran, I think of family. There is nothing more important and she embodies that better than anyone. She truly is the

best and has shown us all that through her actions and
kind words throughout our lives'.

Jen, another granddaughter from Oz and teacher in training,
recently spent time in Gran's home with her boyfriend and found it
a place of love.

'I think of her as giving love. Identity has been the hardest
thing for us in Australia and she provides a key part of that
connection. Gran is timeless. I think that it is why it is easy
not to worry about her. She has so much energy and gets
on with life'.

It is not just her family that Mandi welcomes into her lovely home.
She extends her hospitality to many. How many meals has Mandi
cooked for others over her life? How many has she given to people
that she barely knows just because one of her children, a friend of
a friend, or a bridge contact has put her in touch. Dinner parties or
simple suppers made of unlikely guests turn out to be riotous affairs,
because Mandi is a confident and easy hostess and entertainer as well
as a homely, but fine cook. She takes young people in as lodgers to
help them get started and connects them to others because she is in
touch with the young and takes great delight in doing so. Giving to
others is a key driver for her purpose. Nick wrote:

'I think Mum's heart has always ruled her head . She prides
herself in helping people less fortunate than we are—she
cares about people and always support the underdog'.

Paddy Whack wrote:

'Probably the finest example to demonstrate her generosity
of spirit and hospitality is to mention the English family.
In October 1993, Jo's great mate Howard English died aged
thirty-two on the rugby pitch at Esher. His wife Steph and
their three very young children were living in a tiny house
in South Wimbledon. Without hesitation, Mandi was on the
phone to Marion and Howard English senior in Trearddur
Bay (their permanent residence) to offer her hospitality at
115, thus enabling them to be close to Steph and the children and to come to terms with their grief and the tragic
loss of their only son. Mandi's home became a haven for
them. She put them at ease and made them so welcome.
Howard and Marion were both medics, so they had much in

common, including their love of Trearddur Bay and sailing the same boat, the Myth. Mandi's relationship with Howard, Marion, Steph and all the English family flourished, and they became very loyal friends. Sadly, Marion and Howard have since died, but Steph has kept up her relationship with Mandi. She, Gran, was such an integral part of that very traumatic time in their lives and so typically, a huge comfort and support to them all. So many of our friends love Gran, too many tales to tell here'.

That social confidence and capacity to bring others along with her also gets Mandi invited out a great deal. She knew that Peter would always take her along on business trips, to spend time with her certainly, but also because she was a real social asset, at ease, comfortable and confident with anyone that she met. Her children were no different with her now. It was always good value to have her along. I invited her to every Speech Day whilst I was headmistress and Mandi thrived on these occasions.

On my leaving do from work, Mandi was in her element with the whole family around and buzzing. It was almost as much her leaving do as mine as she had been so much part of it all. She was so much in social mode that she flitted over to James and his Mum, whom she knew well, to admire the baby that they were with. James had shared his eighteenth with Emma, her granddaughter.

'Is this your little one?' she enthused without looking.

'No, it's yours', was the reply as James hadn't got any children at the time and was minding Mandi's great-granddaughter, Matilda, for a moment.

Mandi, of course, carried the moment off with hoots of laughter and proclamations of early madness!

London proved to be a wonderful place to live life to the full again and offered Mandi that sense of belonging, which she had always identified as important and a dense expanse of learning which she loved exploring. It brought her alive.

> *'A man who is tired of London is tired of life'.*
> — Samuel Johnson —

People come to London, via London, from London, and Mandi's

hospitality was indeed second to none.

She started cooking again with real interest and verve and giving dinner parties to new guests that she had met on the Wimbledon circuit, through bridge, the Wandsworth over 50s or the Roehampton Club. Her circle of acquaintances and friendships grew and they were from every class and creed. London offers spice and variety and Mandi thrived on it. She built on previous friendships and she gained respect for her energy and commitment to life.

Mersey her dog was a great reason to get out and about and she would chat to everyone and get to know them. She loved dear old bedraggled and bearded John who would appear at Southfields station, whatever the weather, in his shorts and share his mood of the day with the general public. You watched most sneak by slightly uncomfortably, but not Mandi; they became good friends.

All the shopkeepers came to know her well and she quickly made Southfields her local village. Mandi sees London as a lot of villages that have grown up over the years off the central satellite and she knows many of them well.

She has done most of the guided London walks in her time, starting with Blackfriars in 1991. It was a Friday evening and one of her first outings after losing Peter; the weather was dreadful and she was soon asked if she would share her umbrella with a rather forward balding gentleman in exchange for dinner. Initially this seemed like a pretty good deal, but he spent the rest of the walk and talk getting too close to her under her umbrella and when they got back to The George at London Bridge, she had to make a run for it. He came out of the gents to find that he was going to get wet going home!

It has not stopped her doing so many more though and finding out about Dickens' London, Jack the Ripper's London, Kensington, the palace and the museums, the other palaces and museums, the key history of London, the fire, the plagues, the bombings, the executions at the Tower, Borough Market, Covent Garden, the Chelsea Pensioners and Flower Show, the Thames and the Embankment and so much more. A fair number of these she has done with her daughter-in-law Paddy Whack and both relish these gems of this iconic capital city.

In 2015, I was able to invite her as my guest to a lunch and a gallery viewing with a number of MPs before we went together to Whitehall Court to see where Mandi had grown up. It was one of those days to remember; Mandi's thrill for it all was paramount. Only a year later, she was showing William Earlam around; she took him to St Martin's in the Fields where she had married, and the National Portrait Gallery nearby.

'Gran would often tour me around London and teach me how to use the tube. I dearly loved how she showed me to watch people and study their emotions especially during these times on the tube. I think that guided me in some ways over the years.

She educated most of her grandchildren in one way or another on London and has begun now on the next generation. Her young great granddaughter, Bella, was wide eyed when GG advised her as part of her first visit to London to be sure to go down to the Globe, take in the Golden Hind and stop by the Clink and think about where people who had failed to pay their bills had been strung up alongside the Thames and had to wait until the tide came in and drowned them to remind others not to do likewise. Bella's friends are still hearing the story of the strung up deadbeats that made such an impression upon her'.

Mandi has always had a ball at the All England Club. Tennis was a passion of Peter's for years and it had translated to all of their children. Mandi mastered the game and went on to enjoy it for a fair number of years socially at the Roehampton Club. John Barratt, former Wimbledon commentator and fellow Cambridge tennis player with Peter, had introduced Peter to the All England Club on his arrival in London. On his death, a Trearddur Bay sailing club friend of John and Mandi wrote and told John of Mandi's widowhood and asked him to look after her. Over the years, the Barratts and Mandi have become firm friends and Mandi receives two tickets to Wimbledon annually courtesy of John. Most of her grandchildren as well as many friends have had a wonderful day out accompanying her to the tennis.

As a child who walked out in St James Park with Buckingham Palace always a prime landmark, Mandi has an ingrained respect for the Queen and certain members of the royal family. She admires work ethic, duty, values and commitment and believes that the Queen has steered her family through many choppy waters. She appreciates the standards she has and respects the challenges she faces.

Mandi's diary records her love of London and how she has learned it over the years, genuinely becoming a Londoner. Anyone who drives round London is amazed at her confident lane switching, exact knowledge of where she is going, capacity to choose different bridges to nip one side or other of the river to get to the city or elsewhere, her love of a short cut and immediate rapport with other less friendly drivers on the road. She is not in the least intimidated by a large articulated lorry; those high up drivers are so much easier to make contact with at traffic lights.

Sarah, one of her granddaughters, wrote:

> 'You taught me confidence is everything. Remember mum's birthday party in Notting Hill? You insisted on driving because you would only have a squig of wine. A bottle later you refused to leave your car and Katie and I got in with you. A minute down the road and we hit a drink driving stop check.
>
> 'We're done for', we said.
>
> 'Excuse me madam have you been drinking tonight?' asked the policeman.
>
> 'How very dare you', you said. 'I have my grandchildren in my car', cleverly avoiding the question.
>
> The policeman looked shocked. 'I'm terribly sorry madam do drive on'.
>
> A minute later Katie and I in shock ask, 'Where are we, Gran?'
>
> 'No idea, darlings, had to look like I knew where I was going'.
>
> Truly masterful!'

A genuine nature lover, Mandi has found real beauty, solace and often something greater than herself in London's less frequented glades. Her grandson Charlie picked up on this and wrote:

> 'Gran often talks about hopping off the planet. When people say such things, it's usually a cause of concern but with Gran, it's a frankness and openness about our own mortality that's nothing short of refreshing. I think Mark Twain wrote, 'The fear of death follows from the fear of

life. A man who lives fully is prepared to die at any time,'
and I think it sums up pretty well the place that such comments stem from. One of my fondest memories is walking
with Gran through Richmond Park not far from her house.
We would walk through a beautiful flower garden in the
centre of the park which she said she would often come to
after Grumpy died and spend hours just sitting there. She
would talk about everything that was usually taboo with
an attractive openness and honesty. At fourteen-years-old,
such conversations were usually off-limits, but it really
helped navigate the world and put things into perspective
at that time'.

Every year the Isabella Plantation in Richmond Park, still a secret
to many, draws her to the glorious scent and colours of hidden
rhododendra, camellias and azaleas, which line the ponds and streams.
It is always at its best in late April or early May. Often she takes her
visitors there or recommends would-be bikers to include it on a tour
of Richmond Park. Wimbledon Common, a short walk from her home,
she knows like the back of her hand. When Rachel Nickell was brutally
attacked and murdered in 1992 in front of her three-year-old son, it
might have put Mandi off visiting for a while, but she was undeterred.
Her children would ask her to choose somewhere different, but her
grief was still raw and she used to say she did not care what happened
to her in those early days of widowhood. She and her much loved
Mersey explored Wimbledon Common day after day and found many
a less beaten track. The beauty of the common awakened her senses
again, although the scent was often poisoned by the smell of Mersey
having rolled in fox poo. Having to scrub her dog clean on return
home kept Mandi committed to the down-to-earth business of living
and recovering.

To a large degree, she demonstrated and still demonstrates her
commitment to life through physical fitness and she built up to
walking five miles as a daily habit, which also served her as an explorer
of the capital and indeed the many places she visited. She became very
fit and strong and it was not long before she was entering the very
first walking marathon in London to raise funds for breast cancer.
In 1996, thirteen courageous women in highly decorated bras, led by

Nina Barough, took to the streets of New York to raise funds for breast cancer. It was such a success that Nina ended up putting in two teams into the London Marathon over the next two years, raising thousands of pounds. However, the second time twenty-five team members did not get places, so Nina set up her own twenty-six mile London walk. The idea was to set off at midnight and hand over the baton to the other twenty-five who had got places. The twenty-five walkers grew to sixty-five and Nina ended up doing a double marathon whilst she herself was suffering breast cancer. Mandi joined in those early days and became close to Nina and a great fundraiser herself. Paddy Whack wrote about their walking life together:

> 'Great walkers together, we progressed to powerwalking marathons, for Nina Barough, and her fabulous moon-walk breast cancer charity in London. Gran was viewed as something of a marvel, confidently striding out with me, her daughter-in-law, and my thirty-something mates. Needless to say, Gran was always well ahead and famously gave up on her lodger at the time, Caroline, who was forty years Gran's junior. We powerwalked the New York marathon twice, with gorgeous Bev and then we were beautifully entertained and spoilt in Bev's Connecticut home. Gran was always accepted and cherished as part of the family, no matter where we took her, she was always known as 'Gran'. She always without fail extended such a warm and sincere welcome to our friends and their families, either at Granville towers (as Paddy Whack calls Gran's London home) or at Lamare'.

Ultimately she was to walk six of these marathons, mostly in London, but also two in New York. Although Gran could complete them really quickly, she did recall one time when she had to take longer to sustain her younger companions and another in New York where she had to recite every cautionary verse she knew to keep her companion going.

Mandi relished these walks, London or New York, the speed, the fresh air, the night, the dressing up, the other walkers, the buzz, the competition, the contribution, the sense of making a difference. The physical, mental and spiritual wellbeing that resulted was always so sustaining and it was never a surprise to those that knew her well that she signed up for one after another. It nearly all went wrong in 2005 when Mandi used the Vicks instead of Vaseline on those most sensitive of areas and almost missed her 5.15 am deadline for the need to keep washing and rewashing to lessen the burning that was not coming from overexercise!

I always laugh over the one walking marathon that I did with my mum. I was really looking forward to this mother and daughter moment. It was my first one and I asked how long it might take. Mum thought it would take about seven hours so I duly signed myself up to that category. On the night, I was surprised to find her heading off for a different group to me, only to learn that she had signed up for the fast category and expected to complete it in six hours, which she did not think I could possibly do, so we did the marathon separately! To be fair, it did take me seven and her only six! I was left wondering if some of her mother's genes had rubbed off! Nina gave Mandi a glass triangle as a symbol of appreciation for all her efforts after the last New York Marathon, a gift which she still treasures.

It was not only that Mandi was good at looking after herself physically. She ate well, drank plenty of water, possibly even more wine, did her five-mile march daily and seemed to thrive on this homegrown health package. She had an excellent constitution and people commented on how young she looked for her age. She slept well too and her boundless energy returned. Today, despite a replaced hip, she has not let this discipline falter and, at eighty-five, continues to enjoy a very active life with long and refreshing walks as a regular feature.

Mandi's beloved dog Mersey was a vital companion through grief, spending a fair few nights encompassed in her arms on her bed as a warm, furry substitute for her much loved Peter. Mandi always said that the requirements of having Mersey was key to her recovery. At times when she might have given up, she had the responsibility of her darling pet to consider, a pet that had bound her and Peter together.

Mersey might even have been a hero dog. When toddling William, one of Mandi's grandchildren, managed to bypass all protection, which regrettably did not include a stairgate, and come tumbling down the carpeted but rather steep stairs, Mersey saw him coming and launched herself across the bottom, breaking his fall and in effect catching him. It was a miracle moment.

When the time came for Mersey 'to hop off the planet', as Mandi says, no one could have been more devastated, but this was not a time for more ties, it was a time of freedom, finally a time without accountability and a time to be lived to the full.

Nonetheless, the role of dogs and even cats in her life remained and Paddy Whack particularly commented on her love of their family dogs, Skid, Buzz, Molly, Simba and Hebe as did her son Jo who told this story:

'Mum and I loved our dogs! First was the wonderful Mingo (mum's pornstarname is of course Mingo Hornsby.... work that one out) who provided god knows how many puppies when I was about 4 at Pinhey, then Weasel and later Mersey! In between Mingo and Weasel was of course our fab cat Mumpy! Lived to 21 as I recall and will forever be remembered for peeing all over me in the bunks at Lamare when she took revenge for me pushing her down the bed sheets! Got into a lot of trouble for that one. I always had scratches on me from the Moolie E's claws as she had battles with Weasel when I was a boy. Mumpy always won. They weren't the best of friends at times despite my efforts to roll both the cat and dog down the stairs inside a sleeping bag together in the hope that a combined hardship would do the trick to make them mates...ummm! Weasel became better known as EV Jones and Mum was to bellow this name on one occasion at Lamare one fine summer's day in my early teens. The problem was that EV Jones was also Dad's long standing carpenter living in Holyhead that just so happened to be doing a task for Pop on that very day. Mum in her wonderful style was simply oblivious to her cries for the dog renamed for years as the carpenter and to her shock our diminutive, but good humoured North Walian chippy came sheepishly to our back door together with imposter EV Jones black Labrador to be offered a plate of Chappie. Not ever quite sure how mum got out of that one!'

Throughout the diaries, all the dogs get a mention and Sam and Emma's photo is stuck into the 1994 diary whilst in the bath with their Springer Spaniel, Peg Pog. It amused Mandi hugely and she understood that you would get in the bath with your dog. She certainly influenced her family's love of pets.

There is no doubt that the natural energy in Mandi that defined her as a little girl and which various characters in her life tried to quash at different points sustained her. She came to understand its importance and actively developed a philosophy of positive thinking as part of that emotional and mental wellbeing that she was well-trained in. It was not that she did not see the negatives or understand the downside of a situation, but she chose to be optimistic in her outlook, seek the best in all, and there is no doubt that the law of attraction, real or otherwise, worked for her. Her loo door with its posted sayings actively expresses this philosophy and as she articulated this philosophy, so the number of sayings increased.

Her grandson Fred particularly picks this out when he thinks about what his Gran means to him.

'The main thing I have always found with Gran is more of a feeling. When I am with her, I get the most incredible energy off her. To live with her was amazing. If I had a bad day or she had, we were always there for each other and she could always cheer me up. My time in London was tough mentally and Gran had an infectious positivity that you could not escape even if you wanted to. She, like no one else I have ever met, has an aura about her that lights up any room'.

Gran went out of her way to physically bring him her energy and support in the Alpine bar that he managed in France! Fred is by no means the only one that has said that and Charlie, another grandson, also noted this energy and cited the time his girlfriend visited her:

'My girlfriend Michelle was recently in England and I said she had to meet Gran! She said she would love to pop in for a quick hour. Anyway in a huge testament to such an attractive energy, Michelle spent six hours with Gran and only had to leave because she was late for dinner'.

Loubird, another family lodger, tried to work it out:

'I love Gran's enthusiasm for life, her positive outlook. She leaps out of bed and always has something positive to say and the day is always started positively. It's a no-boundary love, you can talk about anything and everything with no boundaries. For example, I'm naked brushing my teeth and she is in the bath and we are talking about the most ordinary things, such as her missing things, what is in the day, what we are going to achieve and what is round the corner, stories from the past and what we have to look forward to, she tells me something random. We might be having a perfectly normal conversation and it somehow fits it once she has explained it'.

Mandi had been taught from an early age to believe in God and was a regular churchgoer and believer. She first had cause to question the scriptures that had been so indoctrinated into her by her grandmother at fifteen when she heard a lecture on reincarnation with her great friend, Jen Jones. This really caught her attention and never went away.

She next really questioned God and His mysterious ways when she encountered death in Guy's hospital and calls on Him quite naively just to keep her safe, especially when she was driving fast. With the death of her dear patient Jessie, she truly wondered how there could be a God, but her faith remained steadfast, if rather background. It emerged here and there on the way in her life, but it was only on the death of Peter that she really had time to question and work out what held meaning for her beyond the confines of our mortal selves.

Mandi really searched. During the period after Peter's death, she attended philosophy lectures, regularly coming back with her constant questions, but once again it was reincarnation that resonated with her, that chimed with the experiences that she had had and made sense of the range of characters and behaviours that she met and had met in her world. Is heredity responsible for human character? Reincarnation is the only possible explanation. Character, conscience, intuition, aptitudes. They must have evolved through many lives. Have you been born before? The love or hatred of a particular place, passion or country —sometimes it all seems strangely familiar:

'I hold that when a person dies
His soul returns again to earth;
Arrayed in some new flesh-disguise,
Another mother gives him birth.
With sturdier limbs and brighter brain

The old soul take the road again.'
John Masefield. A creed

She came to believe firmly that when a person dies, the old soul takes to the road again, developing, learning, becoming older, wiser on its way. For her, it was not about material wealth, but about battling through life, enjoying, loving when allowed and building that resilience, persisting with the challenges and emerging stronger when required, becoming more determined and more prepared to keep on. For her, it centred around 'reaping as one sows'. Karma made sense. Misfortune comes from your own bad choices. The law sees to justice and it is not for us individually to enact vengeance, nor indeed get involved. Mandi would see it for us to give generously of ourselves and what we have.

All philosophical and biblical quotations from the 1990 diary

The wise man does not lay up treasure; his riches are within.....
The more he gives to others, the more he has of his own.

Mandi recognises her own limits and identifies as a kinesthetic learner first and foremost.

'I hear and I forget, I see and I remember, I do and I understand'.
— CONFUCIUS —

'We can only know what we can know.
The kingdom of heaven is at hand'.
— JESUS, MATTHEW, IV —

You either know or you don't know that you have a faith and she has.

'If one man conquer in battle a thousand times a thousand men,
and if another conquer himself, he is the greatest of conquerors'.
— DHAMMAPADA, 103 – BUDDHA'S PATH OF WISDOM —

Mandi is very aware of her journeying through life, how often she faces her demons and how she seeks self-control.

'What I call happiness exists in the discovery of the true self'.
— Huai Nan Tse Yuen Tao Huin, XIX —

Of course unaccountable fears beset us all at times. Fear, dark, real heights, thunder, open spaces, viruses, and so much more, but love, truth and courage counter that fear and they are the way.

She recognises the importance of taking responsibility, ownership for decisions made, actions taken and consequences incurred. She was very influenced by the Rudyard Kipling poem, which for her meant that we have a free will and need to accept the blame or responsibility ourselves when things go wrong, instead of it always being someone else's fault; this verse shows the free will of man working under the law:

'This was note of the good Lord's pleasure, for the spirit he breathes in man I free; but what comes after is measure for measure and not a God that afflicted thee, as was the sowing so the reaping is now and evermore shall be. Thou art delivered to thy own keeping.
Only thyself hath afflicted thee'.
— Written out at the start of the 2012 Diary from Rudyard Kipling's Men and Machines —

The cycle of birth and life that Mandi regularly saw in life and some of the miracles that she witnessed in mortal life convinced her. She cites gifts that people have and use, such as playing an instrument, a gift for languages, insight as evidence of those who know life. Mandi knows that there is something greater than herself at play, spiritual waves she calls them. Synchronicity often occurs. She will be thinking of a name and then that person is ill or dies or one of her children that she is thinking of just phones. Why does a particular person choose her? The friend who phoned her out of the blue to tell her that her son who had had to be adopted fifty years before had just been in touch and she needed Mandi to work through it with her. Charlie, her grandson, wrote about this:

> 'One of our cousins struggled with a severe form of haemophilia for most of his life that severely impacted on what he could and couldn't do. Gran was out to lunch one day and happened to sit next to a man who was running a medical

trial for haemophilia and ultimately was able to get our cousin onto this trial, which has had a profound benefit to his life. Gran would talk about the coincidence of this chance meeting and the knock on effects it has had. It was a belief in something bigger than herself at play and she says she'll often feel that something/someone is looking out for her in this way. It was one of many stories she would tell in relation to her faith.

This connection to something deeper has been a big source of inspiration for my own spiritual growth and development'.

Mandi attends church regularly; it is a place to contemplate, a place to review those bigger questions, a place to find peace, a place to remember that greater spiritual picture, a place to know that undefined God. She has always supported church life and I rather naughtily played a trick on her back in the late-70s when Mandi was home alone with Jo and it was April Fool's Day. I got a friend to phone: 'Mrs Earlam, I'm Enid Braithwaite and I am phoning as I have just taken over the church cleaning roster and I note that you are down to clean the brass knockers. I am afraid that they do not look as though they have been cleaned for some while!'

Mandi responded to this with a stream of unlikely excuses about her hectic lifestyle and four children keeping her busy and was polishing those knockers within the next half hour! Such is the power of God!

Church is also a place that triggers a lot of her charity work and she supports the church effort to raise money for good causes during Wimbledon week by selling sandwiches to tennis enthusiasts or doing car park duty. Mandi is a such a community person and if there is a street party going on or a volunteer needed, you can count on her. She claims not to be a committee person, but has done her time here too, keen to see a community serve its people through mutual contribution.

Mandi had always loved travel, watching her dear Peter fly round the world whilst she had held the household together, relishing the opportunities she had had to join him on business trips and drinking in the culture of wherever she had gone, filling her diaries with the history, geography and cultural events she attended in the different places.

In the late-70s, she grew tired of Trearddur Bay and longed to see more of the world. Now it was to open up to her. In the last thirty years, she has planned many trips with great excitement and savoured them. Her diaries are full of her adventures. It was a big jump for her to spend money on holidays and she has always been careful to choose modest hotels and economy flights, but she could easily have afforded to travel wherever and how she wanted and it was a mark of the change in her that she gave herself permission to invest in herself.

One of the stories she loves to tell, which seems to boast so much of her recovered confidence, is her bungee jumping in New Zealand after her sixtieth birthday. Invited to jump for free if over sixty or naked, Mandi demanded to know what she would get if she fulfilled both categories. She was in the end politely asked to keep her clothes on, but threw herself off the bridge with unquestioning abandon and lived to tell the tale many times over.

The difference between this kind of danger and the danger that she had seemed to risk in the days and months after Peter's death is that she was actively choosing this danger as a form of exciting living and adventure, freedom. There was control in her choices; previously it was as though she were being controlled by her pain, her grief. She went on to abseil down the side of Bart's hospital as a fund raiser. She opted for innumerable skiing trips with her family, but perhaps the most incredible was the family trip to Aspen which Nick hosted in 2003. Every member of his family was billeted in wonderful villas and he treated each to the slopes, the activities and local experiences, amazing meals and very special and rare time together.

25 DECEMBER 2003

*All my family and their partners, happily married. 13 grandchil-
dren and mi amore, Lorenzo, all under the same roof. Colorado is
beautiful. Twinkling lights abound. Father Christmas came laden
with presents. I don't know if Nick or the little ones were the most
excited!*

The pilgrimage through the Pyrenees covered the 280 miles from Perpignan to Biarritz. It brought with it that real sense of journeying physically, emotionally and spiritually over the seven years that it was completed. Mandi set off with Colin, Peter's former Cambridge friend, and his wife Jenny and a party that they had put together. Ultimately, it was only Mandi and Colin who would make all seven trips.

The start of the first one in September 1997 is vivid in her mind today. When they arrived on 8 September, it was something of a relief. Princess Di had just died and the funeral and drama of that was still going on at the time. Nick and Paige were celebrating sixteen years of marriage and Sarah was just starting her first term at secondary school. Paddy Whack had just been advised that she could have a third baby at home and Mandi was lined up to help. Her friend Sarah was having her house done up and it was not finished yet, so she needed a house to celebrate her fortieth anniversary party in. She had moved in just before Mandi left. Jenny's Mum was taken very ill and she could not make it at the last minute and Lorenzo managed to crash the car on the way. He didn't do the walk, but rather stayed in the hotel, getting to know everyone really well despite not speaking French. The party all had a role. Colin and his friend John were the orienteers, in charge of compasses and the map of the GR10. Sue was Goat One, fit and ready to scamper up the rocks to assess the route, and Mandi was Nurse One, ready with her first aid. They set off, their knapsacks suitably laden with vital provisions and their hiking boots laced up.

9 SEPTEMBER 1997

We began to negotiate the grassy, rocky and heather-covered terrain and drink in the views of the streams tumbling down the mountains into the valleys below as we climb and climb, the tinkle of cowbells and the crickets in the grass, the humming of bees in the wildflowers and garlic, the lizards and beatles. We ate the wild strawberries like the ones we used to grow on my Gran's rockery as a child, bilberries too.

The meal at the gite at the end of the day was hard-earned and much appreciated. Other trips had Lorenzo helping himself to Wayne's car, uninsured for him, and driving himself up the impossibly narrow, spiralling lanes and arriving unexpectedly for dinner. Wayne was a new joiner and fortunately saw the funny side.

On one occasion, all of them sharing the simple room of the gite, Mandi was last into bed, put the light out, only to find a little girl, Victorian-like in her dress, standing before her. 'Hello', she said, putting the light back on, to find the child had gone. Wayne had seen her too and the next day, in his fluent French, he asked the owner about her and the site. It had apparently held a much more established building way back when and the ghost had been sighted many times before. Another time, the expected host got a better offer and went off to the village party leaving the weary travellers with no bed for the night. They lit a fire and made some food and Mandi soon lay down on the heather to sleep under the stars, whilst the less easy-going had a very poor night indeed! Luckily, that was a night of fine weather; they certainly pushed through many a storm and days of high winds, clambering over fallen trees and sodden ground.

The day of the Twin Towers attack in New York, they arrived at their accommodation outside and noticed the flames through the proprietor's window. Initially they thought he was watching James Bond, until finding out what had happened hit them with the hideous reality with what had gone on that day.

Often, Mandi would think how far removed from reality she was while travelling and how those trips restored and strengthened her.

The final arrival at Biarritz was memorable. The three crosses stood to denote the end with Jesus and the robbers to greet them and the wonderful, refreshing sea. She and Jenny immediately stripped to their underwear and plunged in, the hike of the day done and now time to renew the body again. There are too many adventures to tell of these seven years, but they certainly proved to Mandi hers was the power and nothing need stand in her way.

One Christmas in Australia was noteworthy because it almost did not happen. Mandi and I arrived at Dubai airport. I had persuaded Mandi to use the old lady transport to give her a break round the airport. We got from Terminal A to B in record time on the transporter only for Mandi to remember that she had left her passport in the lavatory. I had to walk back, leaving Mandi waiting, but was willingly greeted with the said document when I stuck my hand under the door and shouted out, 'Passport', hopefully! The transporter assistance rather backfired on me there as I had to do the walk to and from the terminal twice! On arriving in Oz, a ten km hike ensued and a first night in bed fully dressed because of the cold and a chicken with all its feathers to keep us company, courtesy of grandson Tom. Mandi never was too sure about the birds and blamed them for her illness which resulted from that trip.

Tom remembered his grandmother for that and other tricks and refers to her affectionately as his 'old friend'. We had an amazing holiday as ever in Oz, Sandringham now familiar for its warm and welcoming Allinson home, wonderful and relaxed hospitality, fabulous coastal walks and swims and unforgettable and precious time spent together.

She accompanied Team Loubird to Paris to welcome her in from her London to Paris fund-raising cycle and was a full-on tourist with the best of them on this trip, partying and whooping into the night to celebrate. A more serious journey of discovery took her to Auschwitz with Jo, PaddyWhack and me. Mandi was both fascinated and horrified and sat shivering in the new warm boots Jo had bought her and her coat on Krakow Square, wondering how those poor prisoners coped in their striped pyjamas in that dreadful place. She is always utterly respectful of any Remembrance Service and never forgets where the freedom she so enjoys came from.

In 2012, Mandi set off to explore Mozambique with her great friend Lucy. She left on Valentine's Day with South African airlines via Johannesburg and changed planes to arrive in Pemba Beach, Mozambique some twenty hours later.

Poverty, litter, smiling, happy people. Colourful, shown beautiful scenery round the ocean, palm trees, the shacks.

She enjoyed discovering geographical facts, such as the fact that Mozambique is six times the size of England and the main commodities are cotton, copper, sisal, maize, sugar and wheat. Twenty-six thousand cotton farmers provide the commodity, each growing it on their allotted patch. This particularly interested Mandi with both of her sons working in the industry and Nick having organised this trip for her. Indeed, one of his contacts met them and looked after them in Mozambique, showing them round Plexus, Nick's cotton company there. Very proud Mum!

After an exciting tour of various sites, they flew in a four-seater plane to a grassy runway with a bus shelter airport on the Quilalea.

SEPTEMBER 2012

Met by a German with a jeep who farms coconut. Greeted by three coloured guys and asked to put on galoshes whilst the greeters put their luggage on their heads. We were then transported on a boat and arrived at the beach to a welcome from the staff. Half a coconut to drink and towels to bathe our exhausted brows. A

briefing and lunch of fresh prawns, samosas, fresh fruit and coco-
nut. Blissful relaxation, the water crystal clear and the birds quite
beautiful. Sundowners went with the stunning sunset. As the only
guests in the hotel we had a quite amazing service from Nelson,
our private butler.

She did get a chance to return to her riding in a fabulous holiday
with Jenny, the friend with whom she did the Pyrenees hikes and
another friend, Sue. The blissful three-day trek of twenty miles a day
along one of the oldest trackways in Europe, the Ridgeway of West
Ilsley near Newbury. Mandi loved Toffee Apple and the gallops, the
pub stops and the walks through the red poppy fields, linseed oil and
blue rape. Grown-up pony club! She has played the odd round of golf
in La Manga, Melbourne, 'Royal' Trearddur and Royal Liverpool. That
childhood training was not in vain after all!

From an early age, Mandi had been labelled as lacking in scholastic
brains, yet she knew that she had a genuine appreciation of the arts.
Her parents had always been theatre goers and she would run to a
theatre with her father or a friend when off duty as a nurse and loved
it. Peter had been an avid classical concert fan, both her parents had
been keen musicians and Mandi herself had been a budding artist.

With London on her doorstep, Mandi began to actively research
what she wanted to see and listen to and the invitations always came
in. When the distorted canvas of grief lifted, Mandi could focus on
other tales, be transported beautifully or otherwise through music
or images and her diaries really began to critically assess the many
works she appreciated. One such description of La Traviata performed
at the Coliseum lingers on Verdi's tragic and resonant tale of society
and morality, his compelling characters and the powerful, moving
and engaging melodies and just how much she loved it. She always
had a book on the go, often an interesting biography, but also a dip
into a favourite book of poetry perhaps, another throwback to her dear
father who had loved poetry just as much as her. All her children had
grown up on Hilaire Belloc and his cautionary verse emerged again
as the grandchildren got older. A fair few of them learned 'Jim' for
poetry competitions and would come and recite proudly to Gran who
would always join in or finish it for them if they got stuck. Emma
was particularly proud of her age ten recitation of 'The Highwayman'
and Gran and she would recite it together with huge passion and ex-

citement. Her book on discovering sex that she kept in the spare room alongside *The Emotional Problems of Living*, *Games People Play*, *Peter Rabbit* and *Topsy and Tim* would be commented on for years to come by family and guests alike; the range of reading that sat in Mandi's library housed in the spare bedroom was certainly unusual.

'No wise man ever wished to be younger'.
— UNKNOWN —

A TIME TO EMBRACE
AND A TIME TO REFRAIN
FROM EMBRACING

We are survivors – For those born before 1940
— WRITTEN BY JOHN O'BRIEN —

We were born before television, before penicillin, before polio shots, frozen food, Xerox, contact lenses, videos and the pill. We were born before radar, credit cards, split atoms, laser beams and ballpoint pens, before dishwashers, tumble dryers, electric blankets, air conditioners, drip dry clothes...and before man walked on the moon.

We got married first and then lived together (how quaint can you be!). We thought 'fast food' was what you ate in Lent. A 'Big Mac' was an oversized raincoat, and 'crumpet' we had for tea. We existed before house husbands, computer dating, dual careers, and when a 'meaningful relationship' meant getting along with cousins, and 'sheltered accommodation' was where you waited for a bus.

We were before day care centres, group homes and disposable nappies. We never heard of FM radio, tape decks, artificial hearts, word processors or young men wearing earrings. For us, 'time-sharing' meant togetherness. A 'chip' was a piece of wood or fried potato, 'hardware' meant nuts and bolts, and 'software' wasn't a word.

Before 1940, 'Made in Japan' meant junk, the term 'making out' referred to how you did in your exams, 'stud' was something that fastened a collar to a shirt, and 'going all the way' meant staying on a double decker bus to the terminus. In our day, cigarette smoking was fashionable. 'Grass' was mown and 'cake' was kept in the coalhouse, a 'joint' was something you ate on Sundays and 'pot' was something you cooked in. 'Rock music' was a fond mother's lullaby, 'Eldorado' was an ice cream, 'a gay

*person' was the life and soul of the party, whilst 'aids' just meant
beauty treatment or help for someone in trouble.*

*We who were born before 1940 must be a hardy bunch when
you think of the way in which the world has changed and the
adjustments that we have had to make. No wonder there is a
Generation Gap today, but...we have survived!*

Mandi's grandchildren know her for all manner of things,
but particularly as a survivor, an adaptable and hardy type who is
constant, careful with what she has and able to make the most of life
in its many guises. This was actually proving very important to her
grandchildren as awareness of the need to sustain our planet and treat
resources as finitely precious hit the public and their private agenda.
All that promise of previous decades had not come to fruition and as
they moved to such as plant diets and taking part in an increasingly
sharing economy, Gran's simple, positive and purposeful way of living
was noteworthy. Her diaries, her loo door and her own individualised
language, as they see it, express her. They find that language quaint
and funny and use it too.

Some of the loo door entries are at the end of the chapters for you
to think about too. They have been added from the '70s when the loo
door sayings began.

Perhaps the individualised language all began with those
nicknames that she had for Peter because all her children have them
too. Perhaps it goes back to her family for her brother is a great one
for making up names too. Her mother was Mip and her father was
Grumpy, though he was not! There is Noodle, Bonzo, Lopsy and
Spriggie, who are her four in order.

She regularly reminds people that she had 'Three under three'
or 'Four under six' and wears this maternal prowess as a badge
of honour. If her house is 'gisly', she will give it 'a mother's do';
'alicing her cushions', and when this is done, the house will be spick
and span again and the cushions beautifully plumped up. If she wishes
to be a bit coy, she will describe herself as being 'nimpy' or name
the person she is speaking to as 'Twidz', some kind of affectionate
nickname and abbreviation of 'Tweedle' which she also regularly uses.
As her guests arrive, she will greet them with what must be a form
of hello, 'Keedoos'. Her eyes will light up as she suggests, 'Shall we
have a squig of wine?', which sounds as though it might be a small

serving, but is a generic term for a glassful at least. If she is musing what you might do next, the musing might begin with the slightly confusing, 'Lettuce with a gladsome mind...' You might then be given one of her excellent stews which will be described as 'Gran's gunge' and is always 'yumpogious'. If you are in a relationship, you are bound to be asked about when you last 'had a jump' or when you are next going to, as Gran places huge importance on a healthy sex life whatever your stage of life and happily and openly discusses it.

Equally if anyone makes a visit to the lavatory and leaves their mark, a rather befuddling 'pomposer stinkador' will feel like a judgement. When she makes a mistake or is once again exasperated with her computer, which she refers to disparagingly as 'the machine', she will announce authoritatively, 'I ought to be locked up' or 'It'll be me next, my friends are dying like flies. I'm eighty-five, you know', or 'Perhaps I should just hop off the planet'. If fun and laughter are getting out of control or perhaps too physical, she will call a halt with the well-known and well-tried, 'Horseplay always ends in tears' or 'Don't be so ridiculous!', all rolled together in a nonsensical way. If she is having a great time or is thrilled with something, then it is 'absolutely wizard'. If surprised or shocked, 'Praise be!' is standard and 'God bless' is a way of saying goodbye or goodnight in person, on the phone or at the end of letters. 'Chobling cheese' has been around so long that Nick named his boat Chobling Cheese as a mark of respect to his mother, as it was originally designed to replace swear words, much as others might say 'Sugar'. It has come to be used as an exclamation of pleasure or surprise. Grandchildren with good eyesight will often be given a pair of tweezers and asked if there are 'any whiskers' that need removing from Gran's chin. Of course they will all be invited to share the latest diary entries too and they all take an interest in Gran's exploits and reports on the family's and world affairs, often seeking out what she has to say about them, unless of course she is 'completely bush' or 'gone barmy' and then everything goes pear-shaped! They will never get through the 'whole kaboosh', there is never time! Australian grandson Charlie, writes of the importance of his grandmother's language in his life, even from so far away.

'Gran has infused my life with storytelling and language.

I've been given many language books throughout my life

but the one that had the most profound effect on my learning was an Italian book that Gran gave me in primary school. She was infectiously passionate about Italian and the way she spoke just made you want to learn. I looked at it every night for weeks until I could count to 1 million in Italian and was very pleased to share this with Lorenzo and Gran who bounced back my enthusiasm in this positive feedback loop. On her most recent trip to Aus, she again punctuated my life with Italian. As we would walk down the street behind lovely women in their active wear, she would announce with the same exuberance as those many years ago 'che bel culo!'

She broke the rules with language and made a rigid necessity something playful and full of joy as she does with most things. It became a matter of not what you said but how you said it. She would make up words and enthuse everyone around her with her signature phrases that we all know and love. Grin is a maverick with words and hearing them leaves you buzzing for hours but it was the stories she told that still have a profound impact on me today. Giving birth on a concrete floor in Africa, having life-saving operations for infected sinuses as a child, completing a marathon in a bikini in the Sahara for charity, bungee jumping, her many tales as a nurse, a marriage counsellor, taking a Purple Heart, her love and tribulations with Grumpy were some of the many stories that she told with so much love and kindness. She shows a zest for life from all her experiences and her openness and entrancing ability to tell these stories are a source of motivation to live life to the fullest and to draw upon in very tough times'.

If you compare Charlie's version of Gran's stories from the diaries, it is a wonderful example of the oral tradition, the value of voice and how stories change as they pass down the generations. Those Moonwalks have become a bikini-clad Gran doing a marathon in the Sahara!

Indeed, Jo has made a bit of a sport of this and light-heartedly and lovingly leads Mum down memory lane in her older years, especially in the knowledge that she does have a habit of repeating herself particularly after a few snifters....

He now invites her to remember all those stories she used to tell him and Paddy Whack when she used to wake them up at 6.00 with a cup of unwanted tea at Lamare with their little ones. Her own hardship at bringing four. 'How many under three did you have? How many under six? Seven O levels? What were they, Mum?' Her uninterested mother-in-law who he and the rest of the family were very fond of. 'What was her degree in? How many stairs did you have to climb up to your Liverpool flat?'

Mandi loves to answer these questions and just giggles when she realises what he is doing. They have a very similar sense of humour.

The whole family will receive a picture of her in the back of their car, head thrown back, catching flies, after an excellent Sunday lunch somewhere. The caption will read: 'Found a corpse!' The VS story is not for telling and would kick up too much of a stink! Jo and Mandi have a very similar love of a joke and her diaries are peppered with his stories and humour. She sees him as very like her in this regard and on the same wavelength and has sometimes regretted for him that he cannot just play his way through life as that is what he is so naturally good at. Equally she has a lot of admiration for the knowledge and skills he has acquired, how he has made his own commodities company work so successfully and built a lovely home with Paddy Whack on the Wirral.

The skills of nurse and counsellor have become intimately interwoven into Mandi's very being. She was innately a caring, compassionate, intuitive and empathetic being, but understood the importance of marrying physical, mental and emotional health years before it became current to do so. Mandi learned in the early '70s that solutions can largely come from the individual themselves and she knew how to put back responsibility to that individual for their own development and recovery in a kind way.

She has never stopped doing that and believes utterly in that unconditional giving. Constant queues of people come to her door and are still lifted by her love, warmth, guidance, shelter and good food and wine before they move on, in some way renewed. Some she knows well through friends or as friends, some are referred to her, many are beloved family, many she picks up on the way and many return for a pick me up. Mandi is essentially a selfless person, but has learned that only by being whole oneself can one truly give to others and the community. Some feed off that wholeness, that togetherness and are mended by it.

Mandi has taught that you have to know yourself first and sometimes give to yourself to find that wholeness in order to be able to be yourself and share yourself. That is partly about being clear about what you value and that needs to include valuing yourself. Mandi had reached that point very convincingly at this latter stage of her life and these values, beliefs and behaviours completely underpin the voice she found and expresses so confidently today.

It took her a long time to be clear that 'Judge not that ye be not judged' was truly one of her values. It sits on her loo door along with many others, but is one that she frequently recites. Mandi grew up being judged, judging, repeating that judgement on herself without knowing how to question it, repeating that pattern on her own children with damaging labels that she ultimately learned to throw off and look at where people were in the moment. She learned that it did not serve her to lock people into where they were rather than where they are. *'I felt for a man who had no shoes and then I saw a man who had no feet'.* Mandi knew that there was always someone worse off than her and it always proved to be a vital perspective.

Her grandson Charlie writes:

> 'I think you're very fortunate to meet someone that oozes love and kindness like Gran does, but to have someone like that as the figure head of your family is beyond a blessing. Mum often ponders that the secret to Gran's outlook and demeanour is that she's always thinking about other people and it's a constant source of inspiration and aspiration.
>
> One of my earlier memories of Gran was when I was 10 years old and had flown solo to the UK to see the family. She took me to the London Dungeon and the London Eye on one of the days. I was never unwell as a child but something in the dungeon set me off as soon as I stepped inside and I began feeling unwell. Gran had just paid about 50 pounds for the tour but didn't bat an eyelid to get me out

of there as I had a turn a minute after entering. She put me
straight in a taxi to get home but I managed to throw up all
over the London taxi's leather seats as soon as I jumped in.
Again there was not a trace of anger, only compassion as
she dealt with situation. I went temporarily blind for about
half an hour and Gran had to walk me from the taxi to the
train station. I think a lot of people may have got frustrated
in that situation but the way she made me feel when I was
very unwell was really pivotal. Acting out of love in adverse
situations has stuck with me to this day and is something
that I hope to emulate in my personal and professional life'.

Mandi is generous and kind, but not to a fault and if you take
advantage, she has learned to let you know clearly where the boundary is. This is an important aspect in recognising why she commands
real respect.

One day whilst walking Mersey, her beloved Golden Retriever,
on Wimbledon Common, Mandi stopped at the Fox and Grapes for a
drink. She settled herself on the bar stool and it wasn't long before
she was chatting to Chris. Chris was looking for somewhere to stay
and was generally struggling with life and could not believe his luck
when Mandi offered him a room. Within a couple of days, he was duly
set up in the back bedroom. Life was much better for him immediately
with Mandi's cooking and excellent hospitality and within a month,
he was fully at home, feeling a lot more content with life, and became
a little over-confident. He paid his meagre rent for the first month, but
told Mandi that he would be late with the second. She reminded him
politely that this was not the basis on which they had made the
arrangement, but he continued to stall. She gave him a clear week's
notice and when he went out early one evening, having made no
effort to rectify the situation, he came back to find he had rather
underestimated her. Everything he owned was neatly lined up on the
garden path and he had to try to win her over from a nearby hotel.
He failed!

Richard and I celebrated twenty-five years of happy marriage
together and no one was more delighted than Mandi who loved her
son-in-law very much. She had helped him transition back in the early
days of marriage from his simple rural background to the sophisticated

urban life that he got drawn into as a bright, high-achieving lad. With a wife then heading up a big and successful prep school, the unexpected death of both his parents, the departure of all his children from home and the banking crisis of 2008, his life was suddenly turned upside down and he then turned his family's life upside down. He began having an affair that was discovered by his children. He turned to Mandi, his mother-in-law, for help. She provided a roof over his head for a month, absolutely understood his mid-life question marks, but would not counsel him, recognising conflict of interest. She found him a counsellor. When he chose to move on in his life from her daughter, she chose to move on too, despite how she had loved Richard. It was a hurt and a choice that would take the whole family years to get over and considerable for Mandi, but she was very clear about where she drew those lines. Mid-life crisis or not, he had made his bed and he could now lie in it.

On another occasion, she had became acquainted with a woman as one of the Wimbledon Senior Wives who had asked Mandi to accompany her on a trip to the Californian desert. Barely knowing her, Mandi set off, a willing travelling companion. The trip was a nightmare. Having picked up the hire car, Ursula was unable to drive on the right side of the road herself, and Mandi had to take over. This was challenging for the domineering and controlling Ursula who then constantly criticised and advised Mandi on her driving. She, the newly self-appointed map reader, soon got them lost down a murky track and would not allow Mandi to step out of the car to ask for help for fear of being hit over the head by hostile natives, which Mandi found utterly ridiculous. They were visiting her friends, so she told Mandi that she would do the talking and Mandi would do the listening. As she slept in and Mandi got up early, Mandi developed a good and natural relationship with her hosts as she would, who were shocked by their friend's appalling behaviour, but could not change it. Mandi recognised that much of the woman's behaviour was driven by fear because when she next drove, she did not exceed twenty miles per hour, caused havoc on the road, and infuriated her host so much that he insisted that Mandi drive, remarking on her extraordinary patience with Ursula.

However, her behaviour was ultimately insufferable to Mandi. The limit came; Mandi quietly changed her ticket, booked the means to return home and did exactly that. She certainly took the wind out of her companion's sails and she was left with some explaining to do on return. Of course, her version of events never did near the truth, but Mandi did not need to say anything as Ursula and her behaviours were well known locally and the wives were surprised that she had even agreed to go.

Mandi nursed dear Lorenzo right to the end, sitting at his bedside and waiting with him until his daughter got to him from Italy to enjoy the fish pie that she had prepared for him and his family. He became very ill the night of their arrival and the family called Mandi back. She blanket bathed him and he came to again, so Mandi went home, but he died shortly afterwards. She knew that he was greatly comforted by his angel close by and she had seen her share of death by this stage of her life. Whilst still so painful to let go of someone she had loved so deeply, she felt more confident that she knew how to this time, knew how to keep Lorenzo safely in her heart and begin again the process of adapting her life to being single. She had never allowed herself to live a married lifestyle again and in many ways therefore it was not too difficult to fill her days with activity, though it was impossible to find her days fulfilling as they had been with Lorenzo. She persisted, giving of herself as she always had, and knowing now to give herself time.

In the round of social activity and just after three weeks looking after Jo and Paddywhack's three, she returned to an invitation to share a bottle of wine with Charles. He had asked his bridge playing friends if they knew any women who were good fun and who loved to walk for miles in nature. They knew just the girl. Mandi returned from her trip and was planting her bedding plants when the call came and typically, she accepted the invitation turning up in her Wellington boots with unkempt hair and an umbrella. When offered the kitchen or the sitting room to enjoy the chilled Chablis, Mandi invited Charles to look closely at her state and her attire and the relaxing kitchen was quickly the chosen venue.

Charles was not at ease socially, though he was an accomplished and interesting character. At times, he was challenged when to join in and when to listen, when to wear his panama hat and when not to, but over the coming years, Mandi was to help him with this and bring out the very best in him; he became confident and less socially gauche with her and he provided a wonderful and generous companion for her and they came to treasure each other dearly. Charles literally treasured Mandi and called her 'precious'; she represented the very essence of happiness to him, a man who had been treated inconsistently by women and for whom trust could not be taken for granted. Mandi was more self-contained in these later stages of her life, but this did not mean that she did not give of herself warmly and it gave her great pleasure to liberate Charles from some of his uncertainties and share his passions and interests with him. Travel was generally on their list and the Destinations Show at Olympia provided a wonderful starting point for discussing where to go next. They have shared some wonderful trips together and Mandi regales the most extraordinary stories of their trip to Oman, sharing a very small tent with Charles, inadequate and not very private washing facilities, surfing sand dunes on trays, bartering for a gorgeous ring for Jen, wearing her turban and rough terrain desert driving in the four wheel drive.

Whilst they both played bridge, they certainly had quite a different approach to it and they only really started to play together when teaching John and myself, quite a number of years into their relationship. Walking together was always a treat and Mandi would write and rave over her ten-mile hikes in Charles' beloved Hungerford, especially when the bluebell carpets abounded. After a fine English tea, Charles would strap her into the passenger side, switch on the heated seat and drive her back to a fresh chilled rosé awaiting in the fridge.

Gardening was a real love for both of them and they would spend hours discussing the quality of their soil or lawns or making vital trips to the Chessington Garden Centre for extended considerations of their needs over rather pleasant breakfasts or lunches. Charles would regularly bring round fresh produce from his garden, delicious runner beans or fresh summer fruits. Mandi is such a fine cook and always has a creative home for the rhubarb or blackberries and Charles would often supplement his home produce with a gâteau from the French delicatessen up the road or indeed try his own hand at cooking or take Mandi out to a number of rather good restaurants locally. Good eating has added much substance to their relationship and it has been greatly enhanced by the many excellent bottles of wine that they have shared together, often reaching a point of uncertainty about where and what they started.

There are many reasons that wine has played such a vital role in Mandi's life, but one of them must be its ability to transport her to another time and another place.

Mention Mateus Rose from Portugal and she wants to put a candle in the unusually shaped bottle or is partying with her friends in the late-70s; Bordeaux from St Emilion and she is with Peter or back at that fabulous wine tasting of February 2015 when she and Charles tasted all the Bordeaux and missed their stop on the way home; Primitivo from Puglia and she is with Lorenzo or the wine tour of April 2017; a delicious rosé from Provence and she is with Charles.

So many wines take her back to stories told in her diaries, to happy and fun times, and wine has become both a conduit to a good time and a thirst for genuine knowledge. She and Charles joined the local Richmond wine club and together travelled the world in search of the best chardonnays, rieslings, pinots and sauvignons as well as the cabernet sauvignons, the merlots, malbecs, pinot noirs, syrahs, and sangiovese.

Mandi already loved her wines and the primitivos and verdecas of Puglia were firm favourites. If ever place, food and wine go together for Mandi, it is there. Staying in the wonderful town of Lecce on that April tour of 2015, a place jammed full of architecture and Roman ruins, she and Charles savoured their first night dinner in the stylish Osteria degli Spiriti. A selection of antipasti including a courgette flan, marinated aubergine and a red pepper souffle whet their appetites. Cherry tomatoes and orecchiette pasta next before moving on to a delicious stuffed beef paupiette, a thin strip of beef rolled and stuffed with vegetables and a rich sauce. This accompanied by beautifully concentrated and balanced reds—a full bodied Negroamaro followed by their top wine—Fanoi, a superb Primitivo. They just managed to squeeze in some feather light cheese cake before staggering to bed and so it went on. They often travelled with the wine club and made some good friends together, learning, sharing and having great fun.

As Mandi approached her mid-eighties, the family were concerned that she was alone in London, approaching her old age. She had Charles and her friends, but no member of her family that could be one hundred percent there for her in the event of a crisis. Others might have begun their old age before their mid-eighties, but not Mandi. Mandi's penchant for a glass or two had led to one or two mishaps, which had given cause for concern as well as some laughter. Firstly, she had had a few glasses of red during a concert outing and missed her footing at the Festival Hall and went tumbling down the steps. Bruised and battered, she found herself in a heap at the bottom of the steps and it was lucky that Paddy Whack and Jo were there to pick her up.

Then there was the night she was going to stay with me to play bridge with some of my friends over the weekend. I had come into London on the Friday to meet her and Matt and his girlfriend in Covent Garden to enjoy an Italian meal out. Matt knew how to give his Gran a good time and had chosen an Italian haunt that he knew she would love. He told the waiters of her love of the food and wines of the country as well as the language and its people and they rose to the occasion with aplomb.

Some three hours later, Mandi left the restaurant steaming with goodwill, good food, good wine and good vibes to share with the general public. I had to stop her sharing these vibes via her umbrella with innocent passers-by on the way to the station and was greatly relieved when we both passed out on the Stansted Express headed for Bishops's Stortford, our destination. On arrival, I woke with a start and had to grab Mandi by the hand and hurry her to the train door. Mandi, still a little asleep, stepped off the train and straight down the gap. One minute her head had been roughly level with mine and the next, it was level with my feet! I, a trained first aider, knew what to do. I reassured my dear mother, whom I still had by the hand, that all would be well and then started yelling for help at the top of my voice, terrified that the train would leave with her trapped beneath the platform. Helpers came running from all directions and Mandi was heaved up from the gap, a little scraped and bashed, but fundamentally intact. A willing sort came over with a bottle which had been flung from Mandi's bag, proffering the half bottle of Beaujolais from the Covent Garden restaurant. Slightly embarrassing, and somehow emphasizing the cause of the whole episode! That weekend we talked as a family about Mum's fun approach to life, but that there was no one there for her or even near her should she have an accident or mishap, and with some reluctance, she agreed to a more watchful approach from her children through her latter years.

She loved her self-contained life and indeed Nick described her as 'fiercely independent', really valuing this quality, but accepted that I would build a flat in half her home over the next year and we would share together. We got on well and there were no real reasons why it would not work, although it would be an enormous adjustment. I was at a crossroads in my life, having retired and divorced, and could take a change and it had the makings of a fun and exciting development to both of our lives.

Mandi and I set about planning the development with the help of Noelle the architect and Mandi began the task of finding herself somewhere to live for six or so months of 2017, the time that the build would last. Out playing bridge one day, she was introduced to Christopher, who was just about to head off on a cruise. Mandi clicked with him immediately and during the banter of the afternoon and over quite a lot of wine, managed to invite herself to stay in his house as housekeeper for the next six months. He literally threw her the keys across the table and invited her to move in. When Christopher returned, the relationship was to blossom into a deep and loving friendship which surprised them both, but which Mandi loved in many ways. Mandi did not want to be his housekeeper, so when Gallina the Russian lady stopped to smell Mandi's gorgeous roses in her garden, little did she know that that chance moment was to result in her telling her life story in Mandi's kitchen and another of those moments which would lead to so much more. In no time at all, she was to become Chris' housekeeper in exchange for board and lodging, rather to Chris' annoyance as he would have much preferred Mandi.

Chris was demanding, but hugely giving too. He was a bright and intelligent man with a deep love and knowledge of the theatre, poetry, music and art that really resonated with Mandi. Night after night they went to one concert or show after another and discussed it either before or after a delicious dinner in some restaurant somewhere. Mandi was back in the centre of London really living a wonderful London life and she thrived on it. She also cooked for him and ran his house, helping him to re-energise it one year after the death of his wife.

There was not as much time for Charles during this period of course and when Charles tried to rail against Christopher's presence, Mandi was firm with him. 'At our age, Charles, we can do what we want. I am friends with you both and I do not have to go through any ridiculous jealousy nonsense'.

Charles was to hear this until he accepted his lot and Mandi knew and loved both men until Christopher died at the beginning of December 2019. Mandi knew that Lockdown and coronavirus would have been too much for him, but yet again she found herself letting go of a much loved man in her life. She grieved with pain for dear Christopher, but life kept renewing as by now she knew it would.

During the development of her relationship with Christopher, her house had changed considerably, following discussion with me who had organised the redecoration of Mandi's part of it and reconfigured the way it was set up completely. It was now divided into two flats, but without any locks on any of the connecting doors. Whilst Mandi lost her old bedroom, spare room and boxroom, two new bedrooms, a large living space, an outdoor self-contained studio and a second floor balcony were added.

It was an enormous change, and after an initial uncertainty, both Mandi and I realised what a rich and unusual opportunity it was to come back to live together as mother and daughter after forty years. The living arrangements worked perfectly for both of us. There were so many parallel experiences in our lives that a mutual understanding of the need for love, excitement, independence, adventure, individual style, acceptance of each other and fun were not difficult to realise and life was the richer for the sharing. A sense of renewal is so often in the air as stories are shared in 115. There was no one more generous than Mandi when I met and fell in love with John. Mandi understood who he was and what he was about very easily and welcomed him so generously into her home that she made it very easy for us to marry. Unsurprisingly, she was chief bridesmaid at our very recent wedding.

Mandi's children were in their fifties and sixties and her grand-children in their thirties and twenties. Nick and Paige still live on the Wirral, not far from the original family home; Nick has reframed, restructured and repositioned Plexus Cotton and works at it with drive and determination. Having founded it around a year after the death of his father, he worked alongside his brother Jo for seventeen years until they could no longer be united in business and are no longer close. Paige works alongside Nick marketing the company, promoting the powerful ethical aspects of it.

'Plexus has involved total commitment—running one's own business to that scale is not for the faint hearted and it has had some great pluses and some major minuses—we should have sold out on my 40th Birthday year when the Company was worth 14 million pounds mostly in cash. However hindsight is 20/20 vision and the last years have been very enriching from a learning point of view if not necessarily from a health and financial perspective.'

Nick reflects further,

'I guess life is a series of choices—you make good ones and you make bad ones but overall I would say that the choices I have made are more positive than negative. I was very lucky in the choices that were made for me such as my parents. Both My Mum and my Dad gave me opportunities—led me in good directions and supported me to the absolute best of their ability. I hope when time looks back I can say that we have tried to do the same with our children.

I think overall my Mum has been the major influence in my life especially in my early years and it is from those years that one establishes one's foundation.

Whatever she has done she has done to the maximum of her ability and never shirked the effort.

She was very unselfish and a real giver and I think that rubbed off on us all—I think we all remember her saying 'if you're not the first one in the pub to buy a drink, you're not my son'.

She is a fantastic person—incredibly unselfish—fiercely independent who has fought through her demons and had so many trials and tribulations and emerged with a completely undaunted spirit. I love her so very much'.

Mandi recognises that she is powerless to do anything about the rift in her sons' relationship, but seeks to enjoy all that she can within the changed boundaries. This acceptance propels her capacity not to judge and remain loyal and confidential to all, something that has come to hold real importance and which Mandi has come to really understand over time even within her own family.

Matthew, her eldest grandson, contemplated the influence of his grandmother more widely:

> 'There's a youtube channel providing a top ten tips for life from some of the world's great successes, it passes down the advice of luminaries like Bill Gates and Steve Jobs. My Gran would be a great person for the show for the lessons she has provided to us.

Many of my favourite Gran moments have come to me through other family members and together with my own have transcended into themes that set apart this spectacular lady in all our lives. I think this can happen when you love someone so much! Where memories have merged, they have strengthened, reminding us who we are, our heritage and offering us principles that help bond our whole family together. My top ten themes are as follows:

1. Granny as a friend, counsellor and empath. There isn't a child, child-in-law or grandchild that hasn't gone through the London soothing factory. I cannot speak for the countless others Gran has nursed back to equanimity through just listening and drawing from them their own emotions. Who is to say how many months and years of emotional toxicity this lady has saved others from through just a warm dinner, her non-judgement and patient kindness? We should all strive to be such a positive influence in others' lives. Her attention to people who have been particularly vulnerable is inspiring.

2. Write and seek wisdom: The world has gone mad in the last twenty years and keeping everything on track is not always easy. Letters, postcards, emails and diary entries are a form of catharsis that have helped us all connect and process things; maybe this was more prominent in a bygone era, but Gran has fostered this in all of us. Whether it is a letter to Dad pinned in his study, this book, or a letter to Gran from Fred, Sam, Sas we all end up seeing; it is a process and discipline that has helped distinguish our family. Gran's loo wall needs no introduction and wherever we put it, the process of compiling wisdom and reflecting on it during times of

need (or just when in the loo) can help renew us all, re-centre us and make us strong again. I will treasure the letters and writings that Gran sent me at school, Paraguay, Texas or wherever...

3. Enjoy life! Whether it is time in the garden, family dinners, wine, G&T, nibbles, going to the theatre, heading on a bus to somewhere you've never been, bungee jumping, seeking love, or playing bridge (enjoyable for Gran, not those trying to learn, I would say!), the simple pleasures! Just enjoy life, and make every day count. The best people in life do this and Gran's get up and go attitude has helped open up frontiers in life for all of us.

4. Anything worth having takes time. The people Gran's children are today, Lamare, that holiday home in North Wales, which took a generation of love and investment, were not overnight successes. They were achieved through a generation spent giving of oneself and working. Even the time Gran has given to her grandkids has always been long and never short. Her diaries were over a lifetime. I think the perspective and successes Gran has had reassure others that life has cycles but being constant and the long road is a better way to meaningfulness in the end.

5. Gran as the lover and welcomer! It feels a bit peculiar to put Gran's lovers in the same headline point as her family's partners, boyfriends and girlfriends (past and present), great grandkids etc but there is something so innate and incredibly special about Gran's ability to welcome and love! It's unconditional wherever she gives it, it compounds and we all live in it because of it. There's no side, only love and we all benefit. It's of course supported by her doctrine for openness, constant communication and willingness to lead from the front in all matters related to the bedroom department. I don't know too many Grans who have attended so many of her grandkids' special moments and less special moments.

6. Quality not Quantity! Whether it is the weekly grocery
    shop that has been managed to perfection to include
    carefully chosen meats, cheeses, juices and everything
    you need to make a wonderful wholesome meal, never
    with waste or buying a pair of shoes, or new item of
    clothing, looking after them, and treasuring them for
    forever, Gran is about quality. Perhaps this way of life
    got lost for a while as things became so fast and quickly
    available, but Gran has not changed and perhaps we
    have something to learn from her. She exemplifies
    gratitude, caring for her things and shows us that less
    can actually be more.

7. Being free from sides makes you light and gives you
    energy and dynamism! It allows you to transcend age,
    class systems and religions. Gran is as comfortable
    with the young friends of her grandchild as she is
    offering her time to dying old parishioners that live
    on her street. It doesn't matter if you are Rastafari,
    Muslim, Hindu, born into high society or from places
    blighted with social problems. There is something to
    learn from everyone and she is keen to find out. How
    many people Gran's age do we know as sophisticated on
    the computer? She may not always speak a politically
    correct language but she certainly embraces inclusive-
    ness and the spirit of giving back to your community'.

8. Stay active, exercise and eat well! (Don't snack, unless
    its nibbles with drinks or a fruit pastille on a long
    journey or in front of the TV). This will also help you
    stay in the same clothes you bought in point 6; control
    your wants, be a bit disciplined, work hard and save
    too. That is a huge part of Gran's secret to success!

9. Life is an adventure, and life is what you make it!
    Whether going off to West Africa, the theatre, swimming
    in the Irish Sea, water skiing at Repulse Bay, dating,
    safari, watching naughty films (I watched Emmanuelle
    4 with Gran when I was about age 13 on channel 5 once
    and she educated me the whole way through. 'That's
    not how they do it in real life, you know!'), getting

pissed regularly, flirting a lot too, going into environments that are tough like counselling or being a nurse,
have a growth mind-set!! Just live, live, live!

10. Family is the most important thing! Celebrate them
with wonderful photos dotted all over your house.

As the news of the need to Lockdown came in at the height of the
coronavirus crisis and Mandi understood the threat to older people,
her first response of lack of concern for her own welfare changed.
It was a realisation that when confronted with her own mortality,
she did care. She was not ready to die yet, not because she was not
fully accepting of herself, others or her lot, but quite simply because
she trusted life to keep renewing, to keep offering her the new and
exciting and she was loving living it. She understood that if it were
her time, then she was ready for it and she accepted that without
complaint or judgement, but equally, if it were not her time, the
pleasures of the everyday were abundant and throughout Lockdown
she did not cease to notice them. New tastes from her cooking, little
birds coming to visit her growing garden, gleaming blue skies and
bright sunshine turning her newly mown lawn bright and lush
green, neighbourly chats across the wall, the sound of trampolining
children from next door, the promise of three great-grandchildren
coming soon, the calls every day from her children, grandchildren
and friends, the sewing project that led to freshly covered dining
room chairs, online trickster bridge, Zoom art classes with the great
grandchildren via art teacher Loubird, the Zoom quizzes which I got
her involved with, the church services, the wonderful differences
certain citizens were making (Captain Moore for one, aged nearly one
hundred), her beloved NHS and clapping outside every Thursday, her
grandson coming to wave from the end of the front path on his bike
and collect the cake that she threw at him, Desert Island Discs for all
the family that granddaughter Katie was leading, great-grandson Seb
learning to read with me, Great Aunt Jen and reading Harry Potter and
writing environmental stories with great-granddaughter Bella with
little sister Matilda listening in.

Mandi chose to protect herself from the virus, accepting all the
help offered her. In this way, she understood once more that her
independence could manifest itself through the choice to look after

and love herself, thereby giving to her adoring family and friends and continuing to inspire those around her for longer.

Carpe diem!

MANDI'S RECIPE FOR HAPPINESS IS THERE FOR US ALL TO FOLLOW ON HER LOO DOOR!

Equal parts of healthy, honest work, recreation and rest, mixed carefully with diligence, contentment, happiness, cheerfulness and even temper. Sift them with determination to get rid of lumps of idleness and despondency. Add the milk of human kindness and spirits of consideration and empathy. Stir gently with unsparing hand. Add a light sprinkling of smiles and colour with illusions. This recipe can be made at home with a little care from everyone.

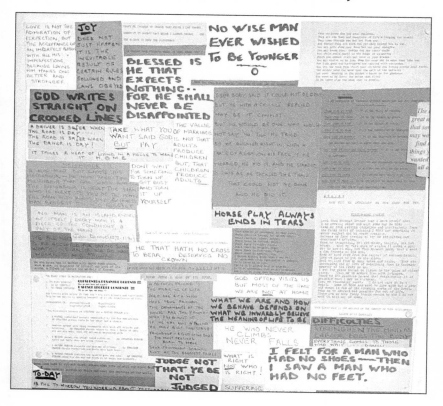

BOOK CLUB DISCUSSION

1. Should we judge Enid, Mandi's mother, for the way that she treated the young Mandi?

2. When did Mandi first gain real self-esteem and how?

3. Which qualities of Mandi do you admire?

4. Is Mandi a woman of her time?
   If so, how?
   If not, why not and in what way is she different?

5. Is Mandi a woman for all time?

6. What does finding her voice mean for Mandi?
   How significant are those early years and attitudes for Mandi over the years?

7. If you were Mandi, which choices would you make differently?

8. Do you find Mandi to be an ordinary, extraordinary woman?

REFLECTIONS

Lightning Source UK Ltd.
Milton Keynes UK
UKHW040648240621
386017UK00017B/109